# The Principles of Writing in Psychology

Visit our free study skills resource at **www.skills4study.com**

## Palgrave Study Guides

Authoring a PhD
Career Skills
e-Learning Skills
Effective Communication for
    Arts and Humanities Students
Effective Communication for
    Science and Technology
The Foundations of Research
The Good Supervisor
How to Manage your Arts, Humanities and
    Social Science Degree
How to Manage your Distance and
    Open Learning Course
How to Manage your Postgraduate Course
How to Manage your Science and
    Technology Degree
How to Study Foreign Languages
How to Write Better Essays
Making Sense of Statistics
The Mature Student's Guide to Writing

The Postgraduate Research Handbook
Presentation Skills for Students
The Principles of Writing in Psychology
Professional Writing
Research Using IT
Skills for Success
The Student's Guide to Writing
The Study Skills Handbook (2nd edition)
Study Skills for Speakers of English as
    a Second Language
Studying the Built Environment
Studying Economics
Studying History (2nd edition)
Studying Mathematics and its Applications
Studying Modern Drama (2nd edition)
Studying Physics
Studying Psychology
Teaching Study Skills and Supporting Learning
Work Placements – a Survival Guide for Students
Writing for Engineers

## Palgrave Study Guides: Literature

*General Editors: John Peck and Martin Coyle*

How to Begin Studying English Literature
    (3rd edition)
How to Study a Jane Austen Novel (2nd edition)
How to Study a Charles Dickens Novel
How to Study Chaucer (2nd edition)
How to Study an E. M. Forster Novel
How to Study James Joyce
How to Study Linguistics (2nd edition)

How to Study Modern Poetry
How to Study a Novel (2nd edition)
How to Study a Poet (2nd edition)
How to Study a Renaissance Play
How to Study Romantic Poetry (2nd edition)
How to Study a Shakespeare Play (2nd edition)
How to Study Television
Practical Criticism

# The Principles of Writing in Psychology

T. R. Smyth

First published 2004 by
PALGRAVE MACMILLAN
Houndmills, Basingstoke, Hampshire RG21 6XS and
175 Fifth Avenue, New York, N.Y. 10010
Companies and representatives throughout the world

PALGRAVE MACMILLAN is the global academic imprint of the Palgrave
Macmillan division of St. Martin's Press, LLC and of Palgrave Macmillan Ltd.
Macmillan® is a registered trademark in the United States, United Kingdom
and other countries. Palgrave is a registered trademark in the European
Union and other countries.

ISBN 1–4039–4236–6

This book is printed on paper suitable for recycling and made from fully
managed and sustained forest sources.

A catalogue record for this book is available from the British Library.

Library of Congress Cataloging-in-Publication Data
Smyth, T. Raymond.
   The principles of writing in psychology / T.R. Smyth.
      p. cm. – (Palgrave study guides)
   Includes bibliographical references and index.
   ISBN 1–4039–4236–6 (pbk)
      1. Psychology—Authorship 2. Report writing. I. Title. II. Series.

BF76.7.S57 2004
808.06615—dc21                                                    2004051504

10  9  8  7  6  5  4  3  2  1
13 12 11 10 09 08 07 06 05 04

Printed and bound in China

To Elizabeth and David

# Contents

## PART 2   SOURCES

## PART 3    WRITING

### PART 5   QUANTITATIVE RESEARCH

# Acknowledgements

It is impossible to give appropriate credit for the content of this book to all of those to whom it is due. No doubt some ideas are the result of a long forgotten conversation with a colleague or a question from a student. I would, however, like to acknowledge the support of my colleagues at the University of Canberra, where I wrote most of the first draft of this book, and to thank Andrew McAleer of Palgrave Macmillan for his help, and the reviewers of the manuscript for their useful comments and suggestions. In particular, I would like to thank Valery Rose and Jocelyn Stockley for detecting and correcting the errors that I made in the manuscript.

Primarily, however, the credit for this book remains with my late wife Patricia and my children, Elizabeth and David. At no small sacrifice to herself, Patricia encouraged me to undertake tertiary studies as a mature student, and continued to support me until her untimely death. Although young when I began my academic career, my children were understanding – and they now, as adults, still encourage and support me.

# A Note to Students

Like you, I once struggled with writing my first essay in psychology. I wondered what and how much to read, what to note and in how much detail, how to organize my notes, and how to plan and organize my paper. I puzzled over when and how to cite sources, whether or not to quote an author, how many sources to use, and what was the difference between a reference list and a bibliography. I pondered over what to include or omit, how to fit the material that I had gathered into the allowed word limit, what was meant by critical thinking, and how to avoid plagiarism. On top of all of this I encountered those frustrating mental blocks when I stared at the paper in front of me for hours, but wrote little or nothing.

When I wrote my first research report, I was faced with the same questions and problems. In addition, I was uncertain about what to include in its various parts, how to write the Method and Results sections, and what was the relationship between the Introduction and Discussion sections.

Like most students, I grumbled about disciplines using different referencing systems, and about lecturers having different ideas about how to write papers. Sometimes I was disappointed with the grade given to my paper, sometimes I disagreed with comments made on it, sometimes I could not read the lecturer's writing, and sometimes I found it a little hard to accept constructive criticism.

Now I know how to do those routine things, like citing references, and I know what to include in the parts of a research report, but writing remains difficult. I still find that planning a paper and critical thinking are hard work. I struggle with deciding what to include and what to omit, and how to write something concisely. I grumble about variations in styles adopted by different journals and editors. At times I disagree with a referee's or editor's comments. When I ask colleagues to read a draft, I occasionally disagree with their comments, and sometimes I find their writing difficult to read. On occasion, I find it a little hard to accept constructive criticism for what it is, and still I sometimes encounter those frustrating mental blocks. Finally, much to my disappointment, I do not find writing any easier. *Plus ça change, plus c'est la même chose.*

Writing a good paper is not easy; it takes time and effort. The key attributes of a good writer are diligence, patience, willingness to accept constructive criticism, and a dedication to simplicity and clarity. A well written paper is easy to read and easy to understand.

T. R. S.

# Introduction

This book offers advice and guidance on the writing of essays, literature reviews, and research reports in psychology. It has been written to cater for (among others) the needs of undergraduate students, and so frequent reference is made to students and to problems that they commonly encounter. On the other hand, the contents of this book apply equally to writing papers at any level. In particular, the advice and guidance offered are equally applicable to writing an article for publication. The only variations necessary are the editorial style adopted by the publisher and the manuscript presentation requirements. These are typically given inside the front or back cover of each issue of journals. In addition, from a conceptual perspective, the advice and guidance offered in this book are relevant to writing any formal or technical paper.

## ▶ Importance

Students often underestimate the importance of being able to write well. A not infrequent comment is something like, "It is the content of a paper that is important, not the way in which it is written." Such a comment reveals a lack of understanding of the necessity for clear communication. *No matter how valuable or useful an idea, it is worthless if it is not communicated effectively*. This often applies equally to knowledge. It follows that the importance of being able to write well cannot be overemphasized.

Moreover, perhaps the most important attitudes, abilities, and skills that students acquire during their university studies are those that are necessary in the preparation and planning of a paper. Essentially, what students are required to do is to identify the problem or question, seek out relevant information and ideas, think analytically and critically, and develop a solution or answer. This is the approach required for a wide range of tasks. The only additional requirement for writing a paper is to present the outcome in a well structured and well written manner.

## ▶ Principles, advice, and guidance

Some principles of writing must be followed. For example, any paper must have a beginning, a middle, and an end; and the structure of a research report must follow the scientific method. In addition, a paper must be written following the accepted conventions of grammar, spelling, and punctuation. The vast bulk of this book, however, is devoted to discussing the principles and logic underlying the preparation, planning, and writing processes; and to offering advice and guidance.

There is considerable scope for individual preference in writing. This extends to areas such as writing style, manner of expressing ideas, and the structure and organization of a paper. Rather than being prescriptive, then, the aim of this book is to provide guidelines within which individuals choose their own paths.

## ► Editorial style

When writing a paper an author must follow some editorial style to ensure consistency, for example, in the citing of sources, presentation of statistics, and format. Moreover, following some particular editorial style relieves the author from having to invent one. One style that is appropriate to papers in psychology is provided by the *Publication Manual of the American Psychological Association*. Because of the wide adoption of this style by psychology departments, the guidance given in this book on editorial style is, with some variations, consistent with it.

Some departures from the APA Manual arise because of its having been written and published in the United States of America. For example, the paper size recommended is the American standard letter size, and imperial units of measure are used when referring to margins. Similarly, the APA Manual uses some terminology, such as "period" for "full stop", which is not used in other countries, and American spelling and date format. As far as is possible, this book is designed to be international in nature.

In addition, the APA Manual was written primarily to cater for authors writing manuscripts for publication. Variation from some requirements in it, therefore, arise because of the inherent differences between manuscripts submitted for publication and papers or theses written by students in the course of their studies. This is recognized in the APA Manual, which recommends that there be appropriate variations.

## ► Local requirements

Although many psychology departments have adopted the APA style as a guide for their students, individual departments may well have some requirements that differ from those given in the APA Manual or this book. Students, therefore, need to check the requirements of their departments. Where these are inconsistent with those of the APA Manual, or given in this book, those of the department involved obviously take precedence. Similarly, those who are writing for other organizations, or for publication, need to check the requirements of the organization, journal, or publisher involved.

## ▶ Using this book

This book has been organized into parts to allow for advice and guidance relevant to a particular writing task to be found as easily as possible. Moreover, to help the reader, there is an element of redundancy in some chapters. On the other hand, it is impossible to include everything that is relevant in any one part or chapter. In particular, Parts 1–3 are applicable to writing any paper, the Introduction and Discussion sections of a research report (Part 5) are literature reviews (which are discussed in Part 4), and much of the advice and guidance on quantitative research reports offered in Part 5 are equally applicable to qualitative research reports (Part 6).

To help the reader to find relevant material, cross-references are included. In addition, a checklist that includes references to relevant parts of this book is provided at Appendix K. This is intended to be used when editing, but it may also be used to find relevant material. Again, however, it is impossible to make cross-reference to everything that is relevant. It will, therefore, be necessary from time to time to refer to various parts of this book, and to use the table of contents or index to facilitate doing so.

Students are busy people, and they typically have only limited time to work on a paper. There is, therefore, a quite understandable tendency to read only that part of a book such as this that is specifically relevant to the task in hand. The importance of Parts 1–3, however, should not be overlooked. These are generic in nature, and apply equally to working on any paper in psychology, and very largely to other disciplines. They are, therefore, broadly relevant to students during their studies, and in their future careers. Students would be well advised to read these chapters carefully and to give some thought to their contents.

# Part 1
# Academic Papers

# 1 Thinking and Writing

It is true to say that often one does not know what one thinks until one has written it. Writing is a discipline that leads to analytical, critical, and logical thinking. A good paper presents a structured argument that is based on sound evidence, and that leads inevitably to a logical thesis or conclusion.

Students are required to write papers such as essays or literature reviews to help them develop the ability to seek out relevant material, to evaluate that material, to think analytically and critically, to develop a reasoned argument, and to present that argument in writing in a scholarly manner. In their future careers students will be required to write papers of various forms that require the same attitudes, abilities, and skills that they developed when writing papers at university. These might include, for example, a position paper for a government department, a report on an investigation, a psychological assessment for a court, or a journal article.

Scholarly style, chap. 3 Scholarly writing, chap. 9

The ability to communicate effectively in writing is highly valued by employers. More important, however, is that *what you write and how well you write it can affect people's lives*. For example, a psychological assessment could influence a decision on whether or not a child is separated from his or her parents, or a decision in a court of law. In other instances, a poorly written paper can, for example, result in a failure to adopt some course of action that might affect people's lives in other ways. It follows, then, that *it is very important to develop the ability to communicate effectively in writing*.

## ▶ Information and ideas

A paper is always written to present a central idea, which can be described as a thesis, or a conclusion; this is developed by an argument based on information and ideas. It follows that the most basic requirement of effective writing is an understanding of these concepts.

Thinking. Your ideas. chap. 9

The meaning of "information"[1] and "ideas" can be long debated, and it can be argued that the two terms are synonymous. For the present purposes, however, it is useful to distinguish between these concepts.

Information can be thought of as what might be described as "factual material". This could include details of the procedure followed in an experi-

---

[1] "Information" also has a specific technical meaning in "information processing theory".

ment, data collected from a study, or the outcome of testing an hypothesis. In turn, information can lead to ideas. For example, information in the form of the outcome of some piece of research can lead to an idea. It follows, then, that *the true value of information is the ideas that result.*

Ideas can be thought of as mental representations of information, but they are not simply a record. Rather, ideas are representations of relationships between items of information and existing ideas. Developing ideas, therefore, involves a careful analysis and synthesis of existing information and ideas, and an examination of relationships within and between information and ideas. For example, information about the pressure and direction of movement of air can lead to the idea that air will flow from an area of high pressure to one of low pressure.

Another form of idea that should be understood is a *construct*, which can be described as an *invented concept*. As an example, gravity is a construct that is used to describe or explain the attraction between bodies. Similarly, intelligence is a construct.

The author of a paper will, of course, be presenting both information and ideas, but these need to be clearly distinguished. *It is the ideas that are important*, rather than the information. *Information is provided only in support of the ideas presented.* Presenting voluminous information – sometimes in minute detail – not only reduces the space available for presenting ideas, it results in the ideas being lost in a morass of information. Only that information necessary to support the ideas presented should be included in a paper.

## ▶ Knowledge

What constitutes knowledge can also be long debated, but again it is useful for the present purposes to distinguish between knowledge and the concepts of information and ideas. Just as information can be thought of as the raw material of ideas, information and ideas can be thought of as the raw material of knowledge.

At a simple level, knowledge obviously means knowing, which can easily be confused with simply remembering. But knowledge is more than this. Knowledge implies not only being aware of, but also understanding, and the ability to reason, to reach conclusions, to solve problems, and to make decisions.

Availability of information and ideas, therefore, does not equate with knowledge. A person who is sitting in a very large library has a great deal of information and ideas available. However, if that person cannot understand the information and ideas, think analytically and critically, reason logically, reach conclusions, solve problems, and make decisions, he or she could not be described as being knowledgeable. Similarly, the same person sitting at a computer, with access to the vast volume of information and ideas available via the Internet, could not be described as knowledgeable. *One of the greatest mistakes of modern time is to confuse information with knowledge.*

The author of a paper is not simply presenting information and ideas, but is addressing some problem or question, and attempting to provide a solution or answer. That is, *the author is presenting knowledge.* Similarly, when students are asked to write a paper they are required to *demonstrate knowledge.* It follows, then, that students must present not only information and ideas: more importantly, they must demonstrate an understanding of the relationships involved, analytical and critical thinking, and the ability to reason logically and to reach valid conclusions.

## ▶ Critical thinking

When you consider the information and ideas that you encounter while reading for a paper, you must do so critically. This *requires the application of knowledge*; which, it has been suggested, requires understanding, and the ability to reason, to reach conclusions, to solve problems, and to make decisions.

It is important to understand that critical thinking does not mean being critical in the commonly accepted sense of commenting that something is, for example, bad or inadequate. *Critical thinking is not an exercise in being pejorative.* Neither does it mean that you should reject information or ideas simply on the basis of "I do not like it, therefore I reject it," or "I cannot understand it, therefore I reject it." Similarly, it does not mean that you should reject a theory because you are of the view that theories are of no practical value. Put simply, theories represent attempts to understand and explain what has been observed: they provide a framework through which to view a problem. Moreover, they allow for prediction, and possibly control. Theories, therefore, do have practical implications and applications: if that were not so, they would be of no value.

*Critical thinking is based on sound scepticism.* You should not simply accept information and ideas as "fact". If you read widely, you will often find that not all authors agree on a given view, and that theories are not always consistent. Adopting a sceptical approach means that you must analytically examine the evidence and reasoning presented. For example, you should consider the evidence that has been advanced in support of an idea or theory, and consider whether or not you think it is valid.

An important point to understand is that critical thinking does not always result in a negative conclusion. It might well be that, as a result of a critical analysis, the conclusion reached is that the information or idea involved is valid. On the other hand, it might be that the result is that there is some doubt on the validity of the information or idea. In this case, there must be some sound basis for this doubt.

## ► Approach to critical thinking

It is impossible to give you a formula to apply, because critical thinking requires a creative approach, as well as at least some knowledge of the area involved, and often a familiarity with at least basic research methods and statistics. As a guide, when you read an author's view on something, or you are examining a theory, ask yourself questions such as:

• What evidence has been put forward in support of this idea or theory?
• Is the evidence valid?
• Is the discussion balanced?
• Is the author's reasoning logical?
• Is the idea or theory consistent with those of others?

When you are reading about a piece of research, you should apply your knowledge of research methods and statistics. Think about aspects such as internal and external validity, and ask yourself questions such as:

• Was the sample random?
• Was there a control group?
• Was the independent variable effectively manipulated?
• Is the instrument used to measure the dependent variable valid?
• Were any differences or relationships observed large enough to be material?
• Is there a possible alternative explanation of the results?

However, *simply asking questions does not constitute critical thinking*. The answer to a question must result in some sound basis for a valid comment.

## ► Spurious criticisms

Simply *inventing* possible answers to questions does not constitute valid critical thinking. As an example, an article might report the finding that, in a sample of university students, the reaction time for a complex task was longer than that for a simple task. This finding could not be validly questioned on the basis that the participants were university students, and that the results cannot be generalized to other people. There is no logical reason to expect that any other group of participants of similar age would produce different results.

Similarly, it is not acceptable to be critical on the basis of grounds that are not supported. For instance, the outcome of a study cannot necessarily be criticized on the grounds that the participants did not respond in a given way because it would contravene some legislation or cultural norm. Legislation differs between countries, and may change over time. For such a criticism to be valid, it would be necessary to show that the particular legislation existed in the given country and at the given time. Similar reasoning applies to culture, which also differs between countries and changes over time.

## ▶ Validity

Another point that needs to be understood is that critical thinking does not necessarily mean questioning the validity of some information or idea. For example, an investigator might report that the outcome of a study suggests that women respond to a particular form of advertising in a particular way. If the investigator restricted the implications to the culture in which it was carried out, it would not be acceptable to question the validity of the study on the grounds that women in a different culture might respond differently. Similarly, because the study was restricted to women, it would not be valid to question it on the grounds that men might not respond in this way. On the other hand, it would be quite valid to suggest that women in a different culture might respond differently, or that men might respond differently. Such suggestions do not question the validity of the original study. Nonetheless, a critical comment has been made. This example illustrates the point that the findings of a particular study might be quite valid and applicable in a particular set of circumstances but not in another, or be quite appropriate to one group but not to another.

## ▶ An example of critical thinking

Some years ago, in France, a study was conducted in which one group of children was given physical exercise activities on one afternoon per week, while another group continued with normal classroom activities. After a period, the academic performance of both groups was assessed, and it was found that those involved in physical activities performed at a higher level than did those who had continued with normal classroom activities. The conclusion reached was that participation in physical activities improved academic performance.

An obvious question that could be raised is whether the children were randomly allocated to the two groups. If random allocation were not used, it is possible that there might have been a pre-existing between-group difference in academic ability. By chance, the children in the physical activity group might have been more academically able than were those in the control group. In any event, the children's academic performance should have been tested before carrying out the experiment. The next obvious question, then, is: was this done?

Another possibility is that two separate classes were involved, and that one was randomly chosen as the experimental group. In this case, it is possible that the teacher of the class that was used as the experimental group might have been a better teacher than was the teacher of the control-group class. Alternatively, the teacher of the class used as the experimental group might have worked harder with the class to overcome the loss of time devoted to physical activity. In either case, the observed between-group difference might have been attributable to a variable other than that which was manipulated.

Finally, there is an apparent weakness in the study. What was required was a third group of children, who were not involved in physical exercise activities and who did not continue with normal classroom activities for one afternoon a week. It is possible to argue that it was not the involvement in physical activity, but rather a break from normal classroom activity, that resulted in the improved academic performance.

## ▶ Basis of assertion

Critical thinking involves questioning the basis on which an assertion is made. When an author makes an assertion it must be supported if the reader is to be convinced of its validity. Obviously, *just because an author writes something, this does not necessarily make it so*. For example, few readers would be convinced by an author's assertion that the earth is flat, or that the earth revolves around the moon. It follows, then, that an important part of critical thinking is questioning the validity of assertions made by authors.

**Basis of assertion by others**, chap. 6

### Citing a source

chap. 6

Sometimes authors support an assertion merely by citing a source. For instance, an author might write:

> Skinner was a behaviourist (McGregor, 2000).

This is a simple, straightforward assertion that is supported by citing McGregor (2000) as the source, and one that would be readily accepted. Similarly, an author might make a simple assertion such as:

> Brain damage often results from severe injury to the head (Tête, 2003).

Again, the author is supporting the assertion by citing a source. In this case the assertion is not particularly surprising, and so is likely to be readily accepted.

On the other hand, not all assertions can be readily accepted. For example, in an article on amnesia an author might write:

> Alzheimer's disease is an hereditary disorder (McKenzie, 2002).

Such an assertion should be treated with some scepticism. The author is merely replicating an assertion made by McKenzie. Moreover, just because McKenzie has made this assertion, this does not necessarily make it so. Critical thinking involves questioning the basis on which the assertion was made. In this example, the only way to do this is to consult the original article or book written by McKenzie.

## Secondary sources

On occasion, *although rarely*, an author will support an assertion by citing a secondary source. For example, an author might write,

> It has been shown that . . . (Turnbuckle, as cited by Calathump, 2004).

*Using secondary sources, chap. 6*

A point that is often overlooked by students is that using a secondary source precludes thinking analytically and critically about the content of that source. By definition, a secondary source has not been read. Therefore, the author citing the secondary source cannot have evaluated that source. Such assertions, therefore, must be treated with caution.

The use of secondary sources is discussed in chapter 6, and an example of the result of not thinking analytically and critically about the content of a secondary source is included. This provides another example of analytical and critical thinking.

*Problems, chap. 6*

## Language

When considering the validity of an assertion, the language used by the author needs to be considered. For example, an author might write:

*Vocabulary, chap. 2*

> It has been *suggested* that Schizophrenia is caused by environmental factors (Galloway, 2002).

Again, just because someone *suggests* something, this does not necessarily make it so. Neither does it make the suggestion valid. The same applies to words such as *thinks, proposed, concluded, thought,* or *argued*. Obviously, the basis on which the author cited made the original assertion must be considered.

## Research findings

In some instances, an author will make an assertion based on research findings. For example, an author might write:

*Research findings, chap. 6*

> Turnbuckle (2003) found that . . .

An assertion of this form is stronger than one based on, for example, "Turnbuckle (2003) *"thinks"* or *"proposes"*. It at least indicates that the assertion is based on some research finding. However, the validity of the research involved needs to be considered. Typically, then, such an assertion should be accompanied by at least a brief description of the research involved. If it is not, the assertion should be treated with caution.

A frequent example of the misuse of "research findings" occurs in advertising in the popular media. Commonly, advertisements for a product will claim that "Research findings show that . . .", or sometimes, in an apparent attempt to gain more credibility, "University studies have shown that . . .". Such claims are obviously worthless. Similarly, any such claim in an academic paper is of no value or credibility. The source must be given so that the research involved can be evaluated.

## Reasoning

**Reasoning,**
chap. 6

Often, an author will support an assertion by a process of reasoning. In this case, *the logic and evidence underlying the author's reasoning should be carefully considered.* Sometimes, a flaw in reasoning will become apparent. For example, the author might not have considered possible alternative explanations of research findings, or might have misinterpreted the premises upon which the reasoning is based. As an example of a flaw in reasoning, students sometimes think that because they achieved a distinction in one discipline they should expect a distinction grade in another. One possible flaw here is that the student might have an aptitude for one discipline but not the other.

### ► Unintentional bias

When reading a report of research, and subsequently citing it in a paper, there is the possibility of unintentional bias. For example, those who are working in the area of physical education might well be predisposed to accept the conclusion that physical activity promotes academic achievement. They might, therefore, tend to overlook some of the possible criticisms of the research reported in the example of the study carried out in France that is given here.

**Objectivity,**
chap. 2

### ► Personal views

Criticism based merely on some personal opinion is not scientifically valid. Rather, and importantly, *critical thinking requires an open mind.* You must understand that just because you hold a particular opinion this does not necessarily mean that it is valid from the perspective of others, or that others are not entitled to have differing views.

## ▶ Familiarity

Some students think that they cannot critically evaluate material that they read because they are not sufficiently familiar with the area. They might, for example, think that they are not sufficiently familiar with the discipline in a general sense, with other research in the area, with the theories involved, or with the nature of the analyses used. However, lack of such familiarity does not preclude critical thinking. For example, no depth of knowledge is required to detect inconsistencies in findings or differences in views between authors, and little knowledge of a discipline is required to detect conclusions that do not follow logically from the data presented, or for suggesting a possible alternative explanation of the findings. Moreover, only limited knowledge of research methods is required to notice a basic flaw in an experimental design, such as the absence of a control group in an experiment.

## ▶ Levels of critical thinking

Critical thinking in the form of detecting a difference in findings or views, or of the absence of a control group in an experiment, might be described as "basic" critical thinking, and this requires no detailed knowledge of the area involved. By comparison, more advanced critical thinking does require a greater level of knowledge. It follows, then, that beginning students cannot be expected to demonstrate "advanced" critical thinking, but they should be able to demonstrate at least a basic level of critical thinking. On the other hand, as they progress through their studies in a discipline, and become more familiar with it, they should be able to demonstrate more advanced critical thinking.

## ▶ Selecting material

Critical thinking also applies to the selection of material to be included in a paper. Some material will be relevant while some is not, and some material will be important while some is not. *It is essential that a paper include only information and ideas that are directly relevant to the subject of the paper.* This does not, of course, mean that material that is counter to the author's thesis can be omitted. The argument and evidence presented in an academic paper must always be balanced.

    Inclusion of material that is marginally relevant contributes little to a

**Objectivity,**
chap. 2

paper, and material that is not relevant merely wastes words, and distracts and possibly confuses the reader. Students often make the mistake of including such material at the beginning of a paper, sometimes in an apparent attempt to justify the importance of the topic under discussion.

### ▶ A reasoned and balanced argument

Simply selecting and presenting information and ideas, no matter how carefully, will not result in a good paper. In the course of developing your thesis or conclusion, you will have convinced yourself of its soundness and validity. The next task is to convince the reader. To do this you must present a reasoned argument that is based on evidence. You might think of this as being similar to the task faced by the prosecutor in a court who is trying to convince the jury that the accused is guilty. Your task, then, is to marshal the evidence, and to present it in a logical sequence so that it will inevitably lead to the jury being convinced of the guilt of the accused. Of course, in a court the prosecutor will present only one side of the argument: The jury will also hear the defence argument. Unlike the prosecutor, then, your task is to present a balanced view; that, is both sides of the argument. You are, in this analogy, "balancing the scales of justice".

A better analogy, then, is to think of yourself as a member of the jury who, having heard both sides, is trying to convince fellow jury members of the validity of your decision. To do this, you must present a balanced argument that is valid, and is based on directly relevant, and sound, information and ideas.

When writing a paper your task is similar. *You must present a balanced argument that is based on sound evidence and logical reasoning.* In addition, you must present the evidence and reasoning in a manner that can be readily understood. This means that you must present the evidence in a logical sequence, weighing it item by item, discarding some and accepting others; until, in the end, the conclusion is obvious.

In a criminal court, sometimes the guilty are found innocent. However, in a criminal court the jury must be convinced "beyond a shadow of doubt". By comparison, in a civil court decisions are made on the balance of probabilities; that is, theoretically, 51% or more either way. Your task when writing a paper is similar: It is to weigh the balance of the evidence. Presuming that you have presented a balanced argument, you have not ignored material that is inconsistent with your thesis or conclusion, and you have demonstrated that the weight of evidence is in favour of it, your argument should be successful.

# 2  Scientific Writing

There are variations in the approach to writing papers in different disciplines. For example, there will be differences in the approach adopted when writing papers in history and in English literature. Psychology is a science, and so papers written in psychology must be written in a scientific manner.

*The aim of scientific writing is to convey information and ideas directly, clearly, concisely, and simply.* In particular, scientific writing requires accuracy and objectivity in both content and use of language.

## ▶ Accuracy

Obviously, any information included in a scientific paper, such as statistics or the procedure followed in an experiment, must be accurate. In addition, ideas must be accurately communicated.

### Detail

Not only must the detail included in a paper be accurate, but also all relevant detail must be included. For example, in a paper on the effects of stress on performance, a student might write:

> Yerkes and Dodson (1908) found that high levels of arousal are associated with poor performance.

While this statement is true, important details are omitted. In particular, Yerkes and Dodson found there was an optimal level of arousal for maximum performance, with both lower and higher levels being associated with lower levels of performance. Moreover, they also found that the optimal level of arousal varied with the complexity of the task, and with the level of an individual's skill. The omission of these details, results in the student's statement not accurately representing the Yerkes and Dodson findings. For example, the original statement written by the student could be taken to mean that there is a simple linear relationship between level of arousal and stress, and that this applies universally.

## Ideas

**Information and ideas**. chap. 1

Communicating ideas accurately requires care. For example, the omission or inclusion of a single word can have a considerable effect on meaning. As an instance, there is a difference between, "Damage to this part of the brain results in . . .", and "Damage to this part of the brain *sometimes* results in . . .". Similarly, the use of the wrong word can affect meaning. For example, whether twins in a study were *zygotic*, or *dizygotic* can influence the interpretation of findings. Simply putting a word in the wrong place can also affect meaning. For instance, consider the following example:

> Use unleaded petrol only in vehicles so marked.

Compare this with:

> Use only unleaded petrol in vehicles so marked.

These sentences have different meanings, resulting from changing the position of the single word *only*.

## Vocabulary

Choice of words is also important in accuracy. Therefore, it is important for the author of a scientific paper to choose words carefully so that the intended meaning is precisely expressed. For example, problems can arise with the use of words such as *large, considerable, substantial, moderate, small*, or *minimal*. A difference that one person thinks of as large, for instance, might be thought of by another as moderate. When used in reporting quantitative research results there is no problem with using such words, because the relevant statistics will always be presented, and so the reader can make his or her own judgement. In other circumstances, however, care needs to be taken.

Such potential problems are not restricted to words that describe magnitude: Care must similarly be taken with the choice of other words. For example, there are differences in meaning between *must, should*, and *could*. As another example, there are differences between *suggested, concluded, found, argued, proposed*, or *postulated*. Again, each of these words has a different meaning. It is important to make the intended meaning clear, and so the word used must be chosen carefully.

## Technical words and terms

Problems can also arise as a result of a word having a commonly accepted meaning, but a different technical meaning when it is used in a specific discipline. Like other disciplines, psychology has its own technical language.

Sometimes the definition of a word given in a normal dictionary differs from the meaning that it is intended to convey when used in psychology, and often within a specific context. Examples of this are *affect*, *mood*, *incidence*, and *prevalence*. These are words that have specific technical meanings in psychology.

A problem that students often encounter arises with using the word *significant*. In common usage it is taken to be synonymous with, for example, *important*, *critical*, or *large*. In psychology *significant* should be used only to refer to statistical findings as in, for example, "There was a *significant* difference between the two mean scores." Perhaps this should be more clearly expressed as, "There was a *statistically significant* difference between the two mean scores," but commonly it is not. The problem is that findings, such as a difference between means, can be statistically significant but quite small, and perhaps unimportant. On the other hand, a large difference might not be statistically significant. One student unsuccessfully tried to overcome this problem by writing, "There was a *significantly significant* difference." Words such as *important*, *large*, *considerable*, or *marked* should be used if that is what is meant.

## Precision

The terms "precision" and "accuracy" are often used interchangeably, in the sense that, for example, a precise measure is an accurate measure. Apparent precision, however, can sometimes give a false impression of accuracy. For instance, it is possible to devise an instrument, such as a questionnaire, to measure some construct such as happiness. Moreover, it is possible that a score derived from such an instrument might be calculated to two decimal places. This would seem to suggest that the measure derived is very accurate. However, it is likely that the items used in the instruments give only an approximate measure. Consequently, although the overall score might be calculated to two decimal places, it remains that it is only an approximate measure. A misunderstanding of accuracy in this way is often associated with, for example, intelligence scores or correlations.

Similarly, an author might convey precisely what he or she means through careful choice of words and use of language, but the evidence or reasoning upon which the assertion is based may be flawed. Although, then, the precision involved might give the impression of accuracy, the assertion may not be accurate.

## ▶ Objectivity

Apart from accuracy, the most important requirement is that *writing a paper must be approached with an open mind*. A paper must reflect the author's

A reasoned and balanced argument, chap. 1

willingness to consider a variety of points of view. This means that a paper, such as an essay or a literature review, must present a balanced discussion of a range of relevant information and ideas. In particular, *information and ideas that are counter to the author's argument must not be omitted*. Moreover, *information and ideas must be examined in an objective manner*. Put simply, a paper must never be biased towards any particular point of view.

Being objective does not, of course, mean that an author cannot argue for a particular point of view, or reach a conclusion. It does, however, mean that an author cannot selectively include or omit information or ideas so as to support that view or conclusion. Similarly, it does not mean that information and ideas can be distorted or misrepresented for this purpose.

## ▶ Values

A problem that sometimes occurs is that authors allow personal values to influence the selection of material that they include in a paper, or their analyses or interpretation of material, which can result in a lack of objectivity. Individuals are perfectly entitled to have an opinion on anything, but this must not be allowed to influence their writing. In particular, authors must not allow their personal values – that is beliefs of what is "right" or "wrong", or "good" or "bad" – to affect their selection of material or their logical reasoning. Scientific writing should be *value free*.

It is, of course, impossible to be completely value free. For example, when selecting sources a judgement must be made on their quality, and some sources will be considered to be "good" while others will not. Similarly, when working on a research report data, will be analysed using what is considered to be the "most appropriate" statistical technique. Such judgements must, however, be distinguished from those that are based on moral or ethical values.

As an illustration, it is perfectly reasonable for a medical practitioner to comment on the physical effects of alcohol consumption, or a psychologist on the psychological effects of trauma in armed conflict. However, it is not acceptable for that person, in the capacity of an expert in the particular field, to comment on, for example, the moral values of drinking alcohol or of armed conflict. Expertise in a particular area does not endow individuals with special qualifications in the making of moral or ethical judgements. In this respect, an expert in some specific area is no more qualified than is anyone else.

Apart from possibly influencing the selection or analysis of material, or the interpretation of research findings, moral or ethical values can also affect conclusions reached. For instance, when writing a paper on juvenile delinquency it would be acceptable to comment on the validity of reported research, or the observed effects of punishment. In contrast, it would not be acceptable to make a comment on the appropriateness of punishment administered, such as "Juvenile delinquents should be punished because they have sinned against society." Similarly, when reporting the outcome of research on long-term unemployed persons, it would be acceptable to comment on the effects of long-term unemployment. On the other hand, it would not be acceptable to recommend that, "The government should take action to overcome this problem for the good of society."

Value judgements of a moral or ethical nature can sometimes be obvious. In other instances, they are less apparent, but are reflected in the use of vocabulary. For example, words such as *good, excellent, bad*, or *careless* reflect value judgements. Such words must be used with care.

## ▶ First person personal pronouns

Pronouns, pronoun agreement, chap. 21

In the quest for objectivity authors have often avoided the use of first person personal pronouns. Of course, this does not necessarily mean that a paper written in this manner is objective: It may simply give the impression of being so. On the other hand, careless use of first person personal pronouns can lead to bias. Therefore, it is important to *use first person personal pronouns, if at all, with care.*

When writing a paper the use of first person personal pronouns is usually superfluous. Unless you attribute an idea or opinion to someone else it is understood to be your own. Therefore, phrases such as "*I* think . . ." or "In *my* opinion . . ." are unnecessary and a waste of words. You could write something like, "*I think* these findings suggest . . .", but the phrase "*I think*" is superfluous. There is nothing wrong with writing, "These findings suggest . . .". For example, suppose you were to write:

> *I think* that the findings of the Deregowski (1972) study show that visual perception can be influenced by culture.

The results of the Deregowski study clearly show that perception can be influenced by culture, and it would be quite correct simply to write:

> The findings of the Deregowski (1972) study show that visual perception can be influenced by culture.

This sentence does not use a personal pronoun, saves two words, and conveys exactly the same meaning.

Yet another problem is that the use of first person personal pronouns can lead to making unsupported assertions. Phrases such as "*I think* . . ." are virtually an invitation to the reader to question what you have written. The immediate and obvious question is, "What makes you think so?" In scientific writing you cannot make an assertion or express an opinion without some supporting evidence. It is not, for example, acceptable to write:

Support. chap. 6

About 6% of ordinary children are abnormally clumsy.

Alternatively, you might write:

*I think* that about 6% of ordinary children are abnormally clumsy.

However, the problem is that, while you might think so, you might be wrong. Some evidence must be provided to support this assertion. You could, therefore, write, for example:

About 6% of ordinary children are abnormally clumsy (Smyth, 1992).

In this sentence you are supporting your assertion by citing Smyth (1992) as a source of this assertion, and no first person personal pronoun is involved.

## *I* and *my*

Sometimes students use *the writer* or *the author* to avoid using the first person personal pronoun *I*. This style should be avoided because it divorces the author from his or her paper. A similar problem sometimes arises when authors refer to themselves when citing themselves as a source. As an example, in an article written by Robertson in 2004, the author might refer to an earlier experiment that he conducted, in the form of, "Robertson (2001) found . . .". This gives the impression that Robertson is referring to someone other than himself. In this instance it would be better for the author to use the first person personal pronoun *I*. The author could, for example, write, "In an earlier experiment (Robertson, 2001), *I* found . . .". The same logic applies to the use of *my*. For example, it would be appropriate to write, "In *my* earlier work (Robertson, 2001) . . .".

### In research reports

It can be argued that in the Method and Results sections of a research report, when the author is reporting something that he or she actually did, the use of first person personal pronouns is appropriate. For example, when reporting an experiment it would be correct to write in the Method section, "*I* tested the participants in two conditions," and the APA Manual suggests that this is preferable to writing, "*The experimenter* tested the participants in two conditions." However, first person personal pronouns must be used with care.

## *We* and *our*

The same reasoning applies to the use of the first person plural pronouns *we* and *our*. Moreover, unless a paper is written jointly with another author, the use of these pronouns is inaccurate.

In addition, there can be other problems with the use of *we*. In particular, authors sometimes write, for example, "*We* know that . . .". The meaning of such a phrase is unclear. In this case *we* could refer to, for example, *scientists*, *psychologists*, or some other group of which the author is a member. The personal pronoun *we* should not, therefore, be used in this manner. If *we* refers to a particular group, the appropriate noun should be used. For example, do not write, "*We* believe . . .", if you mean, "*Psychologists* believe . . .".

Another problem is the use of *we* in, for instance, "*We* can conclude that . . .". This implies that the reader agrees with the author, which is not necessarily the case.

Similarly, the use of *our* can result in ambiguity or uncertainty. For example, "In *our* society . . ." could refer to any society. This can be a problem, especially when papers are read in other countries. It is better to be specific and to write, for example, "In *Australian* society . . .", so that there is no uncertainty.

## *One*

Students sometimes use the indefinite pronoun *one* to avoid use of the first person personal pronoun *I* (or in the rare instance in which it would be applicable, *we*). For example, a student might write, "*One* believes that . . .", or "*One* concludes . . .". Here, the indefinite pronoun *one* is being used as a *false* first person personal pronoun: The student is using *one* to mean *I*, and so is not avoiding the problem. In effect, the student is writing, "*I* believe that . . .", or "*I* conclude . . .". Using *one* as a false personal pronoun in lieu of *I* is generally regarded as poor style, and in some instances as an affectation. This usage, therefore, should be avoided.

In its proper indefinite sense, *one* means everyone, anyone, or perhaps someone. It can, therefore, be used, for instance, to refer to people in general. It is, then, correct to write:

> It is true to say that often one does not know what one thinks until one has written it.

Similarly, it is correct to write, for example:

> On the basis of these findings *one* could conclude . . .

This sentence should be taken to mean that *anyone*, or *everyone*, "could conclude that . . .". In this case the sentence should be written as, for example:

> On the basis of these findings *anyone* could conclude . . .

If this is what is meant, then this is what should be written. More commonly, however, the sentence would be written as:

> On the basis of these findings it can be concluded . . .

## You

A problem is that in everyday speech the personal pronoun *you* is commonly used in lieu of the indefinite pronoun *one*. This leads some students into the mistake of using *you* in this sense in their writing. For example, a student might write something like:

> *You* could be expected to agree with this.

This is improper usage. Employed in this way, *you* refers to the reader, and so does not convey the student's meaning accurately. Moreover, the reader might well disagree with the statement on the grounds that he or she could not be expected to agree with the idea suggested, and might well strongly disagree. In scientific writing, therefore, the personal pronoun *you* must not be used in this sense.

On the other hand, in some particular instances authors can appropriately use this pronoun. When the author specifically wants to address the reader, this usage is acceptable. Notably, *you* is often employed in this book for that purpose. For example, *you* will notice that in some instances advice is offered to *you*. By comparison, when discussing mistakes that students commonly make, *you* is not employed. This avoids the implication that *you* make these mistakes.

## Gender

**Pronoun agreement**, chap, 21

It is quite correct to refer to an individual within a group consisting of both males and females, using a pronoun of the appropriate gender. For instance, when referring to individual participants in discussing the results of an experiment, it would be quite correct to write, "*Her* responses were very accurate." Similarly, when referring to a co-authored article, it is correct to write, for example, "Hulme and *his* colleagues . . .".

Sometimes, however, difficulties can arise, and this is most commonly the case when describing the procedure followed in an experiment in which the participants were both male and female. The following sentence provides an example.

> The participant was instructed to put his hand on the lever that he was required to operate.

Obviously, because both male and female participants were included in the experiment, the above sentence is inaccurate. This could be corrected by replacing *his* with *his or her*, and *he* with *he or she*. The potential problem with this is that the use of *his or her*, and *he or she* becomes rather cumbersome with frequent repetition. Using *he/she* is simply another way of writing *he or she* (and would be pronounced in this way when reading aloud), and so is no improvement. Similarly, *s/he* (which cannot be pronounced when reading aloud) does not help.

Some authorities – but not the APA Manual – recommend using the plural forms *they* and *their*, which are not gender specific, as singular pronouns; as in, for example:

> The participant was instructed to put *their* right hand on the lever that *they were* required to operate.

The problem is that the resulting sentence, as in the example above, is often grammatically incorrect. Both *they* and *their*, which are plural, replace the singular noun *participant*. Also, the singular verb *was* has been changed to the plural *were*, so as to agree in number with *they*, which it immediately follows, and the plural *were* does not agree in number with the singular subject of the sentence (*The participant*). This could have been avoided by retaining the singular verb *was*, but this would have resulted in "they was", which is glaringly incorrect.

The easiest way to overcome this dilemma is simply to write in the plural. Doing this, the example sentence would be written as:

> The participants were instructed to put *their* right hand on the lever that *they were* required to operate.

It might appear that in the above example the use of the singular *lever* is a problem. However, participants in an experiment are usually tested individually, using a single piece of apparatus. Presuming that this piece of apparatus has only one lever, in the example sentence the singular *lever* is correct. Only if more than one lever were involved should the plural *levers* be used. In any case, the apparatus will always be described before the procedure or together with a description of the experimental tasks. No confusion, therefore, should arise.

As a general principle, then, when referring to groups comprising both males and females, writing in the plural is appropriate. This obviates the necessity to write *he or she*, and the grammatical problems that often arise with the use of *they* or *their* as singular forms.

# 3 Style

Style is usually thought of as that which is distinctive about writing, identifying it with the author. This should not be confused with the editorial style adopted by publishers. Writing style refers to the manner of writing, or the way in which information and ideas are presented. This includes the use of words, structure of sentences, variety, and rhythm.

The British ice skaters Torvill and Dean achieved the unprecedented perfect score of 6 from all 12 judges at the 1984 Olympic Games. This obviously required a complete mastery of the skating skills involved. Perhaps more importantly, their mastery of skating allowed them and the judges to concentrate on the artistic elements of their performance. Likewise, outstanding singers such as Sarah Brightman and Plácido Domingo have mastered their art, which allows them to concentrate on interpretation and presentation. In contrast, there are those who typically use elaborate costumes and special effects to disguise their ineptitude.

Similarly, those who write well have mastered the requirements of writing, such as sentence and paragraph structure, and grammar; which allows them to concentrate on presenting their ideas clearly and in a logical progression of thought. Moreover, like skilled performers, they do not resort to ruses such as elaborate or convoluted constructions, and complex language, to hide their lack of writing ability. Rather, *a good author writes in a simple, direct style*. This allows the reader to concentrate on the information and ideas presented, and the logical reasoning involved. Just as a slip on the ice distracts spectators, or a missed note in singing distracts the audience, so too do flaws in writing distract the reader.

## ▶ Scholarly style

*A paper must be written in a scholarly style: in a manner that would be adopted by a learned, or educated person*. Word use, grammar, punctuation, and spelling must be correct. Moreover, the sentence and paragraph structure should reflect an educated mind.

There are those who argue that language is dynamic, or constantly changing, and so what is common usage should be accepted, regardless of any conventions. This is an excuse for lack of knowledge of the English language, and does not provide a justification for blatant disregard of the accepted conventions of grammar, spelling, and punctuation. These conventions have been established over time as an aid to clear and accurate communication. They are, therefore, disregarded at the author's peril.

This does not mean that an author has to be overly pedantic, or that one or two minor errors will be a disaster: Everyone makes mistakes. In addition, there are differing opinions on some points of grammar and punctuation, and there are optional spellings for some words. However, there can be no excuse for errors such as omitting verbs from sentences, misuse of participles, using *that* instead of *who*, omitting the possessive apostrophe, writing *country's* as the plural of *country*, and errors in spelling such as *drawring* or *spersific*. Such flaws clearly show a lack of familiarity with the English language, and carelessness.

Failings such as these are not only distracting, they can also make the author's meaning obscure. Moreover, they cast doubts on the credibility of the author. *The reader of a paper that is not written in a scholarly manner is unlikely to be convinced by the author's argument, or of the validity of any conclusion reached.*

## ▶ New words and new usages

It is, of course, true that any language changes over time. For example, the word *aeronaut*, used to describe pilots in the early days of flying, is no longer used, but the word *astronaut* has entered the English language. Similarly, other words such as *radar*, *television*, and *computer* have entered the language. The advent of the computer, in particular, has resulted in a number of new words. These include, for example, the *Internet*, the *Web*, and *intranet*. In addition, some existing words have taken on new meanings. Such words include, for example, *disc*, *server*, *link*, and *dot*.

As a general rule, new words and usages should not be employed in scientific writing. (An exception is, for example, a new word for a new concept that is defined in a paper.) The potential problem is that the reader might not be familiar with the new word or usage and so might not understand, or might misunderstand, what the author intends to convey. If in doubt, the meaning of a word should be checked in a good quality dictionary, or its usage should be checked in a text on English usage. When a new word or usage has achieved the level of acceptance necessary for inclusion in such sources it may be used.

Care must be taken, however, when referring to a dictionary or a text on English usage. Such sources often include colloquial or regional meanings or usages. This is true in particular of regional dictionaries. It is important in scientific writing to convey meaning precisely. Moreover, scientific papers are read internationally, and often by readers whose first language is not English. Therefore words or expressions that have a colloquial or regional meaning should not be used in that sense in scientific writing.

## ▶ Flaws in usage

Because language changes over time, in some instances what is currently regarded as a flaw in writing will subsequently not be so regarded. For instance, split infinitives have come to be quite common; the most widely known probably being "To boldly go where no man has gone before." However, such deviations from convention usually do not detract markedly from communication. A more common flaw, which can result in misunderstanding, is the misuse of words or expressions, and sometimes abbreviations or symbols. Not infrequently, this results from abuse of language in the popular media, and thoughtless copying by others, some of whom should know better. In some instances, the "new" meaning or usage eventually becomes accepted, while in others it does not.

## Misused words

An example of word misuse is the use of *source* and *conference.* Both are nouns, but in recent time both have sometimes been used verbs; as in, for instance, "These items were *sourced* from," or "The views were *conferenced.*" Similarly, *impact* has come to be used to mean *affect* or *influence*, but when used as a verb it does not mean *affect* or *influence*, and it cannot be used as a noun to mean *influence*. Another example is *call*, which is sometimes incorrectly used to mean "decision", "choice", or "judgement". In time these meanings may come to be accepted. However, until such usages have reached the level of acceptance where they are included in a reputable dictionary they should not be adopted.

The problem with misuse of words is that a lack of clarity or precision can result. In any case, there should be no need for such misuse when the English language already has a more than adequate supply of appropriate words. An educated person will, of course, be aware of this and will use an appropriate word correctly.

Apart from such misuse, words can be used incorrectly in an inexcusable manner. In particular, students on occasion use words with which they are unfamiliar without referring to a dictionary to check their meaning. This can result in the misuse of words, such as *apprehend* instead of *comprehend*. Other examples taken from students' papers are: "Two stages in development are *infantry* and early childhood," "With *retrospect* to this finding," and "The results *collaborated* with the theory." Sometimes students invent words – with bizarre results – such as *sensical*, *incoherable*, and *audial*, which again are examples taken from students' papers.

## Misused expressions

As is the case for words, there are expressions that are commonly but incorrectly used. For instance, "at this point in time" is supposed to mean "now". Perhaps the most outstanding current misuse is "in place", which at best is either incorrectly used or is completely superfluous. For example, "We have plans in place" means that "We have plans", and "There is legislation in place to deal with this" means "There is legislation to deal with this." Often, the meaning of such expressions is obscure, or at least ambiguous. For example, to "take on board" might mean to "incorporate", "consider", or sometimes (especially when used by politicians) even "ignore". Clearly, such expressions should never be used in scholarly writing.

## Clichés

A cliché is a hackneyed phrase such as "springs to mind", or "at the drop of a hat", which is repeated so frequently that it is used thoughtlessly out of context, and becomes meaningless. For example, it has become common in the popular media to describe the scene of a major accident or a disaster as being "like a battlefield". Sometimes the meaning of a cliché can be understood, but often it cannot, or it is unclear. In any event, clichés should not appear in formal writing.

## Jargon

When properly used, "jargon" means the specialized or technical language used by a particular profession or trade. More commonly, however, "jargon" is used to refer to pretentious language, including obscure words, and long and convoluted sentences. Although intended to impress, such language is difficult to understand, and is often meaningless. Jargon, in this sense, should never be used.

## Anthropomorphism (attributing action)

When referring to information in the form of research findings, an important point to remember is that human actions cannot be attributed to inanimate entities. For example, a study cannot *interpret*, evidence cannot *conclude*, and findings cannot *argue*. Students sometimes make the mistake of ascribing actions to inanimate sources by using phrases such as:

| | |
|---|---|
| This article believes | This research thought |
| The report tested | The results found |

On the other hand, inanimate entities can *illustrate* or *portray* something. Therefore, it is correct to use verbs that indicate this, as in:

| | |
|---|---|
| Figure 1 shows | This error pattern indicates |
| These findings support | The results show |

## Abbreviations

chap. 24
Appendices
D and E

Standard abbreviations may be used in scholarly writing. Non-standard abbreviations may also be used, but they must be explained when first used. Such abbreviations should, however, be kept to a minimum. Frequent use of abbreviations can result in confusion. *Experimenter*, *participant*, and *subject* must not be abbreviated as *E*, *P*, or *S*, and *Figure* must not be abbreviated as *Fig*.

## Symbols

Symbols, such as +, −, =, >, or → may be used in mathematical expressions, statistics, or formulae. They must never be used as abbreviations, or in lieu of words.

## Ampersand

Appendices
B and C

The ampersand (&) is used in lieu of *and* only when enclosed in parentheses, as in, for example, "(John & Wayne, 1952)", and in a reference list, as in, for example, "Sellers, P., & Milligan, S. (1961)".

## ▶ **Formality**

A scholarly paper should be written in a formal style. This means that contractions, such as "can't", "don't", or "it's", and informal abbreviations, such as "ad" for advertisement, or "uni" for university, are never used. Similarly, colloquial words such as "gripe", "hassle", or "cobber", and terms such as "write up", and "pear shaped", are not acceptable in formal writing. Similarly, words are never used to convey colloquial meanings. For example, "heaps" should never be used to mean "many". Apart from their casual tone, colloquial terms and their meaning vary between countries and over time.

## ► Writing vs. speech

Sometimes it is suggested that people should write as they speak, and in some instances this might be appropriate. For example, a formal speech could be written and spoken in the same manner. Similarly, a letter to a friend could well be written in the manner in which one would speak to that friend. Commonly, however, writing and speech differ. In particular, the language used in speech is typically more casual than in a formal or technical paper. Moreover, when speaking, people use tone of voice, inflection, and body language (such as a smile), all of which have a marked effect on the listener's interpretation of the meaning of what is said. Obviously, these additional sources of information are not available in writing. In addition, speech is sometimes grammatically incorrect and the content is likely to be rather redundant.

## ► Textbooks

A mistake that students often make is to copy the style used in some introductory or general textbooks. Frequently, such books are written in a somewhat "casual" style. In particular, the authors often use first person personal pronouns and contractions in what can be described as a "conversational" style. Presumably this is done to create a friendly tone to help to engage students' interest.

Textbooks of this type should never be used by students as an example of the style that they should adopt when writing papers such as essays, literature reviews, and research reports, or the formal and technical papers that they will write in their future careers. Rather, students should use as an example the style used in articles published in good quality journals, or specialized academic books.

## ► Expression

*It is critical that the information and ideas involved are clearly expressed in a paper.* Poor written expression will result in confusion and a lack of understanding. For example, the meaning of the following paragraph, which was taken from a student's paper, is not readily apparent.

> The random sample thus studied in this experiment voiced the overall past population statistics, that expressed the serial-like manner in which the brain subjugates information. As a consequence the co-ordination of a response suffers from the time interval, in which mind has to rationalize stimulus alternatives. There is always the factor of the independent variable, the reactionary stimulus, determining the final course of response, namely

depressing the appropriate key, and as a consequence verifying the dependent variable.

Clarity of meaning is best achieved by using a direct and simple form of written expression. Long and convoluted sentences can be difficult to understand, as can be obscure words or terms.

## ▶ Individual preferences

Although the requirements of scientific writing, accepted conventions, and the necessity to write clearly and concisely determine some aspects of writing a paper, there is room for individual preference and style. Formal writing does not need to be dull and boring. Rather, some attempt should be made to write a paper in an interesting manner.

### Rhetorical questions

Presumably in an attempt to create interest, students sometimes use rhetorical questions. These are questions that do not require an answer, and are used only for dramatic effect. For example, a student might write something like, "How do the learning theories of Thorndike and Skinner compare?" Such a question must be followed by the answer, because the student will be making some point. The rhetorical question, then, is unnecessary. It would be better to introduce this comparison using a paragraph topic sentence such as, "There are similarities in the Thorndike and Skinner theories of learning." This makes the point directly, simply, clearly, and concisely. Rhetorical questions waste words, and so should not be used.

### Variety

**Repition,**
chap. 6

Interest can more appropriately, and effectively, be created and maintained by the use of variety in expression. Formal and technical papers do not have to be written using a dry, tedious series of short, abrupt sentences and paragraphs, written with a limited use of language and restricted vocabulary. Rather, you should try to use a style that will stimulate the reader's interest. Monotony leads to boredom. Therefore, you should incorporate variety into your writing by varying the length and structure of sentences and paragraphs. Similarly, you should vary phrasing. For example, a series of "Bloggs (2001) found . . . , Jones (2002) found . . . , and Green (2001) found . . ." becomes tiresome. With a little effort and imagination you can overcome this problem. For example, you could introduce variety by writing something like, "Bloggs (2001) found . . . Similarly, in the Jones (2002) study there was.

. . . In addition, the results of the Green (2001) experiment showed . . .". Although this adds a few extra words, the resulting variety is worth the cost.

The most obvious source of monotony in a paper is unnecessary repetition of words in close proximity. This can be avoided. For instance, do not begin a series of consecutive sentences or paragraphs with the same word. Students often do this when making a series of points. For example, a student might write, "*The* first point to be considered is . . . "*The* second point is that . . ." *The* third point is . . .". Again, with a little imagination this problem can be avoided.

## Alternative words

Tedious repetition can also result from poor use of language and a limited vocabulary. Variety can be achieved by using alternative words with the same meaning. For example, rather than repeatedly writing *experiment*, as in, "Nelson's (2002) experiment . . . , Bion's (2001) experiment . . . , Harvey's (2002) experiment . . .". "This experiment . . .", and so on, you can introduce variety by using, as appropriate, words like *study, research, investigation,* or *work.*

This problem is often encountered in research reports. For instance, frequent reference to the "participants" becomes monotonous. Such repetition can be reduced by using alternative terms. Participants can be referred to, for example, as *adults, children, 8-year-olds, the experimental group,* or *the control group,* among other terms. The following description, for instance, includes unnecessary repetition:

> The mean scores for the adult participants, the mean score for the 12-year-old participants, and the mean score for the 8-year-old participants, are shown in Table 1.

By comparison, this version omits the repetition:

> The mean scores for the adult, 12-year-old, and 8-year-old groups are shown in Table 1.

Another way in which to minimize repetition is to use pronouns, such as *they, their, those,* or *each.* The following example again incudes unnecessary repetition:

> The participants were given 10 trials and the participants' mean scores were recorded. The participants who had at least five correct responses were given 10 more trials, which the participants could perform in their own time.

The obvious repetition could have been avoided by, for instance, writing:

> The participants were given 10 trials and their mean scores were recorded.

Those who made at least five correct responses were given 10 more trials, which they could perform in their own time.

## Caution

Some care is needed when using pronouns in this way. You must ensure that the antecedent for a pronoun (i.e., the noun to which it refers, or which it replaces) is clear. For instance, in the following sentence it is not clear whether it was Sally or Mary who was wrong:

> Mary told Sally that she was wrong.

## A thesaurus

A thesaurus is very helpful for finding synonyms, but some care is needed when choosing an alternative word. There can be subtle differences in the meaning of words and in their usage. You need to make sure that the synonym you choose is appropriate. For instance, if you were to use a thesaurus to find a synonym for *suggest* you would find words like *advise*, *recommend*, or *advocate*. Although it is perfectly correct to write, "The findings of this study *suggest* that children process information more slowly than do adults," it would not be appropriate to write, "The findings of this study *advise* (or *recommend*, or *advocate*) that children process information more slowly than do adults." More suitable alternatives could be *show* or *demonstrate*. On the other hand, just because the findings of an experiment *suggest* something, this does not necessarily mean that they *show* or *demonstrate* that it is so. Similarly, there are differences between *volume*, *quantity*, *amount*, and *number*. You must be confident that the word you choose conveys exactly what you mean.

A useful exercise is to produce your own small, personal thesaurus of words and phrases. You can do this using an ordinary thesaurus and a dictionary, and by taking words and phrases from articles and books that you read. As you encounter new words and phrases you can add them. This makes finding an appropriate alternative word or phrase easier when you are writing.

## ▶ Polish

Apart from using a style that promotes interest, a paper should be written in a polished manner. A paper can be correctly written, from a technical point of view, but still have weaknesses. For example, a sentence might be grammatically correct but long, convoluted, and difficult to read. Usually, it is a good idea to write sentences that are short and to the point. However, an important consideration that should not be overlooked is that *a paper should read smoothly*: Prose has rhythm. Although short sentences can be helpful for clarity of expression, a series of short, abrupt sentences can be monotonous, and interrupt the flow of a paper. By comparison, the judicious use of longer sentences can add variety and rhythm. Similarly, a series of short, abrupt paragraphs will disrupt the flow of a paper. Conversely, long and rambling paragraphs are difficult to read. Manipulating the length of sentences and paragraphs can result in a paper that reads smoothly. Again, therefore, the length of paragraphs should vary.

## ► Conventions

Students should already be familiar with the accepted conventions of writing English prose. There are, however, some particular points that should be emphasized.

### English usage

Use the form of English usage and spelling appropriate to the country in which, or for which, you are writing. The basic difference is between American and what is often described as "Standard English"; although there are some variations between countries in so-called Standard English. You should understand that *science is international*. Papers and books written in one county are read in others, often by readers whose first language is not English. To avoid any possible misunderstanding, therefore, you should avoid any usage that is peculiar to your own country. Rather, you should try to write in what could be described as "International English".

### Tense

Papers should reflect the current state of knowledge; and so they should be written mainly in the present tense, using either the simple or perfect forms. You might, for example, comment that, "These findings suggest . . .", using the simple present tense; or, when describing something that happened in the past, but continues in the present, you could use the present perfect tense and write something like, "Several studies have shown that . . .". However, when referring to past events that do not continue into the present, you should use the past tense. For example, you might write, "Jones (1987) found that anxiety decreased when . . .", "McCloskey (1967) showed that . . .", or "Davis (1979) pointed out . . .". Past and present tenses can be combined. As an example, you could write something like, "Black (1975) *suggested* that . . . , but Jones (2001) *argues* that this view is no longer valid."

**Tense**, chap. 16

## Voice

**Voice**,
chap. 21

Another consideration, especially when referring to existing information or ideas, is the use of voice. For example, the results of a study might be referred to in the passive voice by writing something like:

> This relationship was demonstrated by the findings of the Simpson (2002) study.

Alternatively, this could have been written in the active voice as, for example,

> The findings of the Simpson (2002) study demonstrated this relationship.

As a general comment, it is preferable to use the active voice. On the other hand, there is nothing grammatically wrong with using the passive voice, and authors often use it. For instance, the passive voice is often used in this book. Writing the preceding sentence in the passive voice avoids some potential problems. For example, it avoids the problem that would be present if the sentence were written as, "This book often uses the passive voice." Obviously, a book does not use the passive voice; the author does. In addition, it avoids the use of the first person personal pronoun *I*, as in "When *I* wrote this book *I* often used the passive voice."

## ▶ Editorial style

"Editorial style" refers to the guidelines adopted by publishers, partly on the basis of preference, but also to ensure uniformity in spelling, abbreviations, reporting of statistics, and presentation of figures, tables, and reference lists. Complying with some standard set of style requirements also aids communication. Those who become familiar with a particular editorial style find reading material that is consistent with it easier than that which is not. In addition, following a particular style makes writing easier. Authors do not, for example, have to stop and ponder how to use an abbreviation, or to cite statistics.

A number of style manuals have been published and, although there are some differences, there are many commonalities. There is no reason why a particular style should be preferred to another. Nonetheless, authors must comply with the style adopted by the publisher or organization for which they are writing. Similarly, students must comply with the requirements of the discipline and department in which they are studying.

## ▶ Psychology style

The *Publication Manual of the American Psychological Association* (the *APA Manual*) was written specifically as an editorial style guide for authors submitting articles to APA journals, and a number of other journals in psychology have adopted this style. On the other hand, not all journals have done so, and consequently there are some differences in editorial style, although these are usually minor.

Most psychology departments have adopted the editorial style requirements given in the APA Manual, although typically with some variations. The need for such variation arises mainly because of the inherent differences between manuscripts submitted for publication and papers written by students in the course of their studies. Recommended deviations from, or preferred options in, the APA Manual style requirements, for students' papers, are given in Appendix A.

It is also important to understand that the APA Manual is not *the* definitive work on English usage or writing style (as contrasted with editorial style). In some respects, therefore, the APA Manual should be regarded simply as giving the APA preference, and this should not be slavishly followed. A further point to note is that publishers of books do not necessarily adopt the APA style. When writing papers, therefore, books should not be used by students as a model for editorial style.

Appendix A

## ▶ Local requirements

Individual departments may well have some requirements that differ from those given in either the APA Manual or this book. Students, therefore, need to check the requirements of their departments. Any such requirements obviously take precedence. Similarly, those who are writing for other organizations, or for publication, need to check the requirements of the organization, journal, or publisher involved.

# 4 Academic Standards

Plagiarism and academic dishonesty are regarded very seriously. The penalties involved can include loss of marks, failure in a subject or course, termination of candidature, or removal of a degree. Moreover, in a student's future occupation or profession the consequences are no less serious. Careers have been ruined! It is important, therefore, to understand what constitutes plagiarism and academic dishonesty.

Apart from the question of morality, plagiarism or academic dishonesty are a clear indication of lack of competence. It follows, then, that anyone who is guilty of plagiarism or academic dishonesty is both amoral and incompetent.

## ► Plagiarism

Usually, plagiarism involves copying the work of another author or authors, either in whole or in part, with the deliberate *intention* of misleading the reader into thinking that the work is the writer's own. *It is irrelevant whether or not the work copied has been published, whose work is involved, how much work is copied, or from how many authors work is copied.*

### Copying

In its most extreme form, plagiarism involves *copying the work of another author verbatim*. For example, a student who is required to write an essay could find a journal article that covers a similar topic, copy that article word for word, and submit the copied paper as his or her own work. If the journal article is too long for the word limit imposed, part of the original article is simply omitted. There can be no excuse for this type of plagiarism.

A variation of this blatant form of plagiarism, which is equally inexcusable, is *copying the work of another author with minor changes*. For example, in an essay on anorexia nervosa, a student included the following:

> Where the person is too overweight and usually eats too much, the anorexic is often dangerously thin and does not eat enough. There are some cases of people who are anorexic that are caused by various phys-

ical conditions, for example, in cancer patients who are having chemotherapy which results in nausea and various food dislikes.

A comparison with the following extract from Gleitman's (1991) introductory textbook reveals that it is essentially the same as the material included in the student's essay.

> Where the obese person is too fat and almost always eats too much, the anorexic is too thin (often dangerously so) and eats much too little. There are some cases of anorexia (literally "lack of appetite") that are caused by various organic conditions, for example, in cancer patients undergoing chemotherapy which produces nausea and various food aversions. (Gleitman, 1991, pp. 79–80)

In this example the student has made only minor changes to the wording in Gleitman's book. Consequently, the material included in the student's essay constitutes plagiarism.

As another example, the following paragraph is an extract from a student's paper.

> The couples that are newly married most often settle into their new roles as husband and wife steadily. The difficulties with this transition are more likely to occur when spouses enter a marriage with different expectations about what their new roles are. Unfortunately, a significant proportion of differences in the role expectations appear to be more likely to happen in this era of transition in gender roles.

By comparison, the following is taken from Weiten's (1998) text.

> The newly married couple usually settle into their roles as husband and wife gradually. Difficulties with this transition are more likely when spouses come into a marriage with different expectations about married roles (Kitson & Sussman, 1982; Lye & Biblarz, 1993). Unfortunately, substantial differences in role expectations seem particularly likely in this era of transition and gender roles. (pp. 454–455)

A comparison of what the student wrote and what Weiten wrote shows clearly that the student has essentially copied Weiten's work, changing a few words and omitting the sources cited by Weiten. This, obviously, constitutes plagiarism. Even if Weiten were cited as the source, the close similarity between the student's and Weiten's words still constitutes plagiarism.

## Paraphrasing

A less apparent form of plagiarism is the paraphrasing of the work of someone else and pretending that it is the student's own. Sentences or paragraphs that are rewritten versions of another author's work, but convey the same information and ideas, can also constitute plagiarism *if the original author is not acknowledged*. Again, it does not matter either how much work is paraphrased, or from how many authors.

For example, when writing an essay on impaired motor skill in children, a student might write:

> By comparison with children who are seriously affected, the problems of those who have a minor motor skill impairment can be difficult to identify.

A reader who had read the article by Smyth (1992) would recognize this as paraphrasing the original:

> The problem is that, whilst more severely affected children's impaired performance of motor skills is likely to be evident, it can be difficult to recognize the cause of the difficulties experienced by those who are moderately or mildly affected. (Smyth, 1992, p. 297)

In this example, because the source of the original idea was not acknowledged, the extract from the student's essay constitutes plagiarism. By comparison, had the student acknowledged the idea, for example by simply including "(Smyth, 1992)" at the end of the sentence, there would have been no question of plagiarism.

## Ideas

An important point to note is that *paraphrasing means expressing an idea from another author's work in one's own words*. Clearly, if the source of the idea is not acknowledged, it is understood to be the author's idea. Failure to acknowledge the ideas of other authors, therefore, is plagiarism.

## Another student's work

Of course, *copying or paraphrasing another student's work, either in whole or in part, constitutes plagiarism*. Moreover, in this case the two students involved (i.e., the student who copies or paraphrases the work, and the student who allows his or her work to be copied) would *both* be guilty of academic dishonesty.

In one case, a student who had submitted a research report early lent a copy of it to another student who was experiencing some difficulties. The academic who subsequently marked the reports noticed similarities in the work of the two students. When confronted with this, the second student admitted having copied or paraphrased parts of the first student's report, without that student's knowledge. Nonetheless, both students were found to be guilty of academic dishonesty, and were penalized accordingly. The result was that both failed the course (or subject).

## ▶ Defending plagiarism

Sometimes students, when accused of it, argue that they did not understand what constitutes plagiarism. *Lack of understanding of what constitutes plagiarism is not an acceptable defence.* No reasonably intelligent person can believe that it is acceptable to copy the work of someone else, or to take ideas from another's work, with the intention of presenting the work or ideas as one's own.

In one case, a student copied, with some minor alterations, a considerable volume of material from a book that she had been instructed not to cite as a source. Moreover, she did not acknowledge this source. When confronted with an accusation of plagiarism, her defence was that because she had been instructed not to cite this particular source she had not done so. This defence is obviously not acceptable. Clearly, the intention of the instruction had been that she should not use the particular source, not that she could copy material from it without citing it. Moreover, it is extremely difficult to believe that the student did not understand this.

A defence that is sometimes given is that, while taking notes, the student copied material from one or more sources and then forgot that the material was an exact copy, or paraphrase, when including it in his or her paper. However, for the student to be accused of plagiarism, the material involved would have to be of some volume. Reproducing only one or two sentences in a paper without appropriate acknowledgement would most likely be overlooked at undergraduate level. This applies equally to presenting one or more ideas without appropriate acknowledgement. The student involved, therefore, would have had to have copied, and forgotten that he or she had copied, quite a volume of material, and/or the source of a number of ideas, in which case, *the defence of "forgetting" is unacceptable.*

Another defence that is occasionally offered is that in the student's particular culture copying the work of another shows respect for the author, or some similar justification. *Any such defence is not acceptable.*

## ▶ Detecting plagiarism

Usually, incidences of plagiarism are easily detected. Most commonly, plagiarism is evident because the style and standard of writing are well above that which would be expected of a student. In addition, unless the entire paper has been copied from some source, there will be obvious variations in style and standard in parts of the paper, indicating that some parts are not the student's own work.

Plagiarism is also often detected because the academic involved recognizes the work. It is not uncommon for an academic to have read the work copied, or from which ideas have been taken. There is the story of an academic who suggested to a student that he had copied work from a particular article. When the student denied this, the academic suggested that the student should look at the name on his door and then at the name of the author of the article in question.

An academic who is marking papers is also very likely to notice similarities in the work of individual students. In particular, work that is copied verbatim or ideas that are essentially identical are very likely to be noticed.

A form of plagiarism that is often particularly easy to detect is copying material from the Internet. Obviously, to find appropriate material, the student involved has to search the Internet. Not surprisingly, academics can similarly search the Internet and so find the same material. Moreover, it is often easy to search the Internet for a string of material taken from a paper, and so find the source from which it has been copied.

Apart from recognizing work that has been copied verbatim, or with minor changes, it is often very easy to recognize ideas that have been taken from another author's work, but have not been acknowledged. This is particularly so in the case of ideas that are well known.

## ▶ Avoiding plagiarism

It is easy to avoid plagiarism if you understand what constitutes plagiarism, and this has been explained above. All that you need to do is to follow two simple rules: (a) do not copy the work of others unless you are giving a direct quotation, and (b) always acknowledge the work and ideas of others by citing the source.

## ▶ Unnecessary worry

Some students worry unnecessarily about being accused of plagiarism because they have expressed an idea that has previously been suggested by someone else but, because they are not aware of this, they have not given acknowledgement to that other person. There is nothing new about two or more people having the same idea. Many people have had what they thought was a brilliant and original idea only to find later that someone else "thought of it first". In fact, given the same or similar information, it would be very surprising if only one person ever interpreted it in some given way.

First-year students, in particular, are prone to this concern. After all, they have only just begun their study of psychology. It is, therefore, often difficult for them to know whether or not an idea is original. Academics are aware of this, and no one is going to get excited because a student proposes something that has previously been suggested. However, if the idea in question is one that is well known (but cannot be said to be in the "public domain"), or perhaps features in a textbook to which the student has been referred (for example in a reading list), some question could arise if it is not acknowledged. This would be particularly so if a number of such ideas, or some major idea, were included in the student's work.

## ► Public domain

Some ideas that are long standing and widely accepted can be regarded as being "in the public domain". Including such ideas in your writing without acknowledging a source is not plagiarism. For example, without fear of being accused of plagiarism, you could include in an essay on perceptual ability a comment that, "Of the sensory modalities, vision is generally accepted as being predominant." This is widely accepted and there is no need to credit the idea to anyone. Nonetheless, when expressing such an idea it is preferable to make some comment such as, "It is generally accepted that . . .", or "It is widely known that . . .". This shows that you think that the idea is "in the public domain" and so there is no need for an acknowledgement.

The problem for the beginning student is knowing when an idea can be regarded as being widely accepted in this sense. Sometimes this will be obvious. For example, no one would expect you to attribute to some author the idea that the earth is round, or that the Sun rises in the east. Similarly, if you were to comment that intelligence quotients were originally calculated by dividing mental age by chronological age and multiplying by 100, because this is well known there would be no need for an acknowledgement. In many instances, however, you are likely to be in doubt. You should adopt a simple rule: *When in doubt, acknowledge.* Quite probably you will have found the idea in some book or article, so it is easy to cite the source.

## ► Logical reasoning

If you express an idea based on logical reasoning, and it is sensible to assume that any intelligent person would reach the same conclusion, there is no need to acknowledge the idea. For example, in a paper on movement control you could comment, "In order to successfully reach for and touch an object, an individual must know the location of the object and be able to control his or her movements." This is a logical statement, and there would be no need to acknowledge the idea as being suggested by someone else. Similarly, if you have developed an idea through a process of logical reasoning based on evidence, there should be no problem. In this case, you will have presented the evidence (and cited its source) and reasoning in your paper, and so illustrated how you arrived at the idea.

## ▶ Academic dishonesty

From a student's perspective, academic dishonesty can be defined as *any deliberate act that is intended to deceive those responsible for a student's assessment in regard to his or her level of academic performance.*

### Joint work

Sometimes students work with other students on a paper. Unless they have been instructed to work individually, there is nothing wrong with this. Usually, however, although students may have worked with others on the initial stages of preparation, they are required to submit an individually written paper. A problem then arises if two or more students submit, *as their own individual work*, papers that are essentially the same. For example, although wording and sentence structure differ, the information included, the references cited, the organization of material, the ideas expressed, and the conclusions reached, could be virtually identical. This would constitute academic dishonesty on the part of *all* of the students involved. By comparison, if two or more students were required to write a paper jointly, and that paper were submitted under joint authorship, there would be no question of academic dishonesty.

Another form of academic dishonesty sometimes associated with group work is that a student might not contribute proportionally to the work of the group. For instance, one student might contribute very little to a group research project. But when the resulting research report is submitted, it is so as a group project, under the names of all students involved.

### Getting help

On the other hand, there is nothing wrong with getting help when working on a paper. You are free to discuss your work with academic staff, fellow students, or anyone else. However, with the rare exception of a paper that you have been instructed to write jointly with another student, or other students, you must write a paper on your own. *Having some other person write all or part of a paper, or calculate statistics for a research report, and not acknowledging that other person's contribution, is a form of academic dishonesty.* Submission of such a paper, with the deliberate intention of misleading the reader into thinking that it is completely the student's own work, would be treated in the same manner as plagiarism. Moreover, as for plagiarism, a student who writes part of another student's paper, or calculates statistics for another student, is also guilty of academic dishonesty.

If someone helps you with a paper, you must acknowledge that person's assistance. You could do this by writing an acknowledgement on the title page, or by including a footnote in acknowledgement. If you do so, you cannot be accused of academic dishonesty.

## Having another write a paper

Obviously, if a student were silly enough to have someone else write a paper for him or her, this would constitute gross academic dishonesty. Typically, the rare incidents of this type become evident because the standard of the paper is beyond the student's ability.

## Falsifying data

Another form of academic dishonesty is the falsifying of research data. This is a particularly silly thing to do. In student work, whether or not an hypothesis is supported is usually not important. What is important is how the results are analysed and interpreted. Also, falsification of data is usually very easy to detect.

## Citing sources

Obviously, you must read a reference before you can cite it. A further form of academic dishonesty, then, is citing a source that you have not read – other than as a secondary reference. Sources that you have not read must never be included in your reference list. Usually, incidents of this type become apparent because the student involved omits some important detail, or refers to information or an idea out of context.

# Part 2
# Sources

# 5 Evaluating Sources

A reader will not be convinced by an author's argument unless it is based on accurate information and valid ideas. Authors, therefore, must cite the source(s) of information and ideas included in a paper, and must support assertions made, by citing the source(s) of the information and/or ideas on which assertions are based. This allows the reader to refer to the source(s) to verify or to evaluate the information or ideas involved. Obviously, then, any source cited must be of good quality. It follows that authors must select sources with care.

This chapter suggests an approach to the evaluation of sources. Evaluation of electronic sources involves virtually the same considerations that are applicable to print sources. Therefore, evaluation of print sources is discussed first and in more detail than is the evaluation of electronic sources.

## ▶ Print sources

Most commonly, the sources cited in academic papers are in the form of academic journals and books. Sometimes other material, such as government publications or other non-academic material, may be cited, but this is not common.

## ▶ Abstracts and secondary sources

It is, of course, impossible to evaluate a source without reading it. It follows that a source cannot be evaluated on the basis of reading only an abstract. In addition, obviously a secondary source has not been read, and so cannot be evaluated. Both abstracts and secondary sources, therefore, are of little if any value.

**Abstract**, chaps 14 and 16

**Using secondary sources**, chap. 6

## ▶ Quality control

The quality control exercised by publishers of academic journals and books is usually excellent. By comparison, that exercised by publishers of other material varies considerably.

## Academic journals

Most academic journals use a *peer review* process to assess the suitability of material for publication. When a manuscript is submitted, the editor sends copies of it to experts in the area, who may be referred to as the author's peers. These referees, who are anonymous to the author, assess the manuscript and make recommendations on its suitability for publication. In some instances, to avoid any possible bias, the author's name (or authors' names) is (or are) not revealed to referees. This is referred to as a "blind" or "masked" review.

The editor makes a decision on whether or not to publish an article, based on the referees' reports and editorial judgement. Journal editors will accept for publication only those articles that referees consider to be of good quality and that contribute worthwhile information and ideas. In addition, they will only accept articles that are written in a scholarly manner and that conform to the style requirements of the journal.

Usually, it is quite easy to identify refereed journals. The notes or instructions to authors, which are commonly included inside the front or back cover, will make this obvious. Moreover, refereed journals typically include a list of names of those on their editorial board. Another indication sometimes found in journal articles is a date of original submission and a later date of acceptance for publication of a revised version. Obviously, a revised version would only result if the original manuscript were commented on by referees and the editor.

## Academic books

Editors responsible for publishing books follow a review process similar to that adopted by journal editors. Before making a decision on publishing they send copies of the manuscript, or a detailed proposal, to experts in the area for review. The process is essentially the same as that followed by editors of journals, although the experts involved are usually referred to as *reviewers* rather than referees. As is the case for journal articles, the editor's decision whether or not to accept a manuscript for publication is based on the assessments of the reviewers and editorial judgement. Editors will only accept for publication manuscripts that are of excellent quality, and are considered to make a valuable contribution to the literature.

## Non-academic material

No comparable quality control is exercised in the non-academic arena. This is often not a particular problem in the case of government publications, but it can be in the case of other material. A form of quality control is exercised by editors. However, this usually relates to the likelihood that the publication will sell well. In the case of the popular media, in particular newspapers, editorial control might well also extend to political and other similar influences.

## ► Categories of academic books

Although the quality of academic books is excellent, there are some points that should be considered before deciding to cite them as sources. Academic books can be broadly categorized as those that can be described as *specialized books*, and those that can be described as *general textbooks*.

### Specialized books

Books in this category present a detailed treatment of a subject that represents a limited area of a discipline. They might, for example, present a discussion of research and theory in visual perception, an in-depth discussion of some specific disorder such as depression, or a treatise on strength of effect in statistics. Such books are written for a readership that includes other experts in the area, and they are often used as textbooks at more advanced levels of study. The value of books of this type is that they present an in-depth and detailed discussion, including analysis, evaluation, and critical comment. Therefore, *specialized books are excellent sources.*

### General textbooks

Books that can be described as general textbooks are of excellent quality. However, by definition, they are written at a *generalist* rather than a *specialist* level. This is particularly so for textbooks that are written for use by undergraduate students. Because such books cover a wide area, only a limited discussion of any topic is possible. Consequently, they do not cover material in any depth or detail. Moreover, they are not intended to present a thesis, or to reach a conclusion on any specific topic. Rather, they provide only an overview of the work of others. Therefore, *in effect general textbooks are secondary sources.* Although, then, useful for providing an overview of an area, *books in this category are of no value as sources that could be cited in an academic paper.*

## ► Conference proceedings

Sometimes the proceedings of an academic conference are published in the form of abstracts. Obviously, in this case the work reported cannot be evaluated, as such an evaluation would be on the basis of only an abstract. Therefore, *conference proceedings published in the form of abstracts are of little or no value as a source*. In other instances papers presented are published in full. When this is done the work can be evaluated in the same way in which would be a journal article. Such papers, therefore, may be cited as a source. A point to note, however, is that there might have been no quality control exercised by the organizers of the conference. Moreover, if the material presented is of value it is likely that the author(s) will subsequently publish it as a refereed journal article. When this is so, the subsequently published journal article should be used as a source rather than the conference proceedings.

## ▶ Approach to evaluation

There are two levels of evaluation of sources: *face evaluation* and *specific evaluation*. Face evaluation involves distinguishing – at face value – material that is suitable for academic purposes from that which is not. Specific evaluation involves distinguishing material that is suitable for a particular purpose from that which is not.

## Face evaluation

Usually, face evaluation of sources is quite straightforward. It involves consideration of the nature of the source, the likelihood of an objective and balanced approach, and the vintage of the source.

### Nature of source
Although some other publications can also be valuable for specific purposes, usually the sources that are suitable for use in academic papers are:

- academic journal articles, and
- specialized academic books.

The suitability of other sources is also usually identified with no difficulty. Although often of excellent quality, popular non-fiction works provide only summaries of material, and do not adopt the analytical and critical approach that is needed for academic purposes. Consequently, such publications are of no value. For similar reasons, an encyclopedia is of no value. Dictionaries are of value only for checking the meaning of words and spelling. A point to note is that definitions of concepts provided in dictionaries, including specialized psychology dictionaries, are usually not suitable for use in academic papers. Of course, with rare exception, works of fiction, newspapers, and magazines are of no value.

## Balanced approach

An important consideration when evaluating a possible source is whether or not it is likely to present an objective and balanced discussion of the subject matter. One factor that will influence this is the motivation for publishing.

Some material is published simply to persuade people to favour a political party, or to buy some product. Other material is published to promote the author's view on some subject. For instance, an author might publish a book on child rearing to promote his or her view on how this should be done. Clearly, such publications will be biased in favour of the political party or product involved, or in favour of the author's views on the subject.

The motivation for publishing magazines and newspapers is, of course, monetary gain. Publications in this category, therefore, are unlikely to present views or opinions that are contrary to those of their prospective purchasers. Moreover, it is not uncommon for the content of magazines and newspapers to be influenced by editors' views and those of political parties, among other groups. There is, therefore, a real possibility of bias in such publications.

By comparison, government publications, such as census data and reports of investigations of aircraft accidents, are produced to make information and ideas publicly available. Publications of this type can usually be taken to be objective, balanced, and accurate. On the other hand, some government publications might not be so neutral. For example, it is in the interests of the authors of a report on the completion of a project, and in the interests of the politicians involved, to present a favourable impression. This can also apply to some government investigations, particularly when politicians are involved. Some government publications are, of course, clearly intended to influence public attitude. An obvious example is propaganda (often presented as "information") in time of armed conflict. The conflict in Iraq presents excellent examples of this. Other examples include material motivating people to avoid the risk of contracting diseases such as AIDS, or to conserve energy. Such publications will, naturally, favour the point of view of the government.

Academics are not paid for journal articles. Although they receive royalties for books, these are minimal and do not adequately compensate authors for the considerable time and effort they put into writing a book. The authors of specialized academic books, therefore, do not publish for monetary gain. Rather, they are motivated by the desire to make their research findings and ideas publicly available, and by a sense of achievement. Moreover, it is of no benefit to academics to pursue any particular political or popular viewpoint. Academic articles and books, therefore, are unlikely to be biased.

*Unintentional bias. Personal views, chap. 1*

*Objectivity. Values, chap. 2*

At face value, then, it can usually be assumed that academic publications will present an objective and balanced approach. This is also the case for most government publications, although some need to be considered with caution. By comparison, material published by organizations such as political parties, trade unions, or other groups promoting some particular cause is likely to be biased. The identity of the publisher, and sometimes the author, can often indicate the possibility of an approach that is not objective and balanced.

## Vintage

As a general rule, recently published sources are preferable to those that are older. New publications usually include the most recent (at time of writing) information and ideas. By comparison, in some instances, older publications might include information or ideas that have been superseded. On the other hand, new publications sometimes omit material that, although it might be old, is still relevant. For example, some books on developmental psychology omit the early work of Vygotsky. In some instances, therefore, the vintage of a publication is important, but often it is not.

A point to note here is that, because of the time needed to publish a book, recent material published in journals is often not included in them. This is potentially more of a problem for books that have not been recently published.

## New information and ideas

**Information and ideas**, chap. 1

New information and ideas are continually being published in one form or other. Sometimes new information or a new idea results in completely discarding previously held views. Notable examples are the idea proposed by Copernicus that the Earth revolves around the Sun, Einstein's theory of relativity, and Freud's psychoanalytic theory. Such instances, however, are rare: Most human knowledge results from an accumulation of relatively minor discoveries. Of the vast volume of material that is published, rarely does some new information or a new idea have a dramatic effect on human understanding of the world. The vast majority of academic articles and books are based on existing ideas and findings, adding only little that is new. With very rare exception, any one journal article or book adds little in any field of endeavour; rather, it adds just one small brick to the structure. On the other hand, new findings in a specific area often lead to important ideas that, although not revolutionary, do need to be considered.

The value of an article or book, therefore, should not be discredited purely on the basis of its age. At the same time, it is not wise to rely only on older sources.

There are, of course, instances when only the latest edition of a publication can be used. It might be important, for example, to refer to the most recent data in some area of research. This is also so in the case of manuals such as the *Diagnostic and Statistical Manual of Mental Disorders*, or the *International Classification of Diseases and Related Health Problems*. New editions of such publications incorporate important revisions of information and ideas.

On the other hand, a point that is often overlooked is that information and ideas can be "too new". When new information and ideas are published they are subject to the critical appraisal of those working in the field. Not infrequently, flaws subsequently become apparent. For example, it is not unknown for researchers to find that they are unable to replicate reported findings, or to suggest alternative explanations. Evaluation of new information and ideas takes time. Therefore, new information and ideas, especially if they seem to be particularly surprising, should always be treated with some caution.

## Specific evaluation

Specific evaluation of sources involves a more detailed consideration. One approach to this task is to consider a potential source at two levels of detail, in each of which the author's specific needs and the quality of the source are considered. An *initial evaluation*, in terms of needs and quality, will suggest whether or not the source is likely to be suitable: A *detailed evaluation* will indicate whether or not it is.

### Initial evaluation

At the initial level, the potential suitability of a source is assessed before reading it. This initial evaluation can be made on the basis of the source's relevance to an author's needs and its likely quality.

*Needs*

The first consideration is whether or not the source is suitable for the author's particular needs. For example, the author might be looking for information such as a description of the procedure followed in an experiment, or data such as statistics. Alternatively, the author might be looking for an overview of an area, a description of a model, a critical evaluation of a theory, or a practical application of a theory. Put simply, the author might be looking for information, ideas, or both.

Obviously, the title of a book or journal article should give at least a general idea of the subject matter. An examination of the table of contents and the index of a book allows for a better assessment. In the case of a journal article, an initial evaluation of its contents can be made using the abstract (or summary) of the article.

*Quality*

The second consideration is whether or not the source is of good quality. An initial judgement can be made on the basis of the author, and the reference list or bibliography of an article or book.

A tentative judgement of quality can be based on whether or not the author is likely to be knowledgeable in the area. In academic journal articles and books it can be assumed that the author is so knowledgeable. However, the author's expertise in the particular area might need to be considered. For example, those who have carried out much research in a particular area can be expected to be experts in that area. Such experts can usually be identified on the basis of frequent reference to their work in the literature. Some authors, therefore, are recognized authorities, and so have a high standing in a particular area. Their work, then, tends to be more highly regarded than is that of lesser-known authors, although this is not necessarily a valid judgement.

A point that beginning students need to understand is that the authors of general and introductory textbooks typically present an overview of a large area in a discipline. Such authors will have expertise in one or more of the sub-areas covered, but they will not be expert in all.

Another indication of the quality of a publication is the material cited in support of information and ideas presented. An academic publication will be accompanied by a reference list or bibliography listing the sources to which reference has been made. For a journal article this will be relatively short, but for a book the reference list or bibliography will usually be lengthy. The nature of the sources cited by an author also gives some indication of the likely quality of the work. An exception to this is that books in the form of manuals, such as instruction and style manuals, often have no or relatively short reference lists or bibliographies.

## Detailed evaluation

A detailed evaluation requires careful reading and consideration of the content of an article or book. Only on this basis can an informed decision be made on whether or not the material is suitable for citing as a source.

*Needs*

Although initial evaluation may suggest that an article or book is potentially useful as a source, reading it might indicate that it is not. For example, a description of a theory might not be sufficiently detailed, or the data reported might not be in sufficient detail.

*Quality*

Again, although initial evaluation may suggest that the work is of good quality, detailed reading might indicate that it is not. A number of indicators of quality should be considered.

ACCURACY AND VALIDITY

For a source to be of any value, the information included in it must be accurate and the ideas presented must be valid. Assessing the accuracy and validity of information and ideas presented requires careful consideration of their source.

Accuracy, chap. 2

Sometimes an author will merely present information or an idea and cite the source(s). In this case, the accuracy of that information, or the validity of the idea, can only be assessed on the basis of the apparent quality of the source(s) cited. Obviously, such sources cannot be evaluated themselves without reading them. On the other hand, sometimes the quality of a cited source can be questioned because of evident inconsistencies with other sources. This is likely to become apparent, because anyone working on a paper will have read a number of sources in the area.

Basis of assertion, chap. 1

Basis of assertion by others, chap. 6

Consistency, however, does not necessarily mean that the information or idea is accurate or valid. It is possible for a number of authors to agree on something that is not accurate or valid. For example, a number of authors have proposed similar ideas on the famous Bermuda Triangle, although these are not necessarily valid. A recent example is the wide reporting in the media that the American flag draped over the head of a statue of Saddam Hussein, before it was pulled down, was retrieved from the Pentagon on 11 September. It was not. An example in psychology is that a number of authors have given similar descriptions of the work of Donders in 1869. Reference to Donders' original paper, which was reprinted in 1969, shows that the common descriptions of his work are not entirely accurate.

In other instances the author will cite information and ideas derived from an experiment or study that the author is reporting. When this is the case, the accuracy and validity of the information or ideas can be assessed on the basis of careful and analytical consideration of the experiment or study involved.

REASONING

The author's reasoning should be readily apparent: Information and ideas should be presented in a coherent sequence that leads logically to the author's thesis or conclusion. In addition, the discussion should be internally consistent, and should not include broad, sweeping statements, or ambiguities.

Reasoning, chap. 1

Reasoning, chap. 6

OBJECTIVITY AND BALANCE

Any good source will present an objective and balanced discussion of the subject. An author's task is to weigh the evidence, and to reach a conclusion. Omission of some information or ideas, especially if they are counter to the author's apparent views, is indicative of lack of balance. Similarly, lack of objectivity and balance is evident when an author readily accepts some evidence, but is harshly critical of other evidence that is contrary to the

A reasoned and balanced argument, chap. 1

Objectivity. Values, chap. 2

**Objectivity**, chap. 12
author's apparent views. In addition, lack of objectivity and balance is indicated by broad, sweeping assertions that are often unsupported.

**Value judgements**, chaps 16 and 20
Such indications of lack of objectivity and balance should become evident when working on a paper. Anyone writing a paper will have read numerous sources in the area, and so will detect obviously omitted information or ideas, or the absence of critical comments.

LANGUAGE

Authors of scholarly papers or books will use simple, neutral language. Unnecessarily obscure words or convoluted sentences are used only by authors who are trying to impress, when the content is of little value. Emotive language is indicative of bias. Potential sources that suffer from such flaws are of dubious value, and should not be cited.

ANALYTICAL AND CRITICAL THINKING

**Critical thinking**, chap. 1
An important indication of the quality of an article or book is evidence of analytical and critical thinking. Nothing is perfect. For example, inevitably there are differences in the outcomes of research, sometimes there are alternative explanations of research findings, and often there are differences of opinion on the validity of a particular theory. In addition, there can be flaws in research design or reasoning. A knowledgeable author will be aware of this and will, for example, comment on such differences or suggest alternative explanations. *A source in which the author merely reports what others have found or suggested, is of little value.*

WRITING

chaps. 2 and 3
Any article or book that is likely to be of value as a source in an academic paper, will be well written. It will be well organized; sentences and paragraphs will be well structured; and the article or book will be written in a formal, scholarly style. Colloquialisms will not be found, and there will not be errors in the use of words, grammar, punctuation, or spelling. Flaws in such areas are indicative of lack of ability or carelessness, and cast doubts on the author's credibility. Such flaws will not, of course, be found in the academic literature. No editor would accept for publication a manuscript that was poorly written.

## ▶ Electronic sources

Electronic sources include material available via the Internet, published on CD-ROM, produced on videotape and film, and broadcast on television or radio. Students may well want to cite material available via the Internet, or perhaps published on CD-ROM, but they are unlikely to cite material from the remaining media. A CD-ROM is virtually a book, and so should be evaluated in the same way as would be a book. Therefore, only evaluation of material available via the Internet is discussed here.

## Permanence

Any source cited in an academic paper must be permanently and publicly available. A reader should be able to consult any source cited, to evaluate it, to verify the accuracy of any information or idea referred to, or to find additional information. A point that is important to understand is that, at any time, sites on the Web can be changed, the Uniform Resource Locator (URL) can be changed, or they can disappear completely and permanently. This means that a site that is cited as a source today might change tomorrow, or vanish. Citing an on-line source, therefore, requires careful consideration. In particular, *only sources that can be expected to continue to be available should be cited*.

## ▶ Material available via the Internet

A vast volume of material is readily available via the Internet, and there is a misguided perception that this is the most recent, and therefore the best. Moreover, students can often gain access to material via the Internet more easily than they can from a library. For these reasons, there is a tendency for students to want to use the Internet for sources when working on a paper. It is, therefore, particularly important to understand that *material available via the Internet must be evaluated very carefully*.

## Availability

A point that needs to be understood is that material available via the Internet falls into two categories: that which is publicly available, and that which is not. Confusing this issue is the common acceptance of the terms *Internet*, the *World Wide Web* (commonly referred to as the *Web*), and *on line* as being synonymous. Not all sites to which access can be gained via the Internet are available to everyone. It is important to understand that access to certain materials is restricted to those who have been granted it. In particular, a library must pay a substantial fee for access on line to electronic versions of journals published also in print. No institution, therefore, has on-line access to all of the possible material. Moreover, individuals have access to such material only if granted it by the institution involved.

## On-line journals

There are some journals that are published only on line, and the number so available is likely to increase in the future. This is so because of increases in the cost of publishing, and so the cost to libraries of subscribing to journals in print. At present, some on-line only journals can be described as "in-house" publications. Such journals are published by some organization, or group within it, on the organization's website. Most commonly, at present, on-line journals that are suitable for use as sources are duplicates of print versions.

## Other on-line sources

On-line sources that could potentially be used as sources include sites established by government departments or other reputable institutions. Material available on these sites might include, for example, statistics or reports of investigations. Other material that is published on line must be treated with great caution.

## Educational material

Various institutions, and individuals within institutions, publish material on line for educational purposes. This might, for example, be included on a site for a particular course at a university. For instance, an academic might write a summary of some theory and put this on a site for the benefit of students who are studying a particular course. Material of this type is the equivalent of printed notes that would be given to students in class. Usually such material is in brief summary form, and does not provide an in-depth discussion. Moreover, it is nether publicly nor permanently available. *Educational material of this type, therefore, is not suitable for use as a source in an academic paper.*

## Abstracts

Some databases provide abstracts of journal articles on line. Obviously, an author's work cannot be evaluated only on the basis of an abstract. Rarely, then, is an abstract of any value as a source. *As a general principle, on-line abstracts should not be cited as a source.*

## ▶ Quality control

It is important to recognize that anyone can set up a website, with little difficulty and virtually no cost. Therefore, *virtually anyone can publish anything on the World Wide Web*, and there is no quality control of any kind on most material.

For journals available via the Internet, which are electronic versions of the same journal published in print, the same assessment of quality control is applicable to both media. Obviously, if the journal uses a peer review process, and the electronic version is simply a copy of the print version, then the electronic version has been peer reviewed. On the other hand, for journals that are published only in electronic form (i.e., on-line only journals), whether or not a peer review process is used by the journal can only be assessed on the same basis as it would be for a journal published in print. Some journals published only in electronic form are peer reviewed while some are not.

*Other material that is publicly available via the Internet must be treated with great caution.* Some sites are of excellent quality. For example, sites controlled by government departments usually fall into this category. However, care is needed with material published on line by governments for some purposes, such as propaganda, and with sites controlled by governments in some countries.

Sites controlled by reputable organizations such as universities or research institutions are usually of good quality. However, whether or not such organizations exercise any quality control over material published on their sites by individuals is questionable. Typically, there is no quality control.

## ▶ Evaluating material available via the Internet

Evaluation of material published by electronic means involves the same procedures and considerations that are applicable to printed material. A face evaluation is followed by specific evaluation; which, in turn, involves an initial evaluation followed by a detailed evaluation. However, more care must be taken with the evaluation of sources available on line. In particular, *it is important to treat material that is publicly available with considerable caution, and to evaluate it very carefully.* Although some material published on the Web is of excellent quality, much is of no use to anyone.

### Face evaluation

As for printed material, the face evaluation of sources for an academic paper is usually quite straightforward. Face evaluation of material available via the

Internet involves consideration of the nature of the source, the likelihood of a balanced approach, and the vintage of the source.

## Nature of source

Although some other material can be valuable for specific purposes, in general, suitable sources are:

- on-line refereed journals,
- sites established by government departments, and
- sites established by reputable institutions such as universities.

There are, of course, other sites that might be of some value, but it is impossible to group them under any particular category, and to suggest that any site in a particular category is suitable.

## Balanced approach

A particularly important consideration, when evaluating material available via the Internet, is the reason for publishing. This is particularly so for material that is publicly available. The motivations for publishing material on the Web are essentially the same as those for publishing in print. However, because of the ease of publication, and virtual absence of cost, the Web is an attractive avenue for publication of material that would not be accepted by a reputable publishing house. It is, therefore, particularly important to consider the possible motives for the publishing of any material before considering it as a source.

## Vintage

One of the supposed advantages of the Internet is that it makes the most recently available information and ideas readily and virtually instantly accessible. In some instances this is true, but generally it is not. Academics and other researchers usually make new information and ideas publicly available either by presenting a paper at a conference or by publishing a journal article. Moreover, at present, most on-line journals are duplications of journals published in print, and so will become available at about the same time as the print version. In any event, the same considerations with regard to the vintage of material published in print are applicable to material published in electronic form. Usually, then, the supposed recent vintage of material that is available via the Internet is of no particular importance. On the other hand, there can be exceptions; such as, for example, when recent statistics published by a government department are needed.

## Specific evaluation

As with printed material, specific evaluation of sources involves detailed consideration, and the factors to be considered are essentially the same. There are, however, some differences.

### Initial evaluation

In the same way that an initial assessment is made of print material, the initial evaluation of material available via the Internet involves consideration of the author's needs and the likely quality of the material. Initial evaluation of sources available via the Internet, therefore, involves the same considerations as are applicable to sources published in print. However, when considering an on-line source, particular attention should be paid to the author.

In the academic literature the author's qualifications can usually be taken for granted, but this is not so for authors of material on the World Wide Web. Authors may, or may not, show academic qualifications after their name. Even if they do, there is no certainty that these authors have those qualifications, or that they have been awarded by a reputable institution. It is, therefore, often very difficult, and sometimes impossible, to assess the qualifications of the author of material on the Web.

Often, for publications on the Web, no author's affiliation is given. Sometimes it is apparent. For example, the author of material on a website controlled by some institution can be presumed to be affiliated with that institution. Affiliation with a reputable institution can indicate that the author is appropriately qualified. However, whether or not the institution exercises any quality control over material published on its site cannot be determined: Typically, there is no such control.

### Detailed evaluation

As with print material, detailed evaluation requires careful reading and consideration of the content of the article or paper. The considerations involved in arriving at a judgement when making a detailed evaluation of material available via the Internet are the same as those for printed material.

# 6 Citing Sources

In academic books and journal articles, and often in other material, authors frequently refer the reader to the *source* of some information or idea. Most commonly, this is described as a *reference*. Technically, the *source* is the material to which reference is made (usually a journal article or a book), and referring the reader to the source is the *reference*. However, the terms "reference" and "source" are often used interchangeably and, for practical purposes, they may be regarded as being synonymous. To confuse matters further, referring to a source in this way is usually referred to as *citing* a source. Sometimes, therefore, referring to a source is described as a *citation*.

When you write papers as a student you will similarly find it necessary to refer the reader to various sources. Moreover, in your future career you can expect that you will find it necessary to write papers that are similar in nature, and in which it is necessary to cite sources. It is important, therefore, for you to understand the reasons for citing sources, and to know how to cite them.

## ▶ Availability

Before discussing the citing of sources, however, an important point to understand is that a reader should be able to consult any source cited to evaluate it, to verify the accuracy of any information or idea referred to, or to find additional information. It follows that, *as a general principle unpublished works should not be cited*. There can, however, be some exceptions. In particular, it is acceptable to cite an unpublished thesis (or dissertation). A copy of a thesis is held in the library of the institution in which it was written. Therefore, although perhaps with some difficulty, it is possible to gain access to it. However, a point to consider is that, although it is likely, there is no guarantee that the thesis was passed by the examiners. The work involved, therefore, is not guaranteed to be of good quality. It is also possible that in some research it might be desirable or necessary to refer to an unpublished document such as a personal letter or a diary. Finally, it is acceptable to cite a personal communication, such as from an academic in some institution.

Lecture notes or summaries of material given to students by academics in the course of their studies are unpublished, regardless of the media involved. These should *never* be cited as a source.

## ▶ Sources

The sources cited in a paper typically include journal articles, books, and sometimes material published on the Internet. To avoid unnecessary complexity, the following discussion is restricted to these sources. However, regardless of the nature of the source, the principles discussed are applicable.

Examples of the citing of other sources such as manuals, legislation, newspaper articles, material published by a group or organization, and material with no author name, are given in Appendix B. Also, examples of necessary variations due to, for instance, duplication of authors' names, are included in this appendix.

## ▶ Author–date system

With rare exception (such as the method used by the military), there are two commonly used methods of referring to, or citing, sources. One method is to insert numbers as superscripts at the appropriate point in the text and to give brief details of the source in a footnote. The other method is the *author–date system*, which is used in psychology and many other disciplines.

The author–date system of citing sources is very simple. When a reference is required, the *author's surname (family name) and the year of the publication* of the source are given. The author's Christian or given name(s) and the title of the article or book are not included in a reference. Authors' initials are included only when necessary to distinguish between authors who have the same surname. As an example, if you wanted to refer to an article published by Skinner in 1938, you could simply write, "Skinner (1938)". Similarly, you could refer to a book written by Brebner and Welford, which was published in 1980, by writing, "Brebner and Welford (1980)". Such a reference could take the form, for example, "Greenway (2002) suggested that . . .", or "It has been suggested that . . . (Greenway, 2002)".

Both the author's name (or authors' names) and year of publication of the article or book are given to allow the source cited in the text to be related to the publication details of that source given in the reference list. It is important to understand that Moore (2001) and Moore (2002) are different sources. Obviously, Maguire (2002) and Maguire and Smyth (2002) are different sources, as are Patrick and Fitzmichael (2003) and Fitzmichael and Patrick (2003).

### Edited book

An edited book comprises a number of chapters written by different authors, usually including one or more chapters written by the editor. If you cite a chapter from such a book as a source, you must give the name of the author of that chapter, not the editor – unless, of course, the author of the chapter is the editor. For instance, if a book (published in 2002) were edited by O'Brien and the chapter to which you are referring were written by Aubrey, you would cite this as "Aubrey (2002) argues . . .". Moreover, "Aubrey, J. (2002)" would appear in the reference list, together with the publication details of the edited book.

chap. 8
Appendix C

## Republished book

A book can be republished, perhaps more than once, and sometimes many years after the original publication. In this case, the year of publication of the book consulted is given. If there is some particular reason for doing so, when first reference is made to the source an appropriate comment may be made. For instance, it might be appropriate to write something like, "In his book, first published in 1902, Goldspink (1999) suggested . . .". However, this would be rare. A point to note is that page numbers in a republished book might differ from those in the original.

## Reprint

A book that is reprinted is not republished. Publishers reprint a book when it is out of stock and new copies are needed. The date of reprint, therefore, should be ignored.

## Edition

In contrast with a reprint, a new edition is an altered version of the book. Some material will have been changed and probably some content deleted and/or added. It is, therefore, important to distinguish between editions of a book. The date of publication of the edition consulted must, therefore, be given when citing the book, and both this and the edition number must be given in the reference list.

## Republished article

An unusual situation arises when a classic article is republished. In this case, when citing the source in a paper both years are given, as in, for example, "Donders (1869/1969)"; but only the year of publication of the source that you read (i.e., the article as republished) is included in the reference list. In this example, "Donders. F. C. (1969)" would appear in the reference list. However, a note would be included indicating that the original article was published in 1869.

## Publications in the same year

If two or more sources published by the same author in the same year are cited, an alphabetical character is added to distinguish between the sources, as in, for example, Stephens (2001a) and Stephens (2001b). Obviously, these alphabetical characters also appear in the reference list, as in, for example, Stephens, J. (2001a) and Stephens, J. (2001b).

## Multiple authors

The following notes provide the basic requirements for citing sources when multiple authors are involved. However, there are some differences when authors' names are duplicated in more than one source cited in a paper. Examples of the citing of sources involving multiple authors are given in Appendix B.

### Two authors
When an article or a book is written by two authors, *both authors must be named each time the source is cited*. For instance, an article written by Bond and Twopenny, published in 2003, would be cited each time as:

Bond and Twopenny (2003)

### Three to five authors[2]
If a source has three to five authors, *all authors' names are given when the source is first cited*, as in, for example:

Secombe, Sellers, and Milligan (1968)

Thereafter, the source is cited as, for example:

Secombe et al. (1968)

This use of "et al." is common. The Latin word *et* means *and*, and *al.* is an abbreviation of the Latin word *alii*, meaning "others". Therefore, "Secombe et al." means "Secombe and others". Notice that, because it is a complete word, "et" is not followed by a full stop; but, because it is an abbreviation, "al." is followed by a full stop. Also, note that "et al." is not typed in italics (as it is in some editorial styles).

---

[2] This differs from entries in the reference list, in which "et al." is used if there are more than six authors.

### Six or more authors

In the rare instance when there are six or more authors, only the first author's name, followed by "et al.", is used for the first and all subsequent citations. Obviously it would be disruptive to the text to include a long list of authors' names.

## Possessive case

Often, when referring to sources the possessive case must be used. For instance, when referring to earlier findings in an experiment carried out by Bigglesworth in 1941, the reference would be cited as:

> Bigglesworth's (1941) findings suggest . . .

When two or more authors are involved, the apostrophe is added only to the second, or last, author's name, as in, for example:

> Bigglesworth and Lacy's (1942) findings suggest . . .

or

> Shiraz, Grenache, and Pinot's (2004) findings suggest that . . .

After the first citation, sources written by three or more authors are referred to using only the first author's name, followed by "et al." It is therefore tempting to refer to such a source in the possessive case, after the first citation, as:

> Shiraz et al.'s (2004) findings suggest that . . .

However, *this is incorrect.* As already pointed out, *al.* is the abbreviation of the Latin *alii* (meaning "others") and there is no possessive apostrophe in Latin. Such a source can only be referred to in the possessive case by citing it in full – as, for example:

> Shiraz, Grenache, and Pinot's (2004) findings suggest that . . .

> The Shiraz, Grenache, and Pinot (2004) findings suggest that . . .

> The findings of Shiraz, Grenache, and Pinot (2004) suggest that . . .

> The findings of Shiraz and his colleagues (2004) suggest that . . .

or by citing it using "et al." as in, for example:

> The Shiraz et al. (2004) findings suggest that . . .

> The findings of Shiraz et al. (2004) suggest that. . . .

## Page numbers

When referring the reader to *journal articles* in print (but not quoting) there is usually no need to give page numbers. Typically, journal articles are quite short. Moreover, the nature of the material to which reference is made will indicate the relevant section of the article. For example, the reader would expect information relevant to the procedure adopted in an experiment to be in the Method section of a research report. It should, therefore, be possible to find this information with little difficulty. On the other hand, *if the article is long, page numbers should be given*.

In contrast with journal articles, books are very long, and so finding material in a book is difficult. Therefore, *when referring the reader to a book, the page number(s) should be given* to allow the reader to find the relevant material to which the author has referred. A reference to a book, therefore, would be given as, for example:

> Holmes and Watson (1902, p. 72)

or

> Aubrey and Maturin (1815, pp. 84–87)

*Note*: If an author makes a point at several places in a book there is no need to give every page number involved.

### Exceptions
An exception to this arises when reference is made to an entire book. For example, in the following there is no need to give page numbers:

> Martin (1962) provides a very good cover of the history of psychology.

Similarly, if reference is made to an entire chapter of a book, it may be cited as, for example:

> Sinatra (1959, chap. 2) argues . . .

### Internet material
Similar reasoning is applicable when referring the reader to material available via the Internet. If the article is short, a reader can be expected to be able to find the material referred to with relative ease. In the case of a longer article, however, the reader will need more detail.

If the source is stored in PDF format, and page numbers are available, they should be given as they would be for a printed source. When there are no page numbers there may be paragraph numbers, or the paragraphs can be counted. In this case, the paragraph number is used in lieu of a page number, using the abbreviation "para." As an example, you could refer the reader to a specific paragraph in a journal article by writing:

> Lloyd (2002, para. 15) suggests . . .

When there are no page or paragraph numbers, but there are headings, the reader should be directed to a paragraph under the relevant heading as, for example:

> Webber (2003, Results section, para. 5) noted that . . .

## ► Secondary sources

Critical
thinking,
chap. 1

Sometimes, *but rarely*, you might want to refer the reader to *a source that you have not read*. This is referred to as a *secondary reference*. You might like to think of this as "citing second-hand information". Perhaps the best way to help you to understand secondary sources is to give an example.

Assume that you have read a book written by the well-known Latin scholar Secundus, which was published in 2001. In this book you noted that Secundus cited an article written by Primus (another equally well-known Latin scholar) that was published in 1902. You might, for example, notice that Secundus (2001) cited Primus (1902) in support of an assertion that the study of Latin helps students to understand English grammar and the derivation of many words in the English language. You want to make this point in a paper that you are writing, and you want to cite a source to support your assertion. *Because you have not read the Primus (1902) article you cannot cite it*. Moreover, in spite of a vigorous search, you have been unable to find a copy of the Primus article. Your only option, then, would be to cite Primus by means of a secondary reference. You could do this in the form of, for example:

> Studying Latin helps students to understand English grammar and the derivation of many words in the English language (Primus, as cited in Secundus, 2001, p. 37).

or

> Primus (cited in Secundus, 2001, p. 37) suggests that the study of Latin helps students to understand English grammar and the derivation of many words in the English language.

Notice that, in these examples, it is clear that the *primary source* of the idea is Primus, and that you have cited Primus on the basis of reading Secundus – not Primus. You have read the Secundus (2001) book, but not the Primus (1902) article. Primus (1902), then, is the *primary source*, and you are citing Primus from the Secundus (2001) book, which is the *secondary source*. For this reason *the date of the Primus article is not included in the reference*.

Although it is rare, sometimes you might want to emphasize the point that the original information is very old. In this case, you could write something like:

> As early as 1902, Primus (cited in Secundus, 2001, p. 37) suggested that the study of Latin helps students to understand English grammar and the derivation of many words in the English language.

A point to note is that, because you have not cited it directly, you *do not include the publication details of the Primus (1902) article in your reference list*. On the other hand, because it is the source in which you found the idea, you will have to include the publication details of the Secundus (2001) book in your reference list.

chap. 8

## Multiple secondary sources

It is *not acceptable* to cite multiple secondary sources. For example, it is not acceptable to cite a number of secondary sources as in:

> Seagoon (1975), Eccles (1980), and Bluebottle (1992) (all cited in Moriarty, 2001) have found . . .

If you want to make a point such as that there are several findings supporting something, write, for example:

> Moriarty (2001) cites several studies in which it has been found that . . .

Similarly, *it is not acceptable* to cite a secondary source from several sources. It is not acceptable to write, for example:

> (Erikson, as cited in Sheldon & Kasser, 2001; and Vaillant, 2002)

## ▶ Purpose

Citing a source (i.e., a reference) is sometimes done simply to draw the reader's attention to some idea, or to an article or book. For instance, an author might comment that Pagano (1994) provides a useful discussion of basic statistics, or that Fiske and Taylor (1991) give a good coverage of social cognition. More commonly, however, sources are cited for one or more of the following reasons:

- to give the source of a quotation,
- to acknowledge some idea or work, or
- to support some statement of fact or opinion.

## Quotations

chap. 7

Obviously, the source of any quotations must be given. This is discussed, together with the use of quotations, in chapter 7.

## Acknowledgement

**Plagiarism**
and
**Academic
dishonesty**,
chap. 4

You must always acknowledge the work or ideas of other authors. Imagine that, with considerable effort, you had solved some important problem, and that you had told someone the solution. If that person then published your solution, without acknowledging that it was you who solved the problem, you would justifiably be annoyed. In effect, that person would have stolen your idea. This would be both dishonest and unethical. It is appropriate, then, that you should acknowledge the work and ideas of others.

## Support

Most commonly, sources are cited to support some assertion; that is, to provide supporting evidence. The problem is deciding when such support is needed.

If you are making a statement that you could reasonably expect an intelligent reader to believe, there is no need to provide supporting evidence. For instance, if you were to comment that very young children are awkward or clumsy when performing motor skills such as walking or running, a reader could reasonably be expected to accept the validity of this statement. There is, then, no need to provide supporting evidence.

The problem for the inexperienced is to decide when a reader could reasonably be expected to accept some point, or might be likely to question it. There is no simple solution to this problem. The best approach is to put yourself in the reader's position, and to ask yourself whether you would be willing to accept the assertion without supporting evidence being provided; if you would not, then you must cite some source as evidence. Sometimes you will be uncertain. *When in doubt, cite a source.* You will not be criticized for citing a source when one might not be needed, but you will be criticized for not citing a source if one is needed.

Often you will want to make a statement, or an assertion, that might not be readily accepted. If, for example, you were to suggest that about 6% of ordinary children are abnormally clumsy, the reader might well question this claim. When it is possible that a statement or assertion might be questioned, you need to provide evidence to convince the reader (i.e., support for your statement or assertion). One way of doing this is to cite a source. In the example given, you could cite Brenner and Gillman (1966), who found that

6.9% of a sample of school children were abnormally clumsy. To do this, you could, for example, write something like:

> Brenner and Gillman's (1966) findings suggest that about 6% of ordinary children could be described as being abnormally clumsy.

Citing a source in this way shows that your statement or assertion is based on some evidence, which in this case is the findings of the Brenner and Gillman (1966) study.

## Multiple references

Often, citing a single source in support of some point is all that is required. On the other hand, there are instances when it will be necessary to cite several sources. If you think that a particular point is important, and that it might be questioned even if supported by a single source, then it is wise to cite several to add strength to your assertion. In such a situation there is no answer to the question of how many sources should be cited, but the number will not be large. If you can cite a large number of sources in support of some point, the finding or idea involved must have been widely replicated, or the idea must be widely shared. In this case, the best approach is to comment that the finding is common, or the idea generally accepted, and to cite two or three sources as examples. For instance, if you wanted to argue that often there is a difference between the performance and verbal intelligence scores of clumsy children, you could write something like:

> A common finding is that the performance intelligence scores of clumsy children are lower than those of their verbal intelligence (e.g., Gordon, 1969; Gubbay, Ellis, Walton, & Court, 1966; Wilson, 1974).

Again, the problem for the inexperienced is to decide when more than one reference to a single source is required, and again there is no simple solution. The best approach is similar to that recommended for deciding when a reference is required. Put yourself in the reader's position, and ask yourself whether you would be willing to accept the author's statement, even though it is supported by the citing of a source. Does the statement seem to be surprising, or unlikely? If you think that you would be unwilling to accept the assertion, or that you are in doubt, then it would be wise to cite more than a single source in support of it if you are to convince the reader.

Returning to the example of prevalence of clumsiness in children, if an author suggested that about 6% of ordinary children are abnormally clumsy, and cited Brenner and Gillman (1966) in support, would you be convinced? Do you think that a prevalence of about 6% is likely? Are you just unsure? In this case, the author's claim would be more likely to be accepted if it were supported by more than a single source. The author could cite as additional support the finding of a prevalence of 5.6% by Gubbay (1975) and of 5.7% by Søvik and Mæland (1987). This could be done by writing something like:

> On the basis of the findings of Brenner and Gillman (1966), Gubbay (1975), and Søvik and Mæland (1987), the best estimate is that about 6% of ordinary school children are abnormally clumsy.

Given a total of three separate studies, all of which reported a prevalence of about 6%, would you be convinced that about 6% of ordinary school children could be described as being abnormally clumsy? You might well still be in doubt, but it is clear that you would be more convinced if three sources were cited in support of this claim than if only one were cited.

## ▶ Basis of assertions by others

If you are simply acknowledging the source of some information or idea, you might write something like:

> One theory of cognitive development is provided by Piaget (1957).

As another example, you might comment that:

> Bennet (2000) argued that the level of emotional intelligence in an individual is determined solely by hereditary factors.

More commonly, you will be citing a source in support of some assertion. You might, for example, write something like:

> About 6% of ordinary school children are clumsy (Smyth, 1987).

The problem here is that the reader of your paper is likely to ask, "On what basis did Smyth make this assertion, or reach this conclusion?" and "Why should I believe this figure?" In some instances, then, it is not satisfactory simply to cite a source.

Obviously, before you cite a source in support of some assertion, you need to be convinced of its validity. *Just because another author has made an assertion, this does not necessarily mean that it is valid.* For example, you might have read an article by Bush (2003) in which he claimed that Iraq has weapons of mass destruction, and another by Blair (2003) in which he pointed out that Iraq could mount an attack with weapons of mass destruction within 45 minutes. Before citing these sources in support of some point, you would need to consider the validity of the original authors' assertions. In addition, you should consider the context in which the original author made the assertion. For instance, in the above example it might be that Bush and Blair were referring to a Catholic Mass.

You must indicate to the reader of your paper the basis upon which the original assertion was made. When doing so, care must be taken. Words such as *argued*, *suggested*, *proposed*, *postulated*, *considered*, *thought*, or *believes* immediately raise a question. For example, if you wanted to support the assertion that about 6% of ordinary school children are clumsy, you might write something like:

> Smyth (1987) *suggests* that about 6% of ordinary school children are clumsy.

Again, however, just because an author suggests something, this does not necessarily make it valid. If the reader is to be convinced of the validity of this assertion, more detail needs to be given.

## Reasoning

It might be that the author whom you want to cite supported the original assertion by a process of logical reasoning. In this case you need to convince yourself of the validity of that reasoning. Moreover, you need to make it clear that the author cited made the assertion on this basis. For example, you could write:

> Christie (1910) argued, on the basis of the findings of a number of studies, that . . .

or

> Poirot (1913) *reasoned, on the basis* that no one could have entered the train, that . . .

This allows the reader to make some judgement on the validity of the assertion that you are making.

## Research findings

In yet other instances, the material that you want to cite will be the results of research that has been reported in a journal article. When this is the case you need to convince yourself of the validity of the findings before citing the source. This means that you need to read the article and evaluate it. Presuming that you are satisfied on the validity of the research, you can then cite the findings in support of the assertion that you want to make. When doing so, you should indicate that you are referring to some research findings. You could do this, for example, by writing something like:

> Moriarty's (1910) *findings* suggest . . .

or

> *In their study*, Holmes and Watson (1911) found . . .

Often, it is advisable to give some detail of the research involved. This is especially so if the point that you are making is crucial to your argument. For example, you might write:

> Brenner and Gillman (1966) found that the prevalence of clumsiness in ordinary children was about 6%.

Although it is apparent that Brenner and Gillman arrived at this estimate on the basis of some research, the reader might well question the claim. It would have been helpful if you had written something like:

> Brenner and Gillman (1966) found a prevalence of clumsiness of about 6% *in a survey of ordinary school children*.

This allows the reader to make a better judgement of the validity of the assertion. On the other hand, it might have been better still to give some additional information. You could, for example, have written something like:

> In a survey of 810 ordinary school children, Brenner and Gillman (1966) found a prevalence of clumsiness of about 6%.

Rather than simply citing a source, you have provided additional information to help you to convince the reader of the validity of the assertion that you are making.

## How much detail?

To some extent, how much detail you need to provide when citing a source will depend on the apparent reasonableness of the assertion, and its likely acceptance. The deciding consideration is the importance of the assertion to your argument. If it is critical, you will need to provide considerable detail. For instance, if a prevalence of clumsiness in ordinary children were critical, you might want to provide even more detail than that given in the above example. You might, for example, want to give details of the test used in the survey and the criteria adopted; but this goes beyond simply citing a source.

## Discussion or description

In some instances, you might want to describe, in some detail, a considerable volume of material that is included in the source to which you refer. A not uncommon example is describing a theory. Sometimes students begin the description of a theory by citing a source, and then continue with a lengthy discussion or description of it with no further reference to the source. Clearly, this is not acceptable.

In this situation it is impossible to stipulate how often you need to refer to the source involved. However, throughout the discussion or description it must be clear that you are referring to the source: It is not acceptable simply to cite it at the beginning or end of a paragraph. This means that the source will need to be referred to frequently.

## ▶ Using secondary sources

Any source cited in a paper should be a primary source. That is, it should be the original source of the information or idea referred to. *If the information or idea involved is critical, the use of a secondary source is never acceptable.* In any event, the use of secondary sources is always accompanied by a number of potential problems.

Critical thinking, chap. 1

For papers written by undergraduate students, the use of secondary sources may sometimes be accepted. This is so because library holdings are limited and the source needed might not be available. However, this does not mean that students can use this as an excuse for indiscriminate use of secondary sources. In most circumstances, no more than one secondary source will be accepted. In any event, the use of secondary sources will always be regarded as a weakness.

## Problems

The main problem with citing a secondary source is that you have not read the primary source. Citing such a source is rather like, in a debate with a friend, making some point and supporting it by saying that your mother's uncle told her that he saw it, and she told you that he did, and so it must be true. Obviously, this is always risky. Returning to the immediate problem of citing a secondary source in a paper, a potential problem is that it is possible that an author could have misinterpreted another author's work.

As an example, a number of texts report the classic Donders' (1869) experiment, and explain Donders' subtractive method. In fact, the method by which Donders calculated discrimination time and response selection time is not exactly what is commonly reported. In this case the slight difference is immaterial. Nonetheless, this example illustrates that what is reported about an author's work by another author is not necessarily so.

More commonly, an author might omit some details when citing a source, or might cite a source in support of some point within a particular context, which could differ from the context in which you are writing. Because you have not read the primary source, you could be unaware of such potential problems.

For example, you might read a book on a particular disorder, written by Bond (2003), in which he comments that, "Freiderick (2002) found in her

study that use of medication X resulted in an increase of 27% in the incidence of depression." Because you are writing a paper on depression, and
the increase in incidence referred to is so large, you want to make this point.
When you search for the Freiderick article you cannot find it in your library.
Suppose, then, that you decided to cite Freiderick as a secondary source, and
you wrote in your paper, "Use of medication X has been found to result in an
increase in incidence of 27% in depression (Freiderick, as cited in Bond,
2003)." You would, then, be citing this evidence to support your conclusion
that depression can be associated with some aspect of this medication.

Suppose also, however, that a problem arose when the academic who
marked your paper questioned the validity of the key point that you had
made on the basis of the Freiderick (2002) finding. As it happens, the academic had read the paper, and made the point that in Freiderick's study there
were 10,000 people in the experimental group and 10,000 in the control
group. Moreover, the incidence found in the control group was 30, and that
in the experimental group was 38. While, then, it is true that the difference
was eight additional cases, which is 27% of 30, the incidence in the control
group was 0.30% (i.e., 30 in 10,000) and that in the experimental group was
0.38% (38 in 10,000). Clearly, a difference of 0.08% is not the same as an
increase of 27%. Moreover, there is always the chance of random error. For
example, it might well be that, by chance, eight of those in the experimental
group developed depression for some other reason not associated with the
medication involved. In a group of 10,000 this would not be surprising. As a
result, your conclusion is flawed. Had you read the original article you would
have been aware of this flaw, but because you relied on a secondary source
you were not.

## Referring to theories

A mistake that students sometimes make is to use a secondary source when
they need to refer to a theory. In particular, students sometimes find a
description of a theory in some general textbook (often an introductory text)
and then use that secondary source when discussing the theory. Obviously,
any general textbook will only provide a summary – and typically a very brief
one – of any theory. Using such a textbook as a source, therefore, is quite
unsatisfactory. This is especially so if the theory is central to the student's
paper.

*The only acceptable source, when discussing a theory, is the original author's
work*. For example, if you wanted to discuss Erikson's theory of development
in relation to some topic, you would need to refer to Erikson's work, not to
some secondary source that describes his theory.

If the original author's work cannot be obtained, as a last resort a *specialized source* should be used. For instance, you might be able to find a book

that specifically discusses the theory, or several similar theories, and provides a detailed analysis and discussion of the theory in question. Although not entirely satisfactory, such a book would be a better source than would be a general textbook, such as an introductory text.

## ▶ Placing a reference

Where the reference is given in a sentence or paragraph is important. When you make some comment or assertion that needs to be supported, you must cite the source at that point. *A reference is part of the sentence.* For example, you could write:

> Elliott (2001) found that fatigue detrimentally affected skilled performance.

On the other hand, you could place the reference at the end of the sentence; but, because it is part of the sentence, *the full stop follows the reference.* A common failing in student papers is to end the sentence with a full stop and then to cite the reference, as in, for example:

> It has been found that fatigue detrimentally affects skilled performance. (Elliott, 2001)

In some instances, a reference supports only part of the sentence. For example, an author might write:

> Gerontology, which is a young science (Baltes & Graf, 1996), is demonstrating that positive feelings about older people are emerging.

Notice that, in this sentence, the only assertion supported is that gerontology is a young science. More commonly, however, a source is cited in support of the first part of a sentence, as in, for example:

> Clumsy children have been found not to be able to judge distance accurately (Smyth, 1997), which suggests that they will experience difficulty with tasks requiring accurate reaching.

In this example, the source cited supports only the first assertion (i.e., that clumsy children cannot judge distance accurately). The second assertion, therefore, is not supported, and so must be attributed to the author. Although this can be done, it would have been better to use two separate sentences, as in, for instance:

> Smyth (1997) found that clumsy children cannot judge distance accurately. This suggests that they will experience difficulty with tasks requiring accurate reaching.

Writing the material in this way makes it quite clear that only the first assertion is intended to be supported by the source cited, and that the second is the author's own, based on the first (supported) assertion.

Another flaw that is sometimes found, which is more serious, is giving a

**Your ideas.**
chap. 9

reference at the end of a paragraph in a manner suggesting that it is an after-thought, because the student knows that a source should be cited some-where. In this case, what the student is trying to support or acknowledge by the reference cannot be determined. Consider the following example:

> The prevalence of abnormal clumsiness in ordinary school children has been estimated at about 6%. This represents a large proportion of the population. Moreover, the disorder has been associated with secondary effects. In particu-lar, abnormal clumsiness has been associated with poor self-concept. (Brenner & Gillman, 1966)

In this example, the reference appears at the end of the paragraph, and is not part of the last sentence. Therefore, it supports nothing. It might be that the student intended the reference to support the last sentence. If so, the problem is that Brenner and Gillman (1966) made no comment on the self-concept of clumsy children. So the reference cannot support that assertion. Alternatively, the student might have intended the reference to support the entire paragraph. The problem then is that Brenner and Gillman made no reference to the last assertion, which is part of the paragraph. In fact, the only assertion in the paragraph that can be supported by reference to the Brenner and Gillman (1966) study is that in the first sentence. The para-graph, then, should have been written as, for example:

> The prevalence of abnormal clumsiness in ordinary school children has been estimated at about 6% (Brenner & Gillman, 1966). This represents a large proportion of the population. Moreover, the disorder has been associated with secondary effects. In particular, abnormal clumsiness has been associated with poor self-concept.

This revised version of the paragraph makes it clear that the only assertion supported is the first. Therefore, no support is provided for any other asser-tion in the paragraph.


## ▶ Style matters

Those who are inexperienced with the citing of sources often encounter problems with style. In this sense, style refers to matters such as use of the ampersand, punctuation, where to put a reference in a sentence, and whether it is necessary to repeat a reference continually. The following sections offer some suggestions to help with this problem.


### The ampersand

When citing a source the ampersand is used only when enclosed in paren-theses, as in:

(Alexander & Slim, 1941)

or

(Alexander, Slim, & Wavell, 1941)

When not enclosed in parentheses, *and* must be used, as in:

Alexander and Slim (1941)

or

Alexander, Slim, and Wavell (1941)

## Punctuation

If there are three or more authors involved, a comma is placed before the *and*, or ampersand, as in:

Pinot, Shiraz, and Merlot (2003)

or

(Pinot, Shiraz, & Merlot, 2003)

When several references are cited, authors are separated by semicolons, as in:

(e.g., Christie, 1938; Doyle, 1912; and Haggard, 1914, 1915)

*Notes*:
1. The "and" is optional, but is usually omitted.
2. The dates of different articles by the same author are separated by a comma (not a semicolon), as in the two articles by Haggard in the above example.

## Order of sources

If several sources are cited in parentheses they are listed in the order in which they appear in the reference list, as in:

(e.g., Alexander, 1940; Rommel, 1941a, 1941b; Slim, 1939, 1947)

## Repetition

It is not necessary slavishly to add a reference in the form of name and year to each statement or assertion that needs to be acknowledged or supported.

**Variety,** chap. 3

Such unnecessary repetition soon becomes tedious, for both the writer and the reader. You should, therefore, try to achieve some variety; for example, by referring to the author(s) only by name, using a personal pronoun, or using terms such as *investigator, author*, or *researcher*. For instance, you could write something like, "Smith and Jones (2003) have made a number of observations on these findings. They have commented that. . . . Moreover, Smith and Jones suggest that . . . Further, they argue that . . . On this basis, these investigators concluded that . . .".

As long as the statement or assertion is close to the original citing of the source, and it is completely clear that the statement or assertion is related to that source, there is no need to repeat it formally. For such a clear relationship to exist, *the statement or assertion and the reference must appear in the same paragraph*. Also, it should be obvious that there can be no intervening reference to a different source. For example, if you were to write, "Reavley (1995) demonstrated that . . . , and Roberson (1997) found . . . This study suggests that . . .", then, "This study" can only refer to Roberson (1997), and not to Reavley (1995).

When multiple authors are involved a similar approach can be adopted. In this case, the source can be referred to as, for example, Simpson, Brown, and Jones (2002) for the first citation, and subsequently in various forms. For instance, this source could be referred to as Simpson et al. (2002), Simpson et al., Simpson and his (or her) colleagues, or Simpson and colleagues.

Within a paragraph, as long as no confusion can arise, the year of publication may be omitted after the first reference to a source. For example, you could write something like, "Although Reavley (1995) suggested . . . , Murphy (2001) argued that . . . This suggests that Reavley's reasoning is flawed. On the other hand, Reavley's study clearly showed that . . . It follows that Murphy's argument is not valid."

Similarly, if in a paragraph you refer to only one source, and you refer to only that source in the immediately following paragraph, the year may be omitted, because no confusion will arise. For example, if you were to write, "Charlesworth (2010) found . . . and he argued on this basis that . . .", the immediately following paragraph could begin with, for instance, "Charlesworth also suggested . . .".

Following the same logic, in the case of a book or long journal article, page numbers may sometimes be referred to without giving the author's name and year of publication. For instance, you might write something like, "Alexander and Slim (2002, p. 25) suggest that . . . However, they subsequently acknowledge that this might not always be valid (p. 42)." But, this can only be done when it is perfectly clear that reference is being made to another page in the same source. Usually this means that the second reference must be in the same or immediately following sentence, but in some circumstances it might be in the same paragraph.

# 7 Quotations

Authors sometimes, although infrequently, quote directly from a source. It is important, therefore, to understand the circumstances under which a quotation is acceptable, and how to quote another author's material.

## ▶ Caution

Care is needed when using quotations. In particular, making alterations to an author's words, albeit relatively simple, can lead to a distortion of the original meaning. For example, if you read that a critic had commented of a play at your local theatre, "This . . . brilliant play is in a class of its own," you might well decide to see it. On the other hand, if you knew that the complete quotation was, "This *not very* brilliant play is in a class of its own," you would probably decide otherwise.

Another potential problem with quotations is that the original author's words can be quoted out of context. For instance, a remark that it is quite warm when the temperature is 20°C could be quite valid in mid-winter, whereas in mid-summer this would be regarded as cool. Moreover, this comparison would depend on geographical location. For example, in Darwin, Australia, the temperature is often about 34°C, with little variation.

## ▶ Avoiding quotations

*As a general rule, you should not quote another author directly.* In an extreme case, a paper could be comprised almost entirely of quotations, linked together by a few of the student's own words. If the quotations are appropriately acknowledged this is not plagiarism, but neither is the paper the student's own work. Rather, it is simply a collection of extracts from the work of others.

In any paper, *you are expected to present your own ideas.* Moreover, as a student, what you need to demonstrate is that you can understand the material that you have read, and think about it analytically and critically, *not that you can copy it.* Therefore, you must present information and ideas in your own words. Usually, it is the information or idea to which you are referring, not the original author's words, that is important.

**Information and ideas.** chap. 8
**Your ideas.** chap 9

Students often find it difficult to avoid a quotation. Typically, a student reads something that he or she thinks is important and wants to include in a paper, but finds it impossible to do so without quoting the author directly. The more the student tries, the more impossible seems the task.

To overcome this problem, try to concentrate on the information or idea involved rather than the author's words. Make a brief note of the key points in your own words. Leave this note aside for a time and forget about it. Then, read it and try to express the idea in one or two sentences using your own words. Another approach is to try to describe or explain the idea to a friend.

## ▶ Why quote

On the other hand, there are sometimes circumstances that will require you to quote an author directly. This can arise because you think that a point has been made so clearly and succinctly that it must be made in the original author's words. More commonly, you will want to quote another author because you want to emphasize the content of that author's words. For example, you might want to show that the author made some specific point in a particular manner. Another example is where you might want to give an author's exact definition of something; perhaps to draw the reader's attention to some difference in definitions adopted by two or more authors.

## ▶ Source

If you do decide to quote another author directly, *you must give the source of the quotation*. The reader might, for example, want to verify the accuracy of the quotation, or to consider the quoted material in its original context. To allow this to be done, you must give the source, including the page number(s) (or in the case of on-line material, possibly the paragraph number) from which the material has been quoted.

### Print source

Short quotations (less than 40 words) are included in the normal text of a paper, but are enclosed within *double* quotation marks. You must also give the page number(s) on which the quoted material appears. You could, for example, write something like:

> Although aspects of research in the social sciences can lead to heated debate, "In some social research the values are so uncomplicated or noncontroversial that they almost cease to exist." (Judd, Smith, & Kidder, 1991, p. 5)

Alternatively, this quotation could be presented as:

> Although aspects of research in the social sciences can lead to heated debate, Judd, Smith, and Kidder (1991) comment that, "In some social research the values are so uncomplicated or noncontroversial that they almost cease to exist." (p. 5)

*Note*: The page number(s) always directly follow(s) the quoted material.

Long quotations (more than 40 words) are presented as a separate block of text, which is indented between five to seven spaces from the left-hand margin (not the left edge of the paper), and is *not* enclosed in quotation marks. The page number(s) of the source from which a long quotation was taken is (are) always given in parentheses immediately after the last full stop in the block of quoted material. This block of quoted text is typed in the same typeface as is used throughout the paper. In student papers there is no need to double space long quotations.

## Electronic source

When quoting from an electronic source the same requirements for quoting from print sources apply, with the possible exception of the page number.

If the quotation has been taken from an electronic source that is stored in PDF format, and page numbers are available, they should be given as they would be for a printed source. If there are no page numbers there may be paragraph numbers, or the paragraphs may be counted. In this case, the paragraph number is used in lieu of a page number, using the abbreviation "para.". As an example, you could quote from a specific paragraph in a journal article by writing:

> Taylor (2002, para. 30) suggests that, "There is no need to consider . . ."

or

> It has been suggested that, "There is no need to consider . . ." (Taylor, 2002, para. 30).

When there are no page or paragraph numbers, but there are *headings*, the reader should be directed to the relevant paragraph under the relevant heading as in, for example:

> Rickwood (2003, Results section, para. 5) noted that, "The relationship between . . ."

## Format

A journal article might be published on line in either text or PDF format; or in both. When published in PDF format it is a copy of the print version, and so page numbers will be available. Where possible, therefore, the PDF format should be referred to when quoting.

## ▶ Exact copy

When quoting another author's words you must do so *exactly*. This means copying the original author's spelling and punctuation, including any errors. However, minor changes may be made, some comments may be inserted, and material may be omitted, subject to the following requirements.

### Errors

If there is an error in the original material being copied (e.g., a spelling error) it is not corrected. In this case, insert the Latin word *sic*, meaning "thus", in brackets (not parentheses) immediately after the error. This shows that the mistake was the original author's and that you are aware of it. An example of this is:

> As Twaddle (2002) has commented, "A student's passionate desire to write yet another paper can be attributed to varius [*sic*] motivational factors." (p. 9)

### Insertions

You may insert an explanatory comment into a quotation, but you must indicate this insertion by enclosing it within brackets. Similarly you may add emphasis to one or more of the original author's words by typing them in italics. If you do this, you must indicate that you have done so. In the following example an explanatory note has been inserted, and emphasis had been added to the word *supported*.

> In writing an academic paper, the "task is not so much to present facts, ideas and opinions, but to interpret, criticize and analyze them, while expressions of your [the student's] opinion are expected to be *supported* [italics added] by arguments and evidence." (Bate & Sharpe, 1990, pp. ix–x)

### Omissions

Material may also be omitted from a quotation. Sometimes, part of what the original author wrote is not essential to the idea that you are trying to present, support, or illustrate, and so you want to include only that which is immediately relevant. In this case, that material not important to your purpose may be omitted. When you omit material, you must indicate that you have done so by inserting three full stops, with a space before and after them. This is referred to as an *ellipsis*. As an example, you might have read the following sentence in Fiske and Taylor (1991).

> "Regression is a phenomenon related to prediction from probabilistic information, and is poorly understood by most people." (Fiske & Taylor, 1991, p. 353)

If you wanted only to make the point that regression is not widely understood, you could write:

> "Regression . . . is poorly understood by most people." (Fiske & Taylor, 1991, p. 353)

If the material omitted is the end of a sentence, four full stops are inserted; that is, an ellipsis indicating the omission, and a full stop indicating the end of the sentence. Usually, ellipses are not used either at the beginning or at the end of a quotation.

## References within a quotation

On the rare occasion that material quoted includes a reference, that reference is included in the quotation, because you are copying the material quoted verbatim. However, the source referred to within the quotation is not included in your reference list, because you have not cited it. Of course, if you did cite this source elsewhere in your paper it would be included in the reference list.

## Quotation marks

Short quotations included in text are enclosed within *double* quotation marks. When the quoted material includes words that were enclosed in double quotation marks in the source from which you are quoting, these words are enclosed within single quotation marks to avoid confusion. The following short quotation, for example, includes words that the original authors had enclosed within double quotation marks.

> "Values, however represent a point of view, a judgement that 'this is good and that is bad' which someone else might dispute." (Judd et al., 1991, p. 5)

## ▶ Very short quotations

Sometimes you will want to quote only one, or a few, of an author's words. For example, you might want to comment that:

> Dundee (2000) described crocodiles as being "extremely agile" in their movements.

In such instances there is usually no need to give a page number, although it would not be incorrect to do so. There is no rule to determine what constitutes a "short" quotation, but it would always be less than a complete sentence.

*Note*: Some departments or publishers might insist that page numbers are given for such short quotations.

## ▶ Secondary quotations

*It is usually not acceptable to quote a quotation* given in another author's paper. For example, Startle (2001) might have written:

> It has been suggested that, "students like complying with style requirements" (Waffler, 1999, p. 21).

You cannot simply "quote this quotation". If you find it necessary to include the quoted sentence in your paper, you would need to obtain the Waffler (1999) book or article and to quote from it. If this is impossible, and the quotation is *essential* to your paper, the only way in which the material could be quoted would be to write something like:

> Startle (2001, p. 84) has quoted Waffler (1999) as commenting that, "students like complying with style requirements" (p. 21).

Quoting a secondary source in this way is, however, very unusual. *Such a quotation would be acceptable only if it were essential to your argument, and the original source were not available.* One instance could be where the original source is very old and is not available, or perhaps the material that you want to quote has been translated from another language. You might, for example, want to reproduce a comment made by the ancient Greek philosopher Plato that you have read in some source.

# 8 The Reference List

A reader must be able to refer to any source cited in a paper or a book. The publication details of cited sources must, therefore, be provided. This information is provided in the reference list or bibliography that forms part of any paper.

Do not confuse a reference list with a bibliography. *A reference list includes only those sources cited in a paper.* Conversely, all sources given in a reference list must be cited in the paper. A *bibliography* is a list of all sources consulted when preparing a paper, regardless of whether or not they are cited in it. For papers in psychology, a reference list (*not* a bibliography) is required. Do not include both a reference list and a bibliography.

It is, of course, important that every reference given in a paper must correspond with the source listed in the reference list. In particular, the name of the author(s) and year of publication must correspond *exactly*.

## ► Print sources

Preparing a reference list is quite straightforward. All sources cited in the paper are listed in alphabetical order of the author's, or first author's, surname (family name). Books, journal articles, and any other sources, are not differentiated for this purpose: They are *not* listed separately.

### Detail

Sufficient detail must be included in a reference list so that the reader can find the source cited. This chapter provides guidance for commonly cited sources. Examples of publication details needed for a range of sources are given in Appendix C. If the required guidance is not provided in this book it might be necessary to refer to the APA Manual. In some instances it may be that neither this book nor the APA Manual provides the necessary guidance. When this is so, the principles involved should be applied.

Appendices
C and I

### Journal articles
In the case of a journal article, the title of the article, the name and volume

number of the journal, the issue number if appropriate, and the page numbers for the article are given, as in the following example:

Carroll, W. R., & Bandura, A. (1982). The role of visual monitoring in observational learning of action patterns: Making the unobservable observable. *Journal of Motor Behavior, 14* (2), 153–167.

*Notes*:

1. The issue number is included only when each issue begins at page 1.
2. The issue number is not typed in italics because it indicates the location of the article in the volume, in the same way as page numbers.
3. Some journals give only a month of publication, and do not use volume numbers. In this case, the month of publication is given in lieu of a volume number.

### Books

The *title* of a book, the *city* in which it was published, and the name of the *publisher* must be given, as in the following example:

Ryckman, R. M. (2000). *Theories of personality* (7th ed.). Belmont, CA: Wadsworth.

*Notes*:

1. Although it forms part of the title, the edition number is not typed in italics.
2. The city of publication precedes the name of the publisher, and is separated from it by a colon.
3. Page or chapter numbers are not given for a book. This is unnecessary, because the relevant page or chapter numbers will have been given in the text when citing the source. An exception is a chapter from an edited book.

### Edited book

Unless it has been referred to in its entirety, an edited book will not appear in the reference list. Only the chapter(s) cited in the text will appear, as in, for example:

Luszcz, M. A. (1992). Memory and ageing: Cognitive and functional approaches. In P. C. L. Heaven (Ed.). *Life span development* (pp. 302–328). Sydney: Harcourt Brace Jovanovich.

*Notes*:

1. The page numbers of the chapter must be given.
2. The title of the chapter is not given in italics, but the title of the book is.

## City of publication

The requirement given in the APA Manual is that, for cities within the United States of America, the city and state (abbreviation) should be given in the reference list. In the example above, for instance, the city (Belmont) is followed by the abbreviation for California (CA). For other countries the city, state (or province), and country should be given. The APA Manual includes a list of 17 cities (including 7 in the United States) for which the country need not be given because these are well-known publishing centres.

Clearly, if the city of publication is not well known, then the state or province and country should be given. On the other hand, for well-known cities there would seem to be no need to do so unless some possible confusion might arise (e.g., Cambridge, in England, the United States, or New Zealand). This, however, would seem to be unlikely.

## Multiple cities

Sometimes publishers of books include multiple cities of publication (e.g., London, New York, Rome). In this case, only one (usually the first named) city should be included in the publication details. If in doubt, use the most widely known city.

## No city

Sometimes, publishers do not clearly give the city of publication. In this case, the publisher's address should be able to be found in the first few pages together with the ISBN number. The city of publication can be taken from this.

## ► Electronic sources

Electronic sources are included in alphabetical order together with the other sources listed. They are not listed separately.

A large number of possible sources is available via the Internet. Moreover, changes in the Internet and its use can be expected. It is, therefore, impossible to give other than general advice and guidance on how to present publication details of sources available via the Internet.

## Format

Material can be published on line in either text or PDF format, or in both. When available, the PDF format should be used to find publication details.

## Minimum requirements

The publication details given for an on-line source must include, if available, the author's name and the date of publication (see Appendix C for examples of sources with no author or date), the title of the document cited (or a description of it), and the Internet address at which the source can be found (i.e., the Uniform Resource Locator [URL]). Of these, the most important is the URL. Obviously, if this is incorrect the site involved cannot be located.

### Internet address
The URL must be typed *exactly* as it appears at the site, including all symbols, spacing between characters, and the use of upper- and lower-case letters. If the complete URL will not fit onto a line, the break at the end of the line must occur immediately after a slash, or before a dot. (The "dot" in a URL is not a full stop.) Do not split individual elements of the URL.

### Site address
If a document is one of numerous documents available on a site do not give only the site address. Give the full URL that gives access to the document cited.

### Date of retrieval
A date of retrieval need only be given if the site involved is likely to be changed in the future. In effect, doing so is an indication that the material retrieved was "correct at that date". Once published, journal articles do not change, and so there is no need to give a date of retrieval.

### Database
There is no need to give the database (or "gateway" or "search engine") used to find a journal article. The URL should be all that is required.

## Electronic versions of journals

The majority of sources that are likely to be cited in papers in psychology are on-line journal articles. Most commonly, these will be electronic versions of articles appearing also in print. In this case, publication details of the article should be given as they would be for the print version, with only the inclusion of "Electronic version." As an example, the publication details would be presented as:

> Thompson, J., & Brown, L. (2002). The use of kinaesthetic feedback in movement control [Electronic version]. *Journal of Motor Behavior, 27,* 75–79.

*Note*: As in the case of print journals, the issue number is given only when each issue begins with page 1.

## On-line only journals

If the journal is available only on line, the details shown should be the same as for a journal in print. The only exception is likely to be that the article might not be paginated. In this case, obviously, no page numbers can be given. For a journal available only on line, "Electronic version" (as shown in the above example) should be replaced by "On line".

## ► Presentation

As a separate section of a paper, *the reference list begins on a new page*, under the centred heading "References". Although the basic requirements of a reference list are simple, there are some style requirements that must be followed. However, these are quite simple and should cause no problems:

1. The reference list is typed with a *hanging indent*: That is, the first line of each reference should be aligned with the 35 mm left margin, but each subsequent line is indented by 5–7 spaces.
2. In student papers single spacing should be used within references, but a double space left between references.
3. Sources listed in a reference list are *not* numbered, nor are "bullets" or any other symbols used.
4. Titles of journal articles and books are *not* enclosed in quotation marks, and are *not* abbreviated.
5. In the titles of books and journal articles, a capital (upper-case) letter is used only for the first word of the title, and any subtitle following a colon. Capital letters are used for the main words in the name of a journal.
6. The titles of books (but not the edition number), and the names and volume numbers of journals, are typed in italics. The titles of chapters in an edited book, and the titles of journal articles, are *not* typed in italics.
8. Authors' initials, but *not* given names, are included.
9. The author's initials follow the author's surname, but the initials precede the surname of the editor of a book.
10. All authors' names are given, except when there are more than seven, in which case the first six authors' names are given followed by "et al."
11. When there are two or more authors, the ampersand (preceded by a comma) is used in lieu of *and*.

*Note*: Following the APA Manual style, a comma precedes the ampersand when there are two or more authors. However, when giving a reference in the body of a paper, and there are only two authors, a comma is not used.

## ► Abbreviations

Abbreviations used in a reference list are included in the list of abbreviations given in Appendix D. The abbreviation *e*, for "edition", as in, for example, *3e*, has come to be used by some publishers. This is not used in a reference list. Note the difference between "Ed." (editor) and "ed." (edition). The titles of journals must not be abbreviated in the reference list.

# Part 3
# Writing

# 9 Writing a Paper

In a generic sense, the term "paper" can be used to refer to essays, literature reviews, and research reports (sometimes described by students as laboratory or practical reports); and to other documents, such as a proposal, a report of an investigation, or a journal article. Regardless of the form of a paper, the underlying principles involved in writing it remain unchanged. This chapter provides advice and guidance of a generic nature that is equally applicable to any paper. Further advice and guidance that are applicable to writing an essay, a literature review, or a research report are given in later chapters.

## ▶ Time and effort

*The time and effort involved in writing a paper must not be underestimated.* Writing a paper is always time consuming and difficult. This is as true for experienced writers as it is for beginning undergraduate students. Too often, students do not appreciate the time and effort needed, and expect to be able to write a paper easily and quickly. In particular, they commonly do not understand the need to write and edit several drafts.

chap. 10

## ▶ Thinking

Above all else, *the most important part of the preparation for a paper is thinking*. Again, undergraduate students typically do not understand this. Ideas can only result from careful analytical and critical thinking. This will influence the selection of material included in a paper, and will involve relating information and ideas that are presented in various parts of it. In particular, it is only through this form of thinking that a thesis can be developed or a conclusion reached.

chap. 1 and chap. 5

## Thesis

*You should be able to express your thesis in a single sentence.* For example, your thesis could be something like:

An essay,
A literature
review,
chap. 11

Intelligence is partly inherited and partly influenced by the environment.

or

The cause of depression in young adults is not clear.

Everything in your paper should contribute to developing your argument in support of this thesis. Your thesis, then, gives you direction.

On the other hand, while writing a paper authors sometimes change their theses. In the process of developing a logical argument, and putting on paper the relevant information and ideas in support of that argument, one or more flaws in reasoning sometimes become apparent. As was pointed out at the beginning of this book, writing is an aid to thinking, and it is true to say that often one does not know what one thinks until one has written it.

For example, you might have read relevant literature, thought about it, and developed the thesis that the cause of depression in young adults can be identified. But, when you put pen to paper and develop your argument you decide that you were wrong, and that the cause of depression in young adults is not clear. If this happens, you will have to revise your paper and rewrite your first draft.

## Conclusion

The comments above with regard to a thesis apply equally to a conclusion. However, unlike a thesis, a conclusion usually cannot be written in a single sentence. This is so because a conclusion represents the author's view of the current state of knowledge in the area, and the suggested next step necessary to investigate the problem addressed. Nonetheless, like a thesis, a conclusion gives direction to a paper.

## ▶ Preparation and planning

Of course, before a paper can be written it must be prepared and planned. It is important to understand that *the foundation of a good paper is careful preparation and planning*.

Preparation and planning of any paper will involve essentially the same processes that are involved in the preparation and planning of an essay or a literature review, and these are discussed in chapter 12. Additional requirements for a research report are discussed in chapter 15.

The planning of a paper will result in some structured progression of information and ideas that lead logically to your thesis or conclusion. Moreover, you should have made a list of these key points in note form, in the sequence in which you intend to present the information and ideas involved. This provides the outline structure of your paper.

## ▶ Paragraphs

Paragraphs are the building blocks of a paper. In a well-written paper, paragraphs present ideas in a clear and logical sequence, and each paragraph is linked logically to its successor. The result is that the writer's reasoning is easy to follow.

A paragraph is a group of sentences that relate to an idea and are arranged in some logical order. Often it begins with a topic sentence, which gives the main idea of the paragraph. The remaining sentences provide more information and support the topic sentence by building on it. Sometimes the topic sentence is in the middle of the paragraph, and sometimes it is at the end. It is even possible that the last sentence of a paragraph is the topic sentence of the following paragraph.

In some instances an idea cannot easily be explained in a single paragraph. Consequently, not all paragraphs introduce a new idea; a series of paragraphs can explain different aspects of a main idea. Some paragraphs, therefore, do not have topic sentences.

There is no rule governing the length of paragraphs, but they should not be very long. As a rough guide, a paragraph of more than about three-quarters of a page in length (in double-spaced typing) is probably too long. Short paragraphs can be useful for adding emphasis, but very short paragraphs tend to disrupt reading and so their use should be kept to a minimum.

As a general rule, you should avoid the use of single-sentence paragraphs. On the other hand, sometimes one is appropriate. For example a single-sentence paragraph can be used for particular emphasis of a point, or to introduce a list of points; but this is uncommon.

## ▶ Conclusion

If a paper is well structured, and presents a sound argument in a logical progression of information and ideas, and subsidiary arguments, the conclusion should not be particularly surprising. Nonetheless, it must be presented clearly. A paper is written to present the author's thesis or conclusion. If this is not clearly presented, the paper will fail to achieve its aim.

It is important to understand that in the conclusion you must *summarize* your discussion, not simply refer to it. For example, it is not acceptable to write something like, "The evidence presented shows that . . .", or "The studies discussed suggest . . .". You cannot expect the reader to remember your entire discussion. Moreover, you must show how the evidence leads to your conclusion. Of course, at this point you will be referring only very briefly to information and ideas. Your conclusion, therefore, is likely to include comments such as, "Although Clark (2001) proposed that . . . the findings of Kent (2002) and Lane (2003) are inconsistent with this. In particular, the results of Lane's (2003) study clearly show that . . . Therefore, it can be concluded that . . ."

You might like to think of this as the scene in a murder mystery, in which the detective gathers together all those involved, reviews the clues and evidence, and concludes by dramatically pointing to the guilty party. Clearly, no one would be convinced if the detective merely said something like, "I have examined the evidence and concluded that Colonel Green committed the murder." Similarly, the reader of this murder mystery would not be overly impressed, or convinced, if the author ended the story by writing something like, "The evidence presented in this book clearly shows that Colonel Green committed the murder."

## ▶ Convincing the reader

**Critical thinking,** chap. 1
**Detailed evaluation,** chap. 5

Of course, when you write a paper you are not only presenting your thesis or conclusion, you must also convince the reader of its validity and value. This means that you must not only present existing information and ideas; you must analytically and critically evaluate these. You must, therefore, present your own ideas and support them. Moreover, you must make points clearly.

## ▶ Your ideas

**Support.
Basis of assertion by others,** chap. 6

You cannot simply invent ideas and make comments such as "I think . . ." with no supporting evidence or reasoning. *You must support your ideas by citing appropriate evidence and by logical reasoning.* Moreover, *you must distinguish your own ideas from those of others*. Doing this is largely a matter of expression. For instance, you could write something like:

> Thatcher (2001) found . . . , but in her study she only tested participants using simple tasks. It might well be that participants would respond differently in complex tasks.

The first sentence in this example presents an item of information (i.e., what Thatcher [2001] found), and comments on this (i.e., the observation that she used only simple tasks). This is, presumably, an observation that you have made, because it is not credited to anyone else. The second sentence presents an idea, which is apparently your idea because it is not attributed to anyone else.

As another example, you might write something like:

> Able (2000) found . . . , but Baker (2001) found . . . These findings are inconsistent, which suggests that . . .

In this example the first sentence presents two items of information. The second sentence presents your observation that the findings are inconsistent, and an idea (i.e., "which suggests that . . ."). This must be your idea, because it is not attributed to anyone else.

Usually, however, developing and supporting an idea will involve more than simple statements such as are illustrated above. As an example, you might write something like:

> Loxley (2001) found that stress did not affect accuracy of task performance. In contrast, Sherwood (2002) found that stress decreased performance accuracy. This inconsistency might be attributable to differences in the levels of stress involved. While in the Loxley experiment the level of stress was low, that in the Sherwood experiment was comparatively high. It is possible, then, that the effect of stress on task performance varies with the level of stress.

A discussion of this form clearly shows that the idea that you are suggesting (i.e., that the effect of stress on task performance might vary with the level of stress) is yours. This example is relatively simple (and the idea suggested is not original). Nonetheless, it illustrates the point.

## Information

An important point to note in the above example is that information – in the form of the findings of Loxley (2001) and of Sherwood (2002), and of the levels of stress involved in these studies – is presented first. As was pointed out in chapter 1, information leads to ideas. Logically, then, the information that leads to the idea must be presented first. This represents a clear and logical progression of reasoning. By comparison, students sometimes write something like:

**Information and ideas.** chap. 1

> Jurors generally believe that the more confident are witnesses the more accurate will be their identification of a suspect. This is shown by surveys of prospective jurors' opinions (Brigham & Bothwell, 1983) and in mock jury studies (Wells, Lindsay, & Ferguson, 1979).

An obvious problem with this example is that the idea (that "Jurors generally believe . . .") is presented first. On reading this sentence, the immediate reaction is likely to be to ask, "What makes the author think so?" A reader would have to read the entire paragraph, and then mentally convert it into the reverse order, to follow the author's reasoning. This, then, is an example of what might be described as "upside down" reasoning.

Another problem is that no information leading to the idea is presented. The author merely writes that, "This is shown by . . .". Presumably, then, the idea is not the author's, but rather that of the authors of the sources cited. If so, the author should have written, for example:

> Jurors generally believe that the more confident are witnesses the more accu-
> rate will be their identification of a suspect (Brigham & Bothwell, 1983; Wells,
> Lindsay, & Ferguson, 1979).

or

> In surveys of prospective jurors' opinions (Brigham & Bothwell, 1983) and in
> mock jury studies (Wells, Lindsay, & Ferguson, 1979), it has been found that
> jurors generally believe that the more confident are witnesses the more accu-
> rate will be their identification of a suspect.

## ▶ Making the point

When you present an item of information, or an idea that has been
suggested by some author, you must make clear to the reader why you are
referring to it. Merely presenting information or reporting the ideas of other
authors achieves nothing. Doing so is comparable to walking into a friend's
room and telling him that the temperature today in Arnheim Land is 42
degrees Celsius, or that a friend of yours suggests that piles are developed
as a result of sitting too long at a computer. Your friend would, no doubt,
regard you somewhat quizzically and ask you why you were telling him this.
You must make clear to the reader of a paper how the information or idea
contributes to your argument. For example, in an essay on visual perception,
a student might write something like:

> Connolly and Jones (1970) investigated the ability of children and adults to judge
> the length of a visually presented line, and found that accuracy improved with age.

This sentence quite accurately reports a finding of the Connolly and Jones
(1970) experiment. However, the point that the student is trying to make is
not apparent. The reader would validly ask, "So what?" By comparison, the
student could have written something like:

> Connolly and Jones (1970) investigated the ability of children and adults to
> judge the length of a visually presented line, and found that accuracy improved
> with age, *which suggests that visual perceptual ability improves with age.*

In this case, the point being made is readily apparent. The student is obviously using the Connolly and Jones (1970) finding to support the idea that
perceptual ability improves with age.

## ▶ Clear and concise communication

Given that the aim of a paper is always to communicate information and
ideas, it is obvious that these must be clearly communicated. On the other

hand, *a paper should always be as short as possible*. Consequently, information and ideas must be communicated concisely.

## Clarity

If the information and ideas in a paper are not readily apparent, it is very likely that the reader will either not understand, or misunderstand, what the author is trying to convey. Moreover, a paper that does not clearly convey information and ideas suggests confused thinking. In effect, such a paper indicates that the author does not understand the material about which he or she is writing. What you mean must be expressed directly, clearly, and unambiguously.

*The need for clarity in writing cannot be overemphasized*. If you do not write clearly you will not effectively communicate the information and ideas that you are trying to convey to the reader. For example, the meaning of the following sentence, which was taken from a student's paper, is not clear.

> This result is the verdict of the elderly themselves about their plight and cannot be overlooked as an important source of information relevant to this question.

Another example, again taken from a student's paper, is:

> It would be predicted that probability of recall at a given interval should increase as function of the stimulation or the probability of words correctly recalled will correlate with the frequency of rehearsal.

These examples should illustrate the need to write well-structured sentences that are grammatically correct and appropriately punctuated.

The second requirement of clarity is to *write what you mean*: You cannot rely on the reader being able to draw the inference that you intend from information that you provide. Even if the reader can guess your intended meaning, there will be some uncertainty.

### Familiarity

A point that students often do not appreciate is that because they have devoted considerable time to developing ideas, they are very familiar with them, and with their reasoning. In contrast, the reader of your paper will not be. It is, therefore, very easy to think that something will be obvious to the reader when it is not. *You must consider the reader when you are writing*.

## Concise writing

Concise writing contributes to clarity. Therefore, *a paper should be written in as few words as possible*. You must avoid redundancy, and be economical in your expression. Sometimes a student includes the same information or idea in several different parts of a paper, which wastes words and can confuse the reader. More commonly, however, redundant writing is found in unnecessary repetition, as in the following example:

> There were three experimental conditions in the experiment, and these three experimental conditions were administered to the participants in the experimental group and the participants in the control group in random order. Both the participants in the experimental group and the participants in the control group were tested in all three experimental conditions. Also, the participants in the experimental group and the participants in the control group were tested in random order.

This paragraph could be written in such a way that it conveys the same information, but in a single sentence, as:

> The three experimental conditions were administered in random order, and participants in both the experimental and control groups were tested in random order.

The length of the example paragraph is 72 words, and that of the sentence is 23 words. Therefore, the same information has been provided by the sentence in 32% of the length of the first paragraph.

The unnecessary repetition in the first example is exaggerated to make the point. Consequently, the reduction in length in the revised paragraph is not a good indication of what is commonly possible.

Perhaps a more common problem is simply using more words than necessary to convey information or an idea. The following paragraph, for instance, could be reduced in length.

> Twenty-four participants were used in this experiment. All of the participants were males, and they were aged between 18 and 25 years old. The participants were randomly divided into two groups. There were 12 participants in each group.

This paragraph could be rewritten more economically in a single sentence as:

> The participants in this experiment were 24 males aged 18–25 years, who were randomly divided into two groups of 12.

Again, the revised version (21 words) is considerably shorter than the first (39 words).

## A conflict

On the other hand, being overly concise can result in a loss of information and meaning. For example, when describing the procedure followed in an experiment, a student might write something like:

> The participants were tested in the three experimental conditions, and given practice trials in random order.

Although the sentence is concise, its meaning is not clear, and important information is omitted. To clarify what was done, the description could be rewritten as:

> The three experimental conditions were administered in random order and participants were tested in random order. Before test trials, the participants were given 10 practice trials in the test condition.

Although the revised description is longer, it is clear and provides necessary information.

There can, then, be a conflict between the requirements for conciseness and clarity. When this is so, the clear expression of information or ideas takes precedence. Sufficient detail must be included to make what you want to convey readily apparent.

## ▶ Footnotes

Sometimes footnotes are included in a paper to provide additional information that is not essential to the author's argument. For example, a footnote might be included to clarify some point or to add further detail that is not essential to the argument. In any event, footnotes will always be brief. If the material included is directly relevant and important, it should be included in the body of the paper.

## ▶ Level of writing

Any good author will tailor a paper to the level of knowledge and experience of those who are expected to read it. In academic writing this is usually not a problem, because those who are likely to read a paper can be expected to be familiar with the discipline involved. On the other hand, those who are writing a paper for a more general readership will need to give some consideration to the level at which it can be pitched.

Students often express difficulty with deciding at what level they should write. Typically, they ask questions such as: "Do I have to explain everything?" or "Can I assume that the reader will understand *X*?" As a guide, *assume that your reader has a general knowledge of psychology, and a detailed knowledge in one or more areas*. You can assume, therefore, that your reader is familiar with the discipline and understands, for example, research methods and analyses of data. However, you should work on the assumption that your reader is probably not familiar with the specific subject about which you are writing. It is best to err slightly on the conservative side.

## ► Scholarly writing

Scholarly
style,
chap. 3

A paper must, of course, be written in a scholarly manner. This means that sentences and paragraphs must be well structured, and that the writing complies with the accepted conventions of grammar, punctuation, and spelling. A paper that is not written in a scholarly manner is unlikely to convey effectively the intended information and ideas. Moreover, it casts doubts on the author's ability, and so credibility.

Like anyone else, students will at times be unsure of something and have to check. Similarly like anyone else, students will occasionally make errors in grammar, punctuation and spelling. One or two small errors will be over-looked, but there is no excuse for frequent and glaring flaws.

Students sometimes complain that when writing a paper they were so concerned with grammar, spelling, and punctuation that they could not concentrate on its content. This is not a valid complaint. An educated person should encounter few difficulties. Moreover, *matters of grammar, punctuation, and spelling can be attended to after the paper has been written in final draft form.*

## ► Editorial style

Editorial
style.
Psychology
style.
Local
require-
ments,
chap. 3 and
Appendix A

Apart from being written in a scholarly style, a paper must be written so as to comply with those conventions of writing that are generally accepted in the discipline. Following an accepted editorial style makes some aspects of writing easier, and a paper that follows this style can be more readily understood by a reader who is accustomed to it. On the other hand, failure to comply with the accepted editorial style can be detrimental to clear communication, and indicates lack of care and attention to detail.

As with grammar, punctuation, and spelling, students sometimes complain that they were so worried about editorial style requirements that they could not concentrate on the content of their papers. Again, this is not a valid complaint. The requirements of editorial style are straightforward. Moreover, *editorial style can be attended to after the paper has been written in final draft form.*

## ► Example papers

Sometimes students ask for an example of a "good" paper written by another student to use as a model. However, another student's paper should not be used for this purpose.

Students should be striving to write a paper of the quality of a published journal article. On the other hand, it is unreasonable to expect undergraduate students to achieve this standard. Consequently, even a paper written by a student that is considered to be of "good" quality is not a suitable model.

Another problem is that a paper written on a particular topic will not provide a suitable model for a paper being written on some other topic. Moreover, the approach to a given topic that is adopted by one person is unlikely to be the same as that adopted by another.

Rather than using another student's paper as a model, therefore, *students should develop their approach to writing on the basis of reading a range of articles published in good quality journals.*

## ▶ Word processing

Word processing makes it easy to change text, and so is particularly useful when editing drafts of a paper. However, care needs to be taken when doing so. For example, it is easy to move a paragraph but then to find that it does not lead logically to the paragraph that now follows it. It is also possible, while "cutting and pasting", to cut but forget to paste, resulting in the material being lost.

The most serious potential problem is the possibility of completely losing a document. *Always save a back-up copy of any document on a floppy disc.* Do not rely on a copy on the hard disc. Sometimes the hard disc, or the computer, crashes. If you have a back-up copy on a floppy disc you can use it on another computer.

# 10 Drafts and Editing

*Writing a good paper will always involve a number of drafts*. This is an essential part of the writing process, and it should be looked on as akin to an actor rehearsing a part. A polished performance cannot be achieved without rehearsal, and a polished paper cannot be achieved without writing a number of drafts. Experienced authors write numerous drafts (about 15 or more is common), but about three or four should be adequate for an undergraduate paper.

Some writers try to make the first draft as close to perfect as possible. Others believe that the best approach is to "get one's ideas down on paper" without worrying about minor details. This latter approach is thought to have the advantage of allowing for a free flow of ideas. Certainly, worrying excessively about minor detail distracts from the main task, which *is* to get ideas onto paper. It is better to produce a first draft relatively quickly and to attend to details such as spelling, punctuation, and editorial style later. If you try to make your first draft perfect, you are likely to find that after a considerable period of time you have written very little. This tends to be discouraging. By comparison, if you can see that you are achieving something your motivation to keep working will be greater. Moreover, not being overly concerned with detail can be helpful in overcoming "writer's block".

The best advice, then, is to *write the first draft of a paper without worrying excessively about grammar, punctuation, and spelling; and without worrying about editorial style, or any presentation requirements*. These matters can be attended to when editing the final draft.

Reading a draft with a view to detecting flaws and making any necessary changes is referred to as editing, which falls into two basic categories: editing for content, and editorial editing. The nature of editing will depend on the draft being edited.

## ▶ Editing for content

**The task.**
**The topic.**
**Objectivity,**
chap. 12

Editing a paper for content involves careful consideration of the information and ideas included, and the logical progression of the argument advanced. The aim is to ensure that the paper achieves the desired aim of presenting a valid thesis, or reaching a valid conclusion. This will involve consideration of sentence and paragraph structure, but only in so far as this contributes to a clear and concise presentation of information and ideas.

## First draft

*You should edit the first draft of your paper only for content.* Read your paper carefully, checking for a logical progression of information and ideas that leads inevitably to your thesis or conclusion. Check that everything in your paper contributes to your argument, and that you have made clear the reason for including any information or idea. Make sure that nothing included is irrelevant. In addition, check that you have supported all assertions, and that the points that you are trying to make are clear. In particular, ensure that you have clearly distinguished your own ideas from those of others.

Information and ideas, chap. 1

Your ideas, chap. 9

*The conclusion of a paper is critical.* It must, therefore, be carefully considered. Too often a paper stops abruptly, as though the student involved had suddenly realized that the allowed word limit was reached and so merely stopped writing. The conclusion is that part of the paper in which you summarize the evidence presented, and the reasoning that leads to your thesis or conclusion. If you do not do this well, the reader is left wondering what your thesis or conclusion is, or how you arrived at it.

Thesis conclusion, chaps 9, 13 and 16

Invariably, editing the first draft of a paper will reveal flaws in some or all of these areas. Your task, then, is to revise your paper to overcome the problems that you have detected.

## Length

*It is important to ensure that any paper is written using as few words as possible.* Regardless of the number of words that you have written, you should try to reduce the length of your paper. A concisely written paper will always be better than one that is long and rambling. Moreover, deleting unnecessary material will often allow you to include other material that is relevant, or to expand on some important issue. Always look for anything that is redundant. Try to make your writing simple and concise. Delete any unnecessary adjectives or adverbs.

Concise writing, chap. 9

Word limit, chap. 12

Of course, if your paper exceeds the allowed word length you will have to overcome the problem. Even if you are convinced that everything in your paper is relevant, some material will have to be deleted. This means that you will have to consider carefully all of the material that you have included, and delete any that is not essential to your argument. You will, no doubt, be convinced that all of the material in your paper is essential. However, there will always be some that is of lesser importance and can be deleted.

## Counting words

When counting the number of words in a paper, the title page, abstract (if one is required), the reference list, and any figures or tables are excluded. Similarly, any material included in appendices is excluded. However, this does not mean that material that should be included in the body of the paper can be included in an appendix to circumvent the allowed word limit. If any footnotes are used, these are included in the word count.

You are not, of course, expected to count every word in your paper. Rather, you should count the number of words (including those of one or two letters, abbreviations, and groups of characters such as "1999") in about five or six lines. You can then calculate the average number of words per line and multiply this by the number of lines on the page to estimate the number of words on a page. Multiplying this by the number of pages gives an approximate, but reasonably accurate, number of words for the paper.

Most word processing programs count words automatically. Commonly, this is done by counting the number of characters and dividing by five (the average number of characters in a word). A word processing program, therefore, should provide a reasonably accurate word count.

The number of words on a page can also be estimated on the basis of the page size, margins, spacing, and typeface used. If you use A4 paper, with a 35 mm margin (at the top, bottom, and both sides), use double spacing, and use 12 point Times New Roman typeface, you should find that you have about 290 words on the page.

## Second draft

**Making the point**, chap. 9

Having edited the first draft you must write a second. Before editing this second draft, you should set it aside for a few days and forget it. Invariably, after a little time away from your paper, when you read the second draft you will want to make some changes. For example, something that you thought was perfectly clear when you wrote it might not seem to be so clear when you read it later. On the other hand, do not fall into the trap of exceeding the allowed word limit by simply adding material to clarify something. If you do find that you need to add clarification, you may well have to reduce the number of words elsewhere.

You are likely to encounter a problem if you have not left your draft aside for long enough. Because you will have put a lot of thought into your paper, you will know what you are trying to convey. As a result, some problems might not be apparent to you.

**Detailed evaluation**, chap. 5

Try to read your paper objectively, as though it were a published journal article that you were reading in the library. Question the relevance of material, the logic of reasoning, the organization of information and ideas, and clarity of expression. You might like to think of this as evaluating your paper, as you would that of another author.

Finally, you should check your paper for sentence and paragraph struc-ture. It is very easy to overlook a poorly structured sentence or paragraph when concentrating on the content of a paper. In particular, consider the development of ideas and the logical progression of information and ideas within paragraphs.

**Paragraphs**, chap. 9

## Third draft

When you have edited your second draft, made any necessary changes, and written a third draft, you should check your paper for style and "polish". That is, you should check that your paper is presented in a polished and profes-sional manner. A paper can be correctly written from a technical point of view, but still have weaknesses. For example, a sentence might be gram-matically correct, but long, convoluted, and difficult to read. Usually, it is a good idea to write sentences that are short and to the point.

chap. 3

**A sentence**, chap. 21

You should look for flaws such as inappropriate use of rhetorical ques-tions, beginning a series of sentences with the same word, or sentence structure that is awkward, does not put the emphasis where required, or simply does not read well. Also, you should check that you have not used colloquial expressions, contractions, or first person personal pronouns (except where appropriate). Although these might be relatively minor points, good writing style involves such attention to detail.

It is a good idea to read this draft aloud. Some writers record themselves reading their papers, and then listen to the recording. Often, this will reveal flaws, repetitions, and awkward constructions.

An important point that should not be overlooked is that a paper should read smoothly. If, when reading your paper, you detect a lack of fluidity, you should try to overcome the problem. That is, you should write a fourth draft.

## ▶ Editing for grammar, punctuation, and spelling

When you have written a third draft (or perhaps a fourth) you should have rectified any flaws in content, including flaws in sentence and paragraph structure. At this point, you should edit your final draft for grammar, punc-tuation, and spelling, and for style and presentation requirements.

## Grammar and punctuation

You should have written your paper in a simple and straightforward manner. Grammar and punctuation, therefore, should present no difficulties.

chaps. 21 and 22

Nonetheless, you should check your grammar and punctuation. If your word processing software has the facility, you can use the grammar checker incorporated. However, grammar checkers are not perfect, and can sometimes be misleading. Do not, therefore, blindly accept any corrections suggested by such software.

## Spelling

chap. 23

A mistake such as *hte* instead of *the*, or *fro* instead of *for*, can be attributed to a typing error, but such mistakes should be detected when proofreading. Many spelling errors, however, can only be attributed to laziness and lack of care. Sometimes students even make errors when quoting another author's words (i.e., copying).

When students encounter an unfamiliar word they sometimes attempt to spell it phonetically rather than take the trouble to look it up in a dictionary. This can result in errors such as "metabilism", "curvylinear", or "nural". Even less excusable is an attempt to phonetically spell words that should be familiar. This can result in errors such as "cauze", "posatively", or "insentive". Poor pronunciation can result in even more bizarre errors such as, "approosch", "disguarded", "drawring", "fallicious", "spersific", "floor" instead of "flaw", or even "could of". Although these may seem to be gross exaggerations, they are all examples taken from students' papers.

If you have typed your paper using a word processing program, you will probably have checked your spelling using the built-in spell checker, but you should visually check your spelling. It is surprising how many spelling and typing errors are not detected. In particular, spelling checkers will not detect an incorrectly used word that is correctly spelled. Therefore, you need to look for errors such as *there* instead of *their*, *effect* instead of *affect*, *untied* instead of *united*, and *testes* instead of *tests*.

In particular, you should check the spelling of technical words and the names of authors cited in your paper. You should also check that the spelling that you have used is appropriate to the country in which, or for which, you are writing. Note that, in the reference list, titles and names of journals are spelled as they are published.

## Word choice

**Misused words, new words and new usages**, chap. 3

When you check your spelling it is also a good idea to check the meaning and appropriateness of words, especially any with which you are not entirely familiar. Failure to do so can sometimes result in a lack of clarity, or even a distortion of meaning. For instance, there is a technical difference between the *incidence* and *prevalence* of a disorder.

## ► Editorial style

Editorial style. **Psychology style**. Local requirements, chaps 3, 24 and Appendix A

Check that you have complied with editorial style requirements. In particular, you should check that you have cited sources correctly. If you have quoted an author, check that you have done so correctly, including use of double quotation marks (as applicable) and giving the page (or paragraph) number(s) from which the quotation was taken. Finally, you should check that the style that you have used for abbreviations and numbers is consistent with the style given in the APA Manual.

## ► Figures, tables, and appendices

**Figures and tables**, chaps 18 and 19

**Appendices**, chaps 14, 16 and 20

If your paper includes any figures or tables, check that these have been appropriately referred to in the text. In addition, check that they are presented in accordance with the relevant editorial style requirements. For example, check that figure captions and table headings are correctly presented, including use of italics where required. Similarly, check that any appendices are correctly referred to and presented.

## ► Reference list

chap. 8, Appendix C and Appendix I

Having checked the body of your paper, check the reference list. In particular, check that all sources cited in the text are included in the reference list, and vice versa. Also, make sure that you have included all of the necessary details for sources cited, and complied with editorial style requirements.

## ► Presentation

chap. 25

Check that you have complied with any presentation requirements given. For example, check that you have presented the title page as required.

## ► Final check

When you have printed (or typed) the final version of your paper, make a final check. It is surprising that, in spite of numerous checks, flaws can often still be found. For instance, you might suddenly notice that you have not paginated your paper, or that you have missed some spelling error, date in a reference, or page number from a quotation. If you detect any such flaws, do not correct them in handwriting: Doing so gives an untidy appearance and suggests a lack of pride in a paper.

Finally, check that everything that needs to be included is. For example, make sure that you have included the reference list, or any appendices required. *If you have missed anything, once you have submitted a paper it is too late.*

## ► Checklist

It is impossible to provide a comprehensive checklist that will cater for all papers, because they will vary in type and content. However, one that covers the most common points is provided as Appendix K. Although appendices should be in the order in which they are referred to, this appendix is included at the end of the book for your convenience.

# Part 4

# Essays and Literature Reviews

# 11 An Overview of Essays and Literature Reviews

A paper, whether written by a student or a graduate, is always written to present the author's position on some subject matter. Moreover, it is written to convince a reader of the validity and value of that position. The author must, therefore, develop an argument – which is based on sound information and valid ideas – in support of his or her position. It follows that *a paper must present an analytical and critical evaluation of information, ideas, and theories; and an examination of relationships within and between them.* In particular, it should examine any similarities or differences between ideas, and consistencies or inconsistencies in research findings. Moreover, it should identify any apparent strengths or weaknesses, or flaws in thinking and/or research, and possible alternative explanations of findings.

*Both essays and literature reviews conform to this description.* Often, therefore, no distinction is drawn between them. It is, however, useful to make a distinction based on the purpose of the paper.

## ▶ An essay

An essay is written to address some subject matter or question. In particular, *an essay is written to present a thesis*, which can be thought of as the author's position on the subject or question. This thesis must be supported by an argument that is based on information and ideas gathered from a range of sources. Moreover, it must be based on a synthesis and analysis of the information and ideas involved. Presuming that this has been carefully done, the author's thesis represents his or her final position on the subject.

## ▶ A literature review

Although conceptually similar to an essay, a literature review differs in that it is written to address some specific research problem or question. It does not present a thesis. Rather, *a literature review should reach some conclusion on the current state of knowledge in an area, and suggest the next step in the investigation of the problem or question of interest.* The conclusion reached is not final in the same sense as is a thesis. Moreover, because of its nature, a literature review will be largely based on research findings. The sources referred to in it, therefore, are more likely to be journal articles rather than books. In any event, research findings and theories will predominate.

When the literature review forms the Introduction of a research report it will conclude by outlining the design of the research reported, and (where appropriate) stating the hypotheses to be tested. When it forms the Discussion section of a research report it will, like any other literature review, suggest the next step required to investigate the research problem or question.

## ▶ Similarities

**Scholarly writing**, chaps. 1 and 2

**Scholarly style**, chap. 3

Apart from these differences, essays and literature reviews share many commonalities. Both require a careful determination of the topic, problem or question, and both require a thorough review of relevant literature, which will involve analytical and critical thinking. In addition, both require careful preparation and planning. Of course, essays and literature reviews must be written in a scientific manner, and must be written in a scholarly style.

## ▶ Published vs. students' papers

The essays and literature reviews that students write are similar in content to those published as journal articles in the form of literature reviews, which are often described as review articles. Students, therefore, are well advised to use these as models for their own writing. There are, however, some subtle differences between published articles and the papers that students write. These differences are attributable to the purposes for which a paper is written, and read.

### Published papers

**Information and ideas**, chap. 1

Authors publish journal articles *to communicate information and ideas*, and their articles are read by those who are interested in the area. When writing an article for publication, then, authors will assume that their readers will be familiar with the discipline, and have at least a reasonable knowledge of the subject area. Consequently, they might not discuss an aspect of the subject in detail, because they expect readers to be familiar with it. Moreover, they occasionally make unsupported assertions, which they expect to be accepted by those who are familiar with the area.

## Students' papers

In contrast, *a student's primary aim is to demonstrate knowledge.* This requires the demonstration of an understanding of the information and ideas involved, the ability to think analytically and critically, and the ability to present a soundly reasoned argument that leads to a valid thesis or conclusion. Academics read students' papers with the aim of discovering whether or not the student understands the subject or topic, and demonstrates these abilities. Sometimes, therefore, students must discuss an aspect of the topic or question in greater depth and include more detail than is sometimes found in published articles.

*Knowledge.
Critical
thinking,
chap. 1*

# 12 Preparation for and Planning of a Paper

The most important, and time-consuming, part of writing a paper is preparation and planning. It is critical to allow time for finding and reading sources, noting, thinking, and planning. Moreover, it is important to adopt some systematic approach so that time and effort are not wasted.

This chapter offers advice to help you to prepare for and to plan a paper. The ideas suggested are intended to help you to avoid the pitfalls into which the unwary sometimes stumble, but they are only suggestions. Everyone is different, and how you choose to write a paper is a matter of personal preference.

## ▶ The task

**Criteria,**
chap. 26

*The most basic requirement of any paper is that it fulfils the required task*. It follows that the most serious potential flaw in a paper is that it does not do so. For example, if the task is to write an essay on a particular topic, or to answer a specific question, that is what must be done.

*Before beginning work on any paper it is absolutely critical to ensure that you understand exactly what is required*. This means that you must read very carefully the instructions given to you, and if in doubt, seek clarification. Not only must you ensure that you understand exactly what the topic or question set means; you must also make sure that you understand any other requirements given. Typically these include an allowed word length, the due date, and style and presentation requirements. This is entirely your responsibility. You cannot later claim that you misunderstood something: It is too late.

## ▶ Word limit

**Counting words,**
chap. 10

A word limit is invariably set for students' papers. This is done to encourage students to write concisely, to avoid redundancy, and to include only material that is directly relevant. In addition, a student who writes a longer paper has more scope to develop and present an argument, and to include more material. Setting a word limit, therefore, ensures equity among students.

If a word limit is set by an instruction such as, "Write a paper of 1,500 words," this is usually taken to mean that the number of words written may vary by about 10% either way. Your paper should, therefore, vary between about 1,350 and 1,650 words. By comparison, if the limit is set by an instruction such as, "Write a maximum of 1,500 words," this means that the number of words written must not exceed 1,500 words, and 1,501 words is too many. On the other hand, there is no lower limit.

Of course, words are not counted with complete accuracy and no academic will count every word in your paper. However, you might be required to include a word count on your title page (as is illustrated in the example title page given in Appendix I). Moreover, as a result of their experience, academics can make a fairly accurate estimate of the number of words in a paper.

Attitudes to word limits vary. Some academics will penalize a paper that exceeds the word limit, by deducting marks. Others will simply not read a paper beyond the allowed word length. This is a particular problem if your conclusion section is not read. Finally, some academics will not read a paper beyond the word limit allowed, and will also deduct marks.

## ▶ The topic

Not infrequently, students are given more than one topic from which to choose. If you are free to make a choice, try to select a topic in which you are interested. You will be putting a lot of time and effort into reading for and thinking about your paper, and it is obviously preferable to be involved in a subject that appeals to you.

*Objectivity.*
*Values*,
chap. 2

However, if you have strong views on a particular topic you might be well advised to avoid it. A scientific paper must be written in an objective manner and with an open mind. If you do decide to choose such a topic, you will need to take care *not* to allow your personal values or ethical principles to influence your paper.

## Preliminary reading

Typically, undergraduate students will have little or no familiarity with topics or questions set for papers. Before selecting a topic or question, therefore, it is usually advisable to develop some general familiarity with those given, which allows for a more informed choice. Commonly, this can be done by referring to an introductory or general text. In any event, some familiarity with the area will be needed to allow for a possible, and perhaps necessary, limitation of the topic or question.

### Addressing the topic

Topics can be quite precise. For example, you might be asked to evaluate critically Kohlberg's theory of moral development. When a topic is put in this way you must address it directly. Similarly, if you were asked a specific question, such as, "Does schizophrenia have an hereditary component?", you must answer it. *If you do not address the specific topic, or do not answer the specific question, you will be justifiably criticized, and your paper will fail.*

### Limiting the topic

On the other hand, topics are sometimes phrased in quite general terms. This is usually done to allow students to focus on a specific area of interest. Sometimes the intention is obvious. For example, a topic might be phrased in the form of, "Discuss one or more aspects of . . .", or "What are some important considerations . . . ?" In other instances the intention may not be immediately apparent, but can be assumed because of the broad nature of the topic and the obvious impossibility of adequately discussing it in a relatively short paper. In such instances you will need to limit the scope of your paper. Before doing so, however, you must be sure that this is acceptable. If in doubt, you should seek clarification.

Limitation, chap. 13

For example, it would obviously be impossible to adequately address a topic such as "Discuss the performance of motor skills" in a paper. Given such a wide topic, you would need to narrow your focus. For instance, you might decide to restrict your discussion to the performance of motor skills in early childhood. However, this would still be too wide. A more manageable subject might be the use of visual feedback in reaching. Even this relatively narrow subject could be treated in only a limited way in a typical paper.

### Changing the topic

A very important point to understand is that *limiting the topic in this way does not mean that the topic can be changed*. For instance, if you were required to "Discuss a possible psychological effect of long-term unemployment on adult males," it would be unacceptable to change the topic to a discussion of a psychological effect of unemployment on adolescents or females. Similarly, if you were asked to discuss the aetiology of depression, it would not be acceptable to change the topic to a discussion of the prevalence, importance, or treatment of depression.

## ▶ Applying theory

Sometimes, students are asked to relate some particular theory, or one of their choice, to a problem or question. In this case *the theory must be directly related to the problem or question.* You must show how the theory contributes to an understanding of the problem or question, or can help to provide a solution or answer. It is not satisfactory merely to mention the theory, or to describe it, and then forget it for the remainder of the paper. Frequent reference to the theory would be necessary, and it would feature in the conclusion.

A point to note is that when discussing or referring to a theory, *secondary sources are not acceptable.* If a theory is central to a paper, or contributes in some important way to the discussion, it must be carefully examined. This means that *the original author's work needs to be consulted.* A secondary source such as an introductory or general text is *not* satisfactory.

Secondary
sources,
chap. 6

## ▶ Perspective

It should, of course, be quite evident that a paper in psychology must address the topic from a psychological perspective. On occasion, a student will adopt, for example, a sociological, historical, or economic perspective. Clearly, this is not acceptable. While other disciplines might be relevant to the topic, a student in psychology must examine it from within a psychological framework.

Sometimes students ask if it is acceptable to adopt a particular perspective towards the subject of a paper. For example, a student might ask if it is acceptable to adopt a cognitive, humanist, evolutionary, or feminist approach. Depending on the nature of the topic, it might well be appropriate to adopt a particular perspective. For instance, a cognitive approach to an understanding of some psychological disorder could well be so. However, care needs to be taken when adopting a particular approach, especially if the author has strong personal views on the subject. It is important to acknowledge that alternative perspectives are possible, and to recognize any potential weaknesses in the approach adopted. In any event, *any particular perspective adopted must not detract from the objectivity of the paper.*

Unintentional
bias,
personal
views,
chap. 1

## ▶ Objectivity

Before you begin to work on a paper *you must not have a preconceived thesis or conclusion.* If you do, when you are searching for relevant literature and reading it, you will tend to select only that information and those ideas that support your preconceived position. Moreover, your thinking will be influ-

Objectivity,
values,
chap. 2

**Critical thinking**, chap. 1

enced by this bias, and you are likely to interpret information and ideas to fit with it. *You must prepare and write a paper with an open mind.*

It is only through gathering relevant information and ideas, thinking analytically and critically, and weighing the evidence that you will develop your thesis or conclusion. As you become more familiar with the area, you will start to form a tentative point of view, which you will refine as you read further. However, you must take care to ensure that this does not lead you to a biased selection or interpretation of material. In particular, look for evidence in support of, or counter to, your tentative position. Ultimately, *you must present a balanced discussion.*

**A reasoned and balanced argument**, chap. 1

**Balanced approach**, chap. 5

## ▶ Suggested sources

Academics sometimes give students a short list of suggested sources to help them to begin work on a topic or question. These are always intended to be merely a "start point". Sometimes students try to write papers based solely on these suggested sources, or based largely on them but with the addition of one or two other sources. The main problem with doing this is that students who adopt this approach do not develop their ability to seek out and evaluate relevant sources. From the student's immediate point of view, however, the problem is that, when marking the resulting paper, an academic is likely to view the student as at least lacking initiative, if not being simply lazy. This, of course, is not conducive to being given a good mark.

A more common problem is that suggested sources are not necessarily intended to be used when writing a paper. This is especially a problem when the topic is of a general nature and so must be limited by the student. Depending on any limitations imposed and the approach adopted by the student, the suggested sources might be of no value.

## ▶ Finding relevant sources

Once you have clearly established the topic of a paper, the next obvious step is to seek out sources of relevant information and ideas. Typically, this will involve searching one or more of the specialized on-line databases. It is possible that you might find relevant material by using some "search engine", but this is unlikely. In addition, you will no doubt find the library catalogue useful. A point not to overlook is that you will often find useful sources by examining the reference list or bibliography of journal articles and books that are relevant to the topic. Finally, it is sometimes surprising what can be found by simply browsing through the library shelves.

Searching a database typically produces a very large number of relevant sources. A good search strategy combined with careful choice of keywords will limit sources found to those that are most likely to be useful, but usually the number produced is still quite large. Ideally, all of the potentially useful sources should be subjected to detailed evaluation, but this is obviously unrealistic: Undergraduate students have only limited time available to work on a paper. Realistically, then, all that can be done is to select for detailed evaluation those sources that are obviously important, and a selection of those that seem likely to be so.

Sometimes it can be difficult to find relevant sources in a database. Most commonly, this arises as a result of a poor search strategy or choice of keywords, but it can also result from the use of an inappropriate database. In such instances, the search strategy and keywords used, or the choice of database, might have to be considered. On the other hand, in rare instances it might be that there is only little literature available that is relevant to some specific area. This could arise as a result of some limitation imposed upon a topic or question. In this case, the limitation imposed might have to be reconsidered.

## ▶ Obtaining sources

Typically, the list of potentially useful sources that results from searching a database is lengthy. However, no library will hold all of the sources that appear on this list. Obviously, libraries are restricted by space and available funds. A not uncommon complaint from students is that they have spent considerable time searching a database, produced a long list of sources, and then cannot find them in their library. This problem can be exacerbated if the library's holdings in a particular area are limited. Moreover, if students have left working on a paper until close to the due date, it is likely that they will find that other students have borrowed books or journals that they want to read.

The moral is that you should begin work on a paper as soon as possible. If you do so, you will have time, if necessary, to visit another library or request books or articles on inter-library loan. Moreover, you will avoid the possibility of finding that books or journals are not available because they have already been borrowed. Finally, as a last resort, if you find that it is impossible to obtain suitable sources on the topic you have chosen, or that there are difficulties resulting from any limitation that you have imposed on it, you will have time to choose an alternative topic, or to modify your limitation.

## ▶ Number of sources

Sometimes, students ask how many sources they should read when working on a paper. There is, of course, no answer to this question. Clearly, writing a paper on the basis of one source would constitute inexcusable plagiarism, and using only a small number would not be much of an improvement. At the other extreme, many sources could be consulted, but this is unnecessary: Academics do not expect undergraduate students to know everything about a subject. Another point is that some sources often ultimately prove to be of no value for the particular purpose. The number of sources read, therefore, is typically more than the number cited in a paper. Finally, although relevant, some sources contribute little to a paper. The number of sources that are read when working on an undergraduate paper, therefore, will be somewhere between a very small and a very large number.

You need to read widely if you are to develop an understanding of the topic or question. Obviously, you need to ensure that you include important information and ideas, and by limiting your reading you are likely to miss some. In addition, you need to read widely so that you are exposed to, for example, differing views, or inconsistencies in research findings.

A student sometimes relies heavily on sources in the form of chapters from an edited book. The problem with doing this is that the editor might well have selected authors who share similar views. Moreover, all of the chapters will, of course, have been written at about the same time, and will be based on information and ideas available at that time. More recent information and ideas, therefore, will not be included.

Occasionally, a student will make the mistake of writing a paper that is essentially based on only one source. The student then adds some additional sources with only very brief reference to them – apparently to give the impression that the paper is based on wide reading. Such a strategy will be obvious to the reader. More importantly, *restricted reading will result in a superficial discussion of the topic or question*.

## ► Reading

Reading in preparation for a paper needs to be approached in a *systematic and directed* manner. Obviously, you must restrict your reading to material that is directly relevant to the topic. Use the table of contents and indexes of books and the abstracts of journal articles to identify potentially relevant sources. You will, of course, have evaluated sources at "face" level before considering them to be of potential use for your paper. While reading them you will need to evaluate them more carefully.

chap. 5

As your reading progresses, you will be able to develop a tentative point of view, or position, on the topic or question. This will direct your search for sources and your reading: You will know what you are looking for. Of course, because your initial point of view is tentative, it might well (and probably will) change during the course of your reading and thinking.

A particular point to understand is that while you are reading, apart from evaluating the sources that you read, you must think analytically and critically about the information and ideas involved. In any paper you are expected to present your ideas. It is only through thinking that you will develop ideas. *A paper that merely presents a replication of information and the ideas of others is not a good paper.* You must present your ideas, and *clearly distinguish your ideas from those of others*, if you are to write a good paper.

**Critical thinking,** chap. 1

**Your ideas.** chap. 9

## ▶ Noting

As you read the books and journal articles that you find on the topic, you will need to make notes. Later, you will use these notes when organizing the information and ideas involved. The following suggestions are offered to help you with this task.

### Avoiding plagiarism

If you copy any material verbatim, it is important to make sure that you enclose it in quotation marks. If you do not do so you might copy your note verbatim when writing your paper, and so inadvertently plagiarize someone's work. If you want to quote an author directly, you must do so appropriately. Similarly, you will have to note the source of ideas that you find in the literature so that these can be appropriately acknowledged. Again, you must acknowledge the source of ideas that you find in the literature to avoid the possibility of plagiarism.

**Plagiarism,** chap. 4

chaps 6 and 7

### Detail

When you make notes, try to do so as briefly and concisely as possible. Do not copy large sections of material, and do not photocopy page after page of articles and books. Ultimately, you will have to read all of this and reduce it to a more manageable form. It is better to do so initially.

Concentrate on major points, such as important research findings and implications, and ideas or suggestions. Do not get "bogged down" with detail. As was pointed out in chapter 1, it is the ideas involved that are important rather than information. Try to understand the ideas involved, and note them in your own words, rather than copying verbatim.

On the other hand, there will be instances when you will need to record information. For example, you might want to make a note of the sample size in an experiment, or of the nature of the experimental tasks involved. Similarly, in some instances you will want to make a note of some detail, such as the magnitude of a correlation. You might, for example, want to note that the correlation was only moderate.

In any event, concentrate on the logic and reasoning involved, and the evidence presented in support of assertions or ideas. You will need to use this material when developing your own ideas. Moreover, you will need it when you ultimately write your paper and you are supporting the ideas that you present.

## Publication details

chap. 8 and Appendix C

It is important to record the publication details of any source from which you make a note. When doing so, include the page number(s) or, in the case of on-line sources, possibly paragraph number(s). You will sometimes find that later you want to go back to the source to check something. In any event, you will often need this information when citing sources. Moreover, you will need the publication details when preparing the reference list.

## Organizing notes

How you organize your notes is a matter of personal preference. One approach is to make notes on cards, with individual points on separate cards. This allows for ease of subsequent ordering of information and ideas into some meaningful sequence. An alternative approach is to develop some form of organization early in your note taking, and to head sheets of paper so that they reflect this organization. You can then make notes under the appropriate heading.

Yet another approach is to enter your notes into a database on a computer. A variant of this is to make notes using a word processing program. You can then later use the "find function" to locate notes in a similar manner to that employed using a database. The likely problem with recording notes on a computer, however, is that you need to have the source and the computer together at the same time. If you do not, you will have to make written notes and later enter them into the computer. This involves duplicating the notes, which takes time.

## ▶ Thinking

Critical thinking, chap. 1

You will, of course, have been thinking analytically and critically while reading the various sources that you have found. It is only through doing so that you can develop your own ideas. For example, you might have noticed a flaw in an experimental design, some inconsistency in findings, or a flaw in reasoning. Moreover, you will have made notes of any such ideas. You now have to devote more time to thinking.

Having organized your notes in some preliminary manner, you need to consider "what all of this means". *It is only as a result of careful, analytical, and critical thinking that you will be able to develop a sound thesis, or reach a valid conclusion.*

This does not mean that you have to develop some brilliant, new, and exciting idea. Although it is not impossible, especially early in their studies, undergraduate students are unlikely to have such an idea. On the other hand, it should be possible to develop a thesis or conclusion.

## ▶ Planning

*Planning a paper is the most important part of writing it.* This requires careful thought, and time. In particular, you need to plan carefully the structure of the argument that you will present in support of your thesis or conclusion.

### Information and ideas

The first step in planning a paper is to organize the information and ideas that you have collected into some logical sequence. Looking at the pile of notes that you have made, or scrolling through notes on a monitor screen, your first reaction is likely to be "Where do I begin?" To overcome this barrier, you need to adopt some systematic approach.

Information and ideas, chap. 1

The first step is to organize your notes into groups, each of which has some common theme. For example, you might have several notes on the definition of a particular concept, some on a particular theory, and others on the findings of research in the area. Once you have grouped your notes in this manner, you need to sort the groups into some logical sequence. This forms the basic outline plan for your paper. If you were to give these groups labels, such as "Definitions", "Theory", "Research findings", etc., and list these in the order that you have established, you would have a list that resembles the chapter headings given in the table of contents of a book.

As an example, if you were working on an essay on anorexia nervosa, you might have made notes on therapy, symptoms, definitions of the disorder, cultural influences, and the age of onset. Obviously, the disorder must be defined before it can be discussed, but ordering the remaining points needs some thought. One possible sequence is:

Definition
Symptoms
Age of onset
Cultural influences
Therapy

With the addition of an introduction, and a conclusion, this sequence of headings provides the basic outline for your paper.

## Relevance

**Thinking,**
chap. 9

By this stage of working on a paper, you should have quite a clear idea of your thesis or conclusion. You should, then, go through your notes, group by group, and ask yourself "What does this mean?" and "So what?" If the information or idea does not contribute to your paper in some meaningful way, discard it. Of course, *this does not mean that you discard information or ideas on the grounds that they do not support your thesis or conclusion.* You must present a balanced discussion.

You will, obviously, be very reluctant to discard material that you spent considerable time reading and noting. Nonetheless, if it does not contribute to your discussion of the topic or question in a meaningful way you must do so. For instance, when working on the example topic of anorexia nervosa, you might find that you have noted that: "Patients undergoing chemotherapy often experience loss of appetite." Although victims of anorexia nervosa also suffer from loss of appetite, you would have to ask yourself how this contributes to your paper. No doubt you would decide that it does not. By comparison, a note on the possible influence of advertising on women's eating habits might well be useful.

The inclusion of irrelevant material distracts and confuses the reader. This, obviously, detracts from clear communication. Moreover, it suggests that the author cannot think clearly, and is unable to distinguish between what is relevant and what is not. Finally, because there will always be a word limit for a paper, the inclusion of irrelevant material will restrict the space available for discussion of material that is relevant.

## Specific planning

When you have selected the material that you intend to include in a paper, the next step is to sort your notes into more specific subgroups. This will result in smaller groups of notes relating to specific information and ideas. The process involved is the same as that adopted for the initial sorting. For example, in a group of notes on research findings you might find some in support of a particular view, some against, and some equivocal. The resulting subgroups of notes can then be sorted into a logical sequence. This will produce a sequence of information and ideas that can be labelled, and listed under the originally established main labels, rather like the subheadings under chapter headings in the table of contents of a book.

## ▶ A storyboard

One approach to organizing information and ideas into a suitable sequence is to put the groups and subgroups of notes on a table in some initial order. You can then move these groups, and subgroups within groups, into any other sequence that occurs to you. Alternatively, you can fix your notes to a board using drawing pins, and similarly move them. This approach is similar to the "storyboard" used by those making films ("movies") or documentaries. Using either method, you can easily move your notes into various sequences until you find the most suitable.

## ▶ Art vs. science

Organizing the sequence of information and ideas in a paper is more of an art than a science. There will always be more than one satisfactory sequence. Moreover, often some problem is associated with any given sequence. You might, for example, initially think that the best logical flow is A, B, C, D. However, on consideration you realize that some point within B needs to be made before discussing A. So, you change the sequence to B, A, C, D. On further reflection you might find some problem with this sequence and so change to D, B, A, C. Whatever sequence you choose there is likely to be some problem, and so the eventual sequence selected will be a compromise.

Choosing the "best" sequence of presentation, then, is usually a matter of judgement. This, of course, is particularly so for longer and more complex papers. However, *whatever the sequence chosen it must be logical and easy for the reader to follow*. In particular, *the sequence of information and ideas presented must lead, in a logical progression, to your thesis or conclusion*.

Organizing material in this manner is time consuming. It is, however, the only way to ensure that the information and ideas that you want to include in your paper are presented in a logical sequence. This is essential if your paper is to present and support your thesis effectively.

## ▶ Outline plan

When you have organized the relevant information and ideas into a logical sequence, you have prepared an outline plan for your paper. This plan can be written in the form of a series of headings and subheadings, like the chapter and subheadings in the table of contents of a book. However, you will also need to include other details such as sources, and brief notes of key information and ideas. The list of headings, subheadings, and notes that you make provides the outline plan for your paper.

# 13 Writing an Essay or Literature Review

The writing of papers was discussed in chapter 9, and the writing and editing of drafts in chapter 10. Both of these chapters are, of course, applicable to writing an essay or a literature review. This chapter provides additional advice that is specific to the writing of an essay or a literature review.

chap. 12

Before you begin to write, you will have prepared a plan of your paper in the form of a list of headings and subheadings, together with brief notes. This provides the basic "skeleton" structure. Your task now is to "flesh out" that structure. You must clearly show how the information and ideas that you have listed in your plan lead to your thesis or conclusion. In particular, you will have to convey clearly to the reader your *analysis and critical evaluation* of the relevant information and ideas.

## ► Headings

When writing the first draft of a paper it is a good idea to use the headings and subheadings that you used to plan it. This will help you to follow your plan, to make sure that nothing is missed, and to avoid any possible redundancy. On the other hand, *in the relatively short papers that undergraduate students write there should be no need for headings and subheadings*. The reader should be able to follow the logical progression of your argument without them. You should, therefore, delete headings and subheadings when writing subsequent drafts.

## ► The title

Although not essential, it is a good idea to write the title of your paper first. Doing so helps to focus your thinking, particularly if you have imposed any limitation on your discussion. Sometimes, the importance of the title of a paper is overlooked.

Commonly, essay topics are phrased in the form of an instruction, such as, "Discuss the implications of . . .", or a question, such as, "What are the strengths and weaknesses of Freud's theory of . . . ?" *The title of your paper must not be a reproduction of the instruction or question given*. Rather, your title should concisely describe the topic in no more than about 10 or 12 words. Omit any unnecessary words or phrases such as "A discussion of". Obviously, your paper will present a discussion of the topic. Also, because they might not be readily understood, do not include abbreviations. The following example of a title is too long, and includes unnecessary words.

> A Discussion of the Psychological Effects of Long-term Unemployment on Youths who Have Been Unemployed for More than 12 Months

Apart from the unnecessary "A Discussion of", this title includes a redundancy: Most people would regard unemployment of more than 12 months as being long-term. This title could have been more concisely written as:

> The Psychological Effects of Long-term Unemployment on Youths

A perhaps pedantic point is that the inclusion of the definite article *the* in the original title implies that *all* psychological effects are discussed, which obviously would not be the case. A better title, which leaves open the number of effects discussed, would be:

> Psychological Effects of Long-term Unemployment on Youths

A better title still would be, for example:

> Self-esteem in Long-term Unemployed Youths

This title makes it clear that only one effect of long-term unemployment is discussed, and this only in relation to a particular group.

*Limiting the topic, chap. 12*

   If you have imposed some limitation on your discussion, you should make this clear in your title. For instance, in the above example title it is clear that the discussion will be restricted to a consideration of "Self-esteem".

   The comments above with regard to the title are equally applicable to the title of either an essay or a literature review. By comparison with an essay, however, the topic of a literature review will comprise some research problem or question. The title might, therefore, be something like, "Kinaesthetic Control of Reaching". When the literature review forms the introduction to a research report, the title will, of course, be the title of the research report.

## ► Introduction

The introduction should be no more than about one or two paragraphs in length. Here, you introduce the subject of your paper and establish the context. Basically, you need to provide sufficient information so that the reader knows what the subject of your paper is, and can understand what you mean by any terms that you will subsequently use that might otherwise be unclear.

## Limitation

You should point out any limitation of your discussion in the introduction. Again using the example of an essay on the psychological effects of long-term unemployment, you could write something like:

> It is generally recognized that long-term unemployment can have a number of psychological effects on individuals (Jones, 2003). Of these, perhaps the most important is the effect on the self-esteem of middle-aged males (Thompson, 2004).

These two sentences clearly indicate to the reader that you are aware that there are a number of possible effects, but you are limiting your discussion to self-esteem, and you are giving the reason for choosing to discuss self-esteem. In addition, you are indicating that you are restricting your discussion to middle-aged males.

## Issues, ideas, and concepts

In addition, important issues or ideas should be introduced, and any terms or concepts with which the reader might not be familiar should be defined. You might also have to define a term or concept that you are using in a specific sense. For example, if you were writing an essay on "long-term unemployment", or "below average intelligence", you would need to give your definition of what you mean by the term in the context of your paper.

## Approach

Students are sometimes advised to give an outline of their approach to the topic in the introduction. Often, this advice is taken too literally, resulting in the inclusion of statements such as, "This paper will discuss the use of visual feedback on the control of reaching," or "This paper will review the literature on . . ." and descriptions of the approach adopted such as, "This paper will define the . . . and examine . . . and then . . .", etc. A variant of this approach is to use first person personal pronouns as in, for example, "I will define . . . , then I will discuss . . . , and finally I will demonstrate . . .".

Such statements are unnecessary and merely waste words. The topic of a paper should be evident from the title, and obviously a paper will review the literature. Moreover, the use of the first person pronoun is completely super-fluous: Presumably the author wrote the paper, and not someone else. Another point, although perhaps pedantic, is that making comments in the future tense on what will be discussed, and how, is inappropriate. A paper presents a discussion of the topic: It is not going to do so some time in the future.

As an example, in the introduction to a paper entitled "Antisocial Behaviour in Young Children" a student might include something like:

> This paper presents a discussion of Piaget's, and then Kohlberg's theory of moral development. It then relates these theories to antisocial behaviour in young children. This is followed by a comparison of the two theories. Finally, the validity of the two theories in explaining antisocial behaviour in young children is presented.

Much of this example is unnecessary, and merely wastes words. A better introduction would be something like:

> Both Piaget (1923) and Kohlberg (1967) have proposed that moral development progresses through stages. Antisocial behaviour in young children, therefore, might be explainable in terms of either or both of these theories.

The reader will already know the subject from the title. Moreover, from reading this introduction it would obviously be expected that the paper will present a discussion of Piaget's and Kohlberg's theories of moral development (in that order), that these theories will be related to antisocial behaviour, that some comparison will be drawn, and that some conclusion will be reached on the validity of each theory in explaining antisocial behaviour in children.

As has already been pointed out, in relatively short papers the progression of the author's argument should be such that it is readily followed. Therefore, just as there should be no need for headings to guide the reader, there should equally be no need for directions in the introduction. The introduction to a paper should allow the reader to understand the author's approach without blatant direction.

## Thesis or conclusion

Sometimes a student will include his or her thesis or conclusion in the introduction of a paper. For example, a student might write something like, "It is argued in this paper that high levels of arousal are detrimental to skilled performance." In effect, this is writing the paper "upside down". A paper should lead to the thesis or conclusion. It must end with a summary of the evidence and reasoning presented, thus supporting the author's thesis or conclusion. Obviously, it is only at the end of a paper that this can be done.

*Thesis conclusion, chap. 9*

From another point of view, giving the conclusion at the beginning is virtually an invitation not to read the paper. Moreover, the element of curiosity is removed, which reduces interest. It is rather like telling the reader, on page 1 of a murder mystery, who committed the murder.

*An essay. A literature review. chap. 11*

## Assertions

**Basis of assertion**, chap. 1

**Support**, chap. 6

Another flaw sometimes found in an introduction is the making of unsupported assertions. Obviously, assertions must be supported in the introduction in the same way as they are in the body of the paper. A simple assertion may be supported by citing a source. On the other hand, if supporting an assertion requires a reasoned argument, the point cannot be made in the introduction: rather, it must be included in the body of the paper.

## Relevance

**Selecting material**, chap. 1

Everything in the introduction must be directly relevant to the subject of the paper. Sometimes, students include material that has little or nothing to do with the topic. For example, a student might include in the introduction comments like, "The influence of environment on intelligence has been of interest to psychologists for many years, and numerous studies have investigated this possibility." Such remarks merely waste words.

Students sometimes include material in the introduction in an apparent effort to demonstrate the importance of the subject of the paper. For example, when writing a paper on "The psychological effect of forced unemployment" a student might include material on the reasons for forced unemployment, the proportion of the population affected, the increase in the number of unemployed in recent years, etc. Material that is not directly relevant to the topic should not be included anywhere in a paper. Including irrelevant material wastes words, and can confuse the reader.

## ▶ Body

chaps. 9 and 12

In the body of an essay or literature review you must, of course, present relevant information and ideas in the sequence in which you have planned your paper. You must make your points clearly and concisely, and show how any information or idea included contributes to your argument. Moreover, you must distinguish your ideas from those of others.

When writing an essay or a literature review, *it is important to remember that your aim is to convince the reader of the validity and value of your thesis or conclusion*. To achieve this, you must present the evidence supporting your argument in a coherent manner, with each point leading to the next, and leading inevitably to your thesis or conclusion.

## ► Conclusion

Obviously, in the conclusion section of your paper you present the conclusion that follows logically from the argument that you have advanced. This will differ slightly between an essay and a literature review, but in either it is your central idea. Your paper has been written to present an argument, based on evidence, in support of this central idea. If your paper is well structured, and presents a sound argument in a logical progression of information and ideas, your conclusion should not be particularly surprising. Nonetheless, *you must summarize your argument and evidence at this point.*

   A mistake that students often make is to include irrelevant material in their conclusions. For example, in an essay on the psychological effects of some disorder, a student might include in the conclusion a comment such as, "The government should take action to prevent these problems." In this case, the topic was the psychological effects of the disorder, not what should be done about the resultant problems. Apart from not being relevant to the topic, such comments involve value judgements. Scientific papers should be objective, and value judgements, should not be included.

**Conclusion,**
chap. 9

**An essay.**
**A literature**
**review,**
chap. 11

**Values,**
chap. 2

# Part 5
# Quantitative Research

# 14 An Overview of a Research Report[3]

Not surprisingly, a paper reporting the outcome of a piece of research is written in the same sequence that governed the conduct of the research reported. It follows that, because research is carried out in accordance with the scientific method, it is reported in the same sequence.

## ▶ The scientific method and a research report

Research is always carried out in an attempt to find the solution to some problem, which is described as the *research problem*. Obviously, then, the first step in any scientific investigation is to identify the research problem. When this has been done, the problem is investigated following the scientific method. The six steps of the scientific method are shown on the left of Table 1, and the four main parts (or sections) of a research report are shown on the right. This table clearly shows the relationship between the scientific method and the sequence of the parts of a research report.

Although Table 1 implies that the scientific method comprises a sequence of discrete steps, this is not quite true. In practice, there is overlap between the first two steps (i.e., identifying the research problem and reviewing the literature). Similarly, when hypotheses are involved, there is overlap between developing the hypotheses and designing the research.

## ▶ Format

Because it is written following the logical progression of the scientific method, the format of a research report is largely fixed. With only minor variation, the format of a simple research report is as shown in Box 1. One variation of this is sometimes found when the results and discussion sections are brief. In this case, both may be combined under the heading "Results and Discussion".

---

[3] Sometimes the research reports written by students are referred to as "Laboratory Reports" or "Practical Reports".

TABLE 1   *Steps of the Scientific Method Compared with the Parts of a Research Report*

| Step of the scientific method | Part of the research report |
|---|---|
| 1. Identify the research problem | Introduction |
| 2. Review the literature | |
| 3. Design research to investigate the problem | Method |
| 4. Carry out the designed research | |
| 5. Analyse the results | Results |
| 6. Interpret the findings | Discussion |

*Note*: Because not all research is designed to test hypotheses, no reference is made to hypotheses in this table. When hypotheses are involved, developing them is an integral part of designing the research.

A comparison of this format with Table 1 shows that the main body of a research report (comprising the Introduction, Method, Results, and Discussion sections) follows the same sequence as does the scientific method. The only additions are the Title and Abstract, which have been added to the beginning, and the References and Appendices sections, which have been added to the end.

In research reports in which multiple experiments are involved, the format is only a slight variation of that adopted for a single experiment. Such reports essentially comprise a series of reports of individual experiments in

**Box 1**   Format of a simple research report

Title

Abstract

Introduction

Method

*Participants*

*Apparatus*

*Procedure*

Results

Discussion

References

Appendices (if any)

the format applicable to a simple research report. This series of simple reports is preceded by a *general introduction* to the series, and is followed by a *general discussion* of the outcome of the series of experiments. An outline of the format of such a report is illustrated in Box 2.

**Box 2**   Format of a research report involving multiple experiments

Abstract

General introduction

Experiment 1
Introduction
*Method*
*Participants*
*Apparatus*
*Procedure*
*Results*
*Discussion*

Experiment 2
Introduction
*Method*
*Participants*
*Apparatus*
*Procedure*
*Results*
*Discussion*

General discussion

References
Appendices (if any)

*Note*: The results and discussion for individual experiments can sometimes be combined under the heading "Results and Discussion".

## ▶ Parts of a research report

Each part of a research report fulfils a particular function. The following notes provide an outline of the contents of the parts of a research report.

## Abstract

The abstract of a research report presents a concise summary of its contents. It should succinctly present the research problem, describe the research that was carried out and its results, and state the conclusions reached. Put another way, the abstract should tell the reader what the problem was, what was done, what was found, and what this means. In some journals the abstract is described as a "summary" and is presented at the end of the research report.

## Introduction

Put briefly, the Introduction to a research report is a literature review that presents a research problem and a review of the current state of knowledge in an area, and outlines some research (and where applicable the hypotheses to be tested) that can be used to investigate the problem.

Usually the research problem arises from reading the literature. For example, when reporting research, authors often comment on weaknesses in their studies or questions that remain unanswered, and suggest the next step that logically follows from their investigation. In other instances, reading the literature carefully and analytically reveals, for example, a flaw in reported research that was apparently not detected by the investigator(s) involved, or inconsistencies in findings that pose a problem or a question. Although, then, the first step in the scientific method is to identify the research problem, and the second is to review the literature, these two steps are interrelated and cannot be separated.

## Method

The Method section of a research report describes in detail the research being reported. This includes a description of the participants (or subjects), any apparatus or materials (such as questionnaires) used, and the procedure followed in the research.

## Results

Obviously, the Results section presents the results of the research being reported. It presents a description of the results in the form of a concise summary of the data collected and, where appropriate, the statistical outcome of testing the hypotheses involved. It does not include any interpretation of the results, or any comments on their implications.

## Discussion

The Discussion section presents an interpretation of the outcome of the research and its implications. In particular it relates the findings to the research problem. To achieve this, the research findings must be related to the information, ideas, and theory referred to in the Introduction. This section concludes by summarizing the outcome of the research and by suggesting the next step required to investigate the research problem.

## References

As for any scientific paper, a research report is accompanied by a reference list. This is simply a list of all sources cited in the report.

## Appendices

Sometimes, although not often, appendices form part of a research report. Appendices are included to present information that the reader might wish to see, but that is not essential to an understanding of the report. For example, if a brief questionnaire were used in the research it might be reproduced as an appendix.

## ▶ Introduction and Discussion

The Introduction and Discussion sections of a research report are literature reviews. Moreover, the Discussion must, obviously, follow logically from the Introduction.

A literature review, chap. 11

## Two literature reviews

One way of looking at a research report, then, is to think of it as comprising two related literature reviews – the *Introduction literature review*, and the *Discussion literature review* – that "sandwich" the Method and Results sections. Looked at in this way, the *Introduction literature review* provides a review of the existing state of knowledge *before* the reported research was carried out, and the *Discussion literature review* provides a review of the *new* state of knowledge *after* the reported research was carried out.

## One literature review

An alternative, which is perhaps more appropriate, is to think of a research report as a single literature review comprising the Introduction and

Discussion, but interrupted by the Method and Results sections. From this viewpoint, the Method and Results sections merely provide evidence – in the form of research findings – which is referred to in the same way as would be any research carried out by any other investigator.

## Qualification

Although useful, neither analogy should be taken too literally. A "free standing" literature review commonly does not propose a research design (and if appropriate the hypotheses to be tested); at least not in any detail. By comparison, the "Introduction literature review" in a research report does. In addition, a "free standing" literature review would usually be considerably longer than the Introduction in a research report. Only material that is necessary to develop the research problem being investigated, and clearly leads to the research being reported, can be included in the Introduction to a research report. There is not the scope to provide the detailed discussion that would be presented in a separately written literature review. For similar reasons, the "Discussion literature review" will be shorter than a "free standing" literature review.

## ▶ Published vs. students' research reports

The research reports that students write are similar in content to those published as journal articles. Students, therefore, are well advised to use these as models. There are, however, some subtle differences between published articles and the research reports that students write. These differences are attributable to the purposes for which a paper is written, and read.

## Published reports

**Information and ideas**, chap. 1

Authors publish journal articles *to communicate information and ideas*, and their articles are read by those who are interested in the area. When writing an article for publication, then, authors will assume that their readers will have at least a reasonable knowledge of the area. Consequently, the Introduction to a published research report is often quite brief, and lacking in some details. Moreover, authors sometimes do not clearly state their hypotheses: They expect that readers will be able to deduce these from the information and ideas provided in the introduction.

## Students' reports

In contrast, *a student's primary aim is to demonstrate knowledge.* This requires the demonstration of an understanding of the information and ideas involved, and of analytical and critical thinking. Consequently, the Introduction to a research report written by a student may not be of the sometimes brief form found in published journal articles. In addition, students must clearly state their hypotheses, and make clear the logic and reasoning on which hypotheses are based.

Knowledge, critical thinking, chap. 1

# 15 Preparation and Planning of a Research Report

As for any paper, the most important and time-consuming part of writing a research report is preparation and planning. This chapter provides advice and guidance on the overall preparation and planning of a research report. However, the preparation and planning of the Introduction and Discussion sections involves the same considerations as are involved in any literature review, and these are discussed in chapter 12. They are not, therefore, duplicated in this chapter.

## ▶ The task

**Criteria**, chap. 26

Before beginning the preparation and planning of a research report, *it is absolutely critical to ensure that you understand exactly what is required.* Obviously, a research report involves writing a report of the research that was carried out and its outcome. Before beginning its preparation and planning, however, three essential elements must be clearly determined and understood. These are:

- the research problem,
- the research design, and
- the hypothesis tested.[4]

An author who is writing a report on research that he or she designed and carried out will, of course, be intimately familiar with and understand these three critical elements, the information and ideas involved, and the theoretical context of the research. In contrast, students typically are not, and do not.

## ▶ Students' research reports

The research reports that undergraduate students write (sometimes referred

---

[4] It is, of course, possible for multiple hypotheses to be tested in an experiment. However, for simplicity, in this chapter reference is made usually to only a single hypothesis.

to as *laboratory* or *practical* reports) are typically a report of an experiment that has been designed for teaching purposes, and that has been carried out in class. Consequently, the research problem, the research design, and the hypotheses tested will have been predetermined. In some instances the research problem and hypothesis will be explicitly given to students, while in others they might not. Sometimes the students will be familiar with the research design, because they themselves carried out the research and participated in it. By comparison, it might be that the students simply acted as participants, and some perhaps in only one of multiple groups. Students, therefore, might not be familiar with the overall design. In any event, before doing anything else, the research problem, the research design, and the hypothesis tested must be clearly understood.

When these three key elements have been identified and understood, the students must then find the information (usually in the form of research findings) and ideas that led to the experiment. In particular, the information and ideas involved must be put into some theoretical context. In doing this, students will find themselves in a somewhat artificial position. They have to write a research report as though they, as individuals, had identified the research problem or question, developed the hypothesis to be tested, and designed and carried out the research. Consequently, students have to "work backwards" by finding relevant material in the literature to show that there is a research problem (that which was investigated); and a potential solution, based on some theoretical grounds, that leads to the research reported.

## ▶ Replication

Often, experiments (or studies) used for teaching purposes are a replication, or partial replication, of some published research. Students might well be referred to the article in which the original research was reported, or this may be readily evident. Writing a report of such a teaching experiment does not involve simply paraphrasing the original article, or using only the information and ideas included in it. Usually, the original research will have been modified in some way. In addition, the original article will typically be quite old, and more recent ideas and research findings, and perhaps theories, will have to be considered. In any event, merely paraphrasing the original research report would defeat the learning objective involved, and would essentially constitute plagiarism.

## ▶ Theoretical hypothesis

There is a difference between *a theoretical and an experimental or research hypothesis*. Although the distinction is not always made, it exists and it needs to be understood. A theoretical hypothesis, not surprisingly, is developed on the basis of some theoretical grounding. Specifically, it is a proposed or suggested relationship between two or more concepts. For example, it might be hypothesized that, "Leadership is associated with group performance." More specifically, it might be hypothesized that, "Good leadership results in high levels of group performance." Of course, such an hypothesis must be supported by logical reasoning that is based on sound evidence in a theoretical context.

In particular, the logical reasoning that leads to the hypothesis should follow an "If A then B" form. For instance, the reasoning in the leadership example given could be of the form, "If good leadership results in high levels of group performance, then performance of a group with a good leader will be superior to that of a group with a poor leader." This reasoning leads logically to a prediction of the form, "A will be greater than B." An alternative form of hypothesis could be, "There will be a substantial relationship of A with B." Not all hypotheses, however, are so straightforward. For instance, it might be predicted that "A will be greater than B, but only when . . .". In any event, the logical reasoning leading to the hypothesis must be clear.

A point that is often misunderstood is that the theoretical hypothesis is that which is being investigated. It is put as a tentative solution, or partial solution, to the research problem. However, invariably a theoretical hypothesis cannot be directly tested. In the first place, the terms used typically lack precision. For example, leadership can be defined with relative ease, but "good leadership" cannot. Similarly, although performance can be readily defined, its meaning will vary with context. For example, there will be differences in the concept of performance in piano playing and in solving a mathematical problem. It follows that, for an hypothesis to be testable, it must be expressed in specific and precise terms.

## ▶ Operational definitions

Typically, before an hypothesis can be written an *operational definition* of one or more of the variables involved must be given. For example, leadership could be defined as being that which is measured by some specific test. Moreover, good leadership could be defined as being identified by some particular score on this test. Similarly, performance must be related to some specific task. For instance, performance could be related to the ability to solve some problem of a particular nature, such as crossing an obstacle. This ability must, of course, be quantifiable. The unit of measure selected could be, for example, time required to cross the obstacle; and completion defined as all members of the group involved having done so.

Defining variables in operational terms leads to an experimental or research hypothesis. This, obviously, is the hypothesis that is tested in the research. The theoretical hypothesis, then, is tested indirectly by testing the experimental or research hypothesis. The logic is that, if the experimental or research hypothesis is supported, then so too is the theoretical hypothesis.

## ▶ Research or experimental hypothesis[5]

The experimental or research hypothesis is a clear, precise statement of the expected outcome of the research. In the leadership example given, this could, for instance, take the form:

> The group in the good leadership condition will cross the obstacle more quickly than will the group in the poor leadership condition.

*You must be able to write your research or experimental hypothesis clearly and precisely before you begin to write your research report.* Your research revolves around this. If your hypothesis is wrong there will be a fatal flaw in your research report.

## ▶ Research design

It is important to understand that *experimental or research hypotheses are specific to the research involved*. The research must be designed to test the experimental or research hypothesis. When preparing for a research report written on the basis of a teaching experiment, then, students will again have to "work backwards" to determine how the experiment was intended to test the research or experimental hypothesis.

### Variables

Research designed to test an hypothesis will involve manipulating some *independent* variable (or variables) and measuring some *dependent* variable (or variables). These must be clearly identified. In the example given, for instance, the independent variable is leadership, which is being manipulated by putting a "good" leader into one group and a "poor" leader into the other. The dependent variable, which is being measured, is the time required for all members of each group to cross the obstacle.

---

[5] Although relatively minor, there is a distinction between research and experimental hypotheses. Not all research is experimental in nature. Therefore, hypotheses that are tested in non-experimental research should be referred to as research hypotheses. By comparison, hypotheses that are tested experimentally can be referred to as experimental hypotheses. On the other hand, it is quite appropriate to refer to hypotheses that are tested in an experiment as either research or experimental hypotheses.

## Statistical analyses

chap. 17

In research of the type considered here, the testing of an hypothesis will always involve statistical analyses. Typically, students are not given specific advice on this, and they encounter difficulty with deciding on the analyses needed. This difficulty arises largely because the students have not designed the research. An integral part of designing research is selecting suitable statistical analyses. On the other hand, with a little thought, students should be able to decide what analysis is needed to test the hypothesis involved.

### Descriptive statistics

**Descriptive statistics**, chap. 17

*The calculation of descriptive statistics will always be necessary.* Most commonly, these will be in the form of means and standard deviations. These provide a summary of the data. For instance, in the example given, the necessary descriptive statistics would obviously be the mean obstacle crossing time for the two groups, together with standard deviations

### Inferential statistics

**Inferential statistics**, chap. 17

In addition, *the calculation of some inferential statistic will be necessary* (with very rare exceptions). The nature of the hypothesis involved will determine the necessary statistic. An appropriate inferential statistic to test the research or experimental hypothesis in the example given would, obviously, be a simple Student's $t$ test.

In other instances, the appropriate inferential statistics might, for example, involve a one-way analysis of variance with planned comparisons. This would be appropriate if, for example, there had been three groups: good, average, and poor leaders.

### Calculating statistics

Of course, having decided on the necessary statistics, these must be calculated, and the outcome of the experiment determined. In particular, whether or not the experimental or research hypothesis was supported must be determined.

## ▶ Planning

Once you have completed your preparation, you are in a position to plan your research report. This involves planning the content of the Introduction, Method, Results, and Discussion sections.

In effect, you are "telling a story", but a research report is not a complete historical account of all of the events involved. For example, a pilot study can reveal a flaw in a questionnaire or the apparatus used, or that participants had unusual difficulty with performing an experimental task. As a result of such problems, modifications might have had to be made to the research as originally conceived. Also, there is a large amount of administrative work, such as obtaining permission from parents for their children to participate in a study, and obtaining ethics approval. Details such as these are not reported.

Put simply, when you write a research report you are telling the reader what the research problem was, how you investigated it, what the outcome was, and what this means. You must, then, carefully plan the Introduction and Discussion sections of your report to "tell your story" effectively. In particular, *the Introduction and Discussion sections must be planned together so that they form an integrated whole.*

## Introduction and Discussion

As for any literature review (or any other paper), you have to plan the sequence in which you will present the information and ideas in the Introduction and Discussion sections. In particular, you must plan these sections so that the Discussion follows smoothly from the Introduction, and that the reader can readily follow the logical progression of the information and ideas involved. There is, of course, always more than one sequence of writing any paper that will be effective. However, the underlying structure of the Introduction and Discussion sections of a research report is essentially predetermined by the logic involved. A possible structure, in a general form, is:

chap. 12

Introduction
1. Introduce the research problem.
2. Develop a possible solution.
3. From this possible solution, derive a research question.
4. Outline a research approach to investigate this question.
5. From this approach, derive a theoretical hypothesis.
6. Describe, in outline, research to test this hypothesis.
7. From this research design, develop a research hypothesis.

Discussion
8. Describe the outcome of the research.
9. Discuss how the findings relate to the research problem.
10. Discuss any other implications of the findings.
11. Indicate any flaws, weaknesses, or possible alternative explanations.
12. Suggest the next step required to investigate the research problem.

Within this underlying structure there is, obviously, a need to organize the information and ideas involved into a logical progression. How this is done will depend on the material involved and personal preference. In any event, *it is essential to discuss the theoretical context within which the research problem was investigated, and to clearly relate this to the problem, its investigation, and the outcome.*

## Method

The structure of the Method section of a research report is largely predetermined. This should follow the sequence of Participants (or Subjects), Apparatus (or Materials), and Procedure. In some instances, however, there can be variations to this structure. For example, if a relatively complex experimental task were involved it might be preferable to use a heading such as *Apparatus and Experimental Tasks* under which the apparatus and its use are described. Apart from such variations, planning the structure of the Method section should be relatively straightforward.

## Results

The first step in planning this section of a research report is to decide what results need to be reported. Where hypotheses are involved, the results of testing those hypotheses must, of course, be included. It might also be valuable to include other findings, but this section of a research report should not be used as an opportunity to demonstrate the author's knowledge of analytical techniques. *Only those results that are necessary, and any others that are important, should be included.*

### Structure
How you organize the Results section will depend on the circumstances and on your personal preference. As a general principle, it is important to organize this section so that the reader can understand why you analysed your data in the manner that you did, and can easily follow your analyses.

### Complex analyses
When analyses are complex, some thought needs to be given to the order in which the outcome is reported. For example, when a one-way analysis of variance is used, the first result to be reported is the outcome of this analysis. This is followed by the results of testing of the planned comparisons involved. Similarly, when a two-way analysis of variance is used, the first result that should usually be reported is the presence or absence of any interaction, followed by reporting the results of testing for main effects. In some circumstances, however, the opposite order might be more appropriate.

### Subheadings

Subheadings can help the reader to follow your Results sections. For instance, if you were reporting the analyses of two different sets of scores, say reaction time and movement time, you could use *Reaction Time Analysis* and *Movement Time Analysis* as subheadings under which to report the results of these analyses.

It can also be helpful to use paragraph headings under these subheadings. For example, if you were to report preliminary testing of some statistical assumptions, you could use as a paragraph heading *Statistical assumptions*. Similarly, if you decided that it was necessary to use some data transformation procedure, such as converting raw scores to standard scores, or to logarithms, you could use *Data transformation* as a paragraph heading.

### Presentation

Planning this section of the report will also involve making decisions on the most suitable method of presentation. For example, in some instances it might be more appropriate simply to present statistics in written form, while in others it might be preferable to use a table, and in yet other instances it might be better to use a figure. Sometimes a combination of forms of presentation will be appropriate. For example, some statistics might be presented in the text, but others presented in the form of a table, and a figure might be used to illustrate some relationship. The deciding consideration is that results must be reported simply and clearly.

### Figures and tables

The use of figures and tables is discussed in detail in chapter 18, but a few comments are appropriate here. In particular, it is worth emphasizing that figures and tables are included in the Results section only if they achieve some purpose. Moreover, this purpose must be made clear in the text. As a general principle, a figure or a table should not be used if the information involved can easily be reported in writing.

## ► Multiple hypotheses

If multiple hypotheses are involved, some care needs to be taken in planning the sequence in which they are presented, tested, and discussed. Ideally, they should appear in the same sequence in all sections of the report. This allows the reader easily to relate the hypotheses in the Introduction to the testing of them in the Results section, and interpretation of the outcome in the Discussion. If it is not possible to do this, some thought needs to be given to the most appropriate sequence to be used in each section so that the reader can readily follow your research report.

## ▶ A storyboard

In chapter 12, it was suggested that one approach to the planning of a paper is to use a "storyboard". This approach is particularly useful when planning a research report. In particular, statistics and rough drafts of figures or tables can be placed on the storyboard so that their relationship to the text can be readily seen. Moreover, it allows for planning the sequence of information and ideas, in the Introduction, that lead to the hypotheses; the sequence of reporting results; and the sequence of information and ideas in the Discussion. This facilitates planning the report so that it forms an integrated whole.

## ▶ Length of parts

Sometimes, students seek advice on the relative length of parts of a research report, by asking, for example, "Should the Introduction be about half of the report?", or "Should the Discussion be longer than the Introduction?" There is no correct answer to such questions. In some instances the Introduction will be longer than the Discussion, and sometimes it will not. Similarly, sometimes the Method section will be short, and sometimes it will not. As a rough guide, however, when reporting a single experiment, the Introduction and Discussion sections should comprise the bulk of the report, and generally the Introduction will be somewhat longer than the Discussion.

# 16 Writing a Research Report

This chapter is written on the assumption that the research being reported involves a single experiment that is designed to test a single hypothesis. However, the advice and guidance provided are equally applicable to research involving multiple experiments and hypotheses, and can be generalized to research of a non-experimental nature.

Before beginning to write a research report you will have planned the content and structure of the Introduction, Results, and Discussion sections. You might well not have planned the Method section, but this is straightforward. It now remains to write the research report so that its parts are integrated to form a unified whole.

Writing the Introduction and Discussion sections involves the same approach as is applicable to any literature review. On the other hand, writing the Method and Results sections involves a somewhat different approach. Essentially, these are narratives of what was done and what was found in the research reported. Writing a research report, therefore, involves two somewhat different approaches.

chap. 13

The parts of a research report are not necessarily written in the sequence in which they appear. However, for convenience of referral, they are discussed in that sequence in this chapter. In addition, although the research reports that students write are typically based on research that they did not design, the discussion in this chapter assumes that the author will have designed and carried out the research involved.

## ▶ Information and ideas

It is important to bear in mind when writing a research report that, like any other paper, it is the ideas involved that are important. Information is provided only in support of those ideas. By its nature, a research report must include a considerable volume of information – in particular, in the form of details of the method used, and statistical analyses. If care is not taken, a research report can easily become a morass of information in which the ideas involved are lost. It should be possible to read and understand a research report by reading only the Introduction and Discussion

Information and ideas, chap. 1

sections. Moreover, these sections should include only necessary information.

## ► Format

The format of a research report and the relationship of this format to the scientific method are discussed in chapter 14. For convenience, however, the structure of a research report involving a single experiment is reproduced here.

Headings and subheadings are always used to identify the parts of a research report, with the exception of the Title page, the Introduction, and the Appendix section. Although other headings or subheadings may sometimes be more appropriate, those that are commonly used for a report involving a single experiment are as shown in Box 3.

**Box 3**  Headings for a simple research report

|  |
| --- |
| Method |
| *Participants* |
| *Apparatus* |
| *Procedure* |
| Results |
| Discussion |
| References |

## ► Title

A title should summarize the main idea of a report in no more than about 10–12 words. Unnecessary words or phrases, such as "An experimental investigation of", should not be included. Similarly, information that can reasonably be inferred should be omitted. Finally, because they might not be readily understood, abbreviations are not used in a title. The following example of a title is unnecessarily long, and includes redundant information:

> An Experimental Investigation of the Effects of Practice in a Visual Aiming Task in a Sample of Human Participants

This title could be more concisely written, but still convey the same essential information. For example, it could be written as:

> Practice Effects in a Visual Aiming Task

# ▶ Abstract

Put simply, the abstract of a research report should present a clear, concise summary of the essential elements of the research reported, written in *a single paragraph of no more than 120 words*. It is important because it will be read first, and so it tends to create an initial impression of the content of a paper. Moreover, an abstract must make sense independently of the article it summarizes. It must, therefore, be written with care.

As a guide, the abstract should concisely describe what the research problem was, what was done, what was found, and what this means. An important point to consider is that a reader cannot be expected to understand references to, for example, "the complex task", or "Condition 1", which are not explained until the Method section of a report. Similarly, terms with which the reader might not be familiar should not be included unless they are explained. Sources may be referred to in the same manner as in the text, but to save space, multiple-authored articles may be referred to using the abbreviation "et al." For the same reason, other abbreviations may be used, but any non-standard abbreviations or acronyms must be explained. Also to save space, Arabic numerals are used for all numbers, except those beginning a sentence.

# ▶ Introduction

The first step in a research report is to introduce the area of research. For instance, if you were reporting an investigation of a problem associated with learning abilities, you would need to make this clear. In addition, you will have to define any concepts or terms with which the reader might not be familiar. In particular, you will have to give an *operational definition* of any construct, such as intelligence, to which you refer. You have to make clear exactly what you mean when you refer to particular concepts or constructs in the context of your report.

## Research problem

Having introduced the area of research, you need to present the problem to be investigated. As an example,[6] you might have read an article in which it was reported that adults are better at mental arithmetic than are children. This presents a research problem, which can be expressed in the form of a question. In this case, obviously the question is, "Why are adults better at

---

[6] The example used here is contrived, and is intended only for illustrative purposes. Consequently, there are flaws in it.

mental arithmetic than are children?" To find a possible solution to this problem, or an answer to the question, you would need to consult the relevant literature.

In this example, suppose that on reading the literature you found that short-term memory is sometimes thought of as "working memory", in which material is held for a short time while it is being used or processed. Clearly, the ability to hold material in short-term memory (or working memory) is important in mental arithmetic, and so any deficit would be expected to affect performance in this skill. Therefore, it occurred to you that the difference in mental arithmetic ability between children and adults might be attributable to a difference in their ability to hold material in short-term memory.

You then read in another paper that material can be held in short-term memory for longer periods if it is rehearsed. In yet another article that you read, the author reported the finding that young children do not spontaneously rehearse material in order to hold it in short-term memory, but that they can be trained to do so. Using this information, you could propose a tentative solution to the problem that you have identified. In particular, your proposed solution would be that the observed difference in performance in mental arithmetic between children and adults might be attributable to a difference in the ability of adults and children to hold material in short-term memory.

## Theoretical hypothesis

In the above example you could suggest that there is a relationship between ability to retain information in short-term memory and performance in mental arithmetic. In particular, you could suggest that because children do not spontaneously rehearse material in short-term memory it is lost, and so their ability to perform mental arithmetic is detrimentally affected.

You cannot, of course, simply propose a theoretical hypothesis on the basis of a guess or intuition. While it is true that a researcher can have a "hunch", invariably this is based on knowledge and experience and, with some thought, the logic and reasoning underlying the idea will become apparent. You must provide evidence, in the form of research findings, ideas, and theory, to suggest that your solution might be valid.

## Research question

Your theoretical hypothesis leads logically to a specific research question. In this example, the specific question is, "Does the absence of rehearsal of material in short-term memory in children account for the observed difference in mental arithmetic ability between adults and children?" This becomes your specific research question. To investigate this question, you need to propose a suitable research design.

## Research design[7]

Obviously, the experimental design you describe is that which you actually used, but at this point you are arguing for the use of this design as though the experiment had not yet been carried out. Your aim is to convince the reader that this is a valid and appropriate design that can effectively be used to investigate your theoretical hypothesis.

Consistent with this aim, *your outline experimental design should be as brief as possible*. A detailed description of the experiment is given in the Method section. All that you need to provide here is a brief description to allow the reader to evaluate your design at a conceptual level, and to understand your research hypothesis. In the example given here, you could propose that the mental arithmetic ability of a group of children be tested, that these children be trained to use a rehearsal strategy, and that their mental arithmetic ability be tested again after this training.

## Research or experimental hypothesis

Having given an outline of your experimental design, you need to state your research hypothesis. In brief, a research hypothesis states exactly what you expect to find. Therefore, *your research or experimental hypothesis is specific to the experiment*.

You cannot, however, merely state your hypothesis. *It is essential that you explain the logical reasoning that leads to any hypothesis*. This involves reasoning of the form, "If A, then B." In this example, you could argue that, if the absence of rehearsal of material in short-term memory in children accounts for their poor performance in mental arithmetic, as compared with adults, then training children to rehearse material in short-term memory should result in improved mental arithmetic ability.

However, *you must express this prediction in operational terms*. For instance, in the example given you could hypothesize that, in a group of children, "The number of correct responses in a test of mental arithmetic will be greater after training in a rehearsal strategy than before such training."

---

[7] For teaching purposes, beginning students are sometimes required to include in the Introduction, under a subheading, a more detailed description of the research design. When this is done, care needs to be taken to ensure that this is not a partial duplication of the Method section.

*A research or experimental hypothesis must be stated clearly and unambiguously, in a single sentence.* Moreover, *it is important to be consistent in the wording of an hypothesis.* Sometimes students re-word an hypothesis when it is referred to in the Results section, and again in the Discussion section. The reader is then confronted with two or three versions of wording, which might constitute two or three different hypotheses. This can lead to a confusing situation in which, for example, the hypothesis given in the Introduction is not that tested in the Results section, and this in turn is not the hypothesis referred to in the Discussion. Especially when more than one hypothesis is involved, this can result in total confusion, and a fatal flaw in the research report.

## Multiple hypotheses

It is, of course, possible to test more than one hypothesis in an experiment, and this is commonly done. Rarely, however, are more than two or three hypotheses tested in one experiment.[8] The basis on which each hypothesis is founded must be clearly explained. Proposing a large number of hypotheses, therefore, makes writing a coherent introduction difficult.

Often, when several hypotheses are proposed, each is developed in a separate "subsection" of the Introduction. When this is done, it can be helpful to the reader if you re-state all hypotheses at the end of the Introduction. For example, you could write something like, "In summary, this experiment was designed to test the following hypotheses: . . .". If you do this, do not number the hypotheses and subsequently refer to individual hypotheses only by number. Doing so makes it difficult for the reader, who, later in your report, must keep referring back to the Introduction to decipher what you mean by "hypothesis X". In addition, you too can become confused, with potentially disastrous results. *Each time that you refer to an hypothesis you must write it in full.*

## ► Method

Having stated your research hypothesis, you then need to describe how you tested it. This section of the report should be written as briefly and concisely as possible, but it must provide sufficient detail so that the reader can evaluate the validity and appropriateness of the method used. Also, although it is unlikely, it is possible that another investigator might want to replicate your experiment. The detail you provide should be sufficient to allow for this.

Students often find difficulty with deciding how much detail to give in this

---

[8] For teaching purposes, students might sometimes be required to test a relatively large number of hypotheses. In this case, the emphasis is likely to be on the students' ability to test hypotheses, rather than to support them in the Introduction.

section. The best approach is to pretend that you have designed the experiment, but that someone else will carry it out. If you have written the Method section well, you should be able to give it to any reasonably competent person, who, having read it, should be able to carry out your experiment as you did. You must, therefore, provide sufficient information so that this person can do what is required.

On the other hand, you do not need to give every minute detail. For example, if in your experiment the participants were seated, there is no need to mention that they were seated on chairs (unless, of course, this was not the case). Similarly, there is no need to explain that the participants were allowed to leave the room when the experiment was finished. Anything that you can take for granted that a reasonably intelligent person would infer can be omitted. Do not, however, write this section like a "shopping list" or a "recipe". Also, do not write in note form. *The Method section of a research report must be written in normal English prose.*

A problem often encountered by students is that they are unsure about what to include in each subsection of this section. There is some flexibility with regard to what is included in the various subsections. To a large degree this is a matter of judgement and common sense. Commonly, the subheadings of the Method section are:

- *Participants*
- *Apparatus*
- *Procedure*

When no apparatus is used (for example, in a study in which the data were collected using questionnaires or a paper and pencil test) the subheading *Apparatus* is replaced with *Materials.*

Other headings can be used. For example, if the participants were required to perform complex experimental tasks you could decide to describe these under a separate heading, following your description of the apparatus used. An appropriate heading would be *Experimental Tasks.* Alternatively, you could decide to describe the experimental tasks and apparatus together under the combined heading *Experimental Tasks and Apparatus.*

The following sections outline the information that should be included under the three common headings (*Participants*, *Apparatus*, and *Procedure*). You should be able to generalize the principles involved to any other subheadings that you may choose to use.

## Participants

In the past, this section of a research report was headed *Subjects*, but the APA Manual now recommends that the heading used should be *Participants.* People should be referred to as *participants*, and not as subjects. However, when discussing research design or statistical analyses the conventional statistical terms "within-subjects" or "between-subjects" are used.

Under this heading, the participants should be described as concisely as possible. The detail required will vary, but will always include how participants were selected, and their age and sex. Authors commonly give the mean and range for age. It is better to give the range rather than standard deviation, because it gives the youngest and oldest ages in the group(s), which could he important in some circumstances. This information can often be given in one or two sentences. For example, you could write something like:

> The participants were 40 volunteers (20 males and 20 females) from an under-graduate psychology class. The mean age of the participants was 19 years 6 months (range 18 years 4 months to 21 years 2 months).

When deciding what, if any, other information to include in your description of participants, you should ask yourself if there is anything about them that could have affected the outcome of your experiment in a manner that was not intended. For example, a hearing deficit could affect the outcome of an experiment involving responding to an auditory stimulus, or a visual deficit responding to a visual stimulus. In such instances you would have to comment on the hearing or visual ability of the participants. For example, you might well have tested the participants' hearing and vision. In this case you would describe the testing procedure used, and any criteria adopted.

On the other hand, there is no need to include anything about participants that could not have influenced the outcome of your research. For instance, if some of the participants had red hair, this is rather unlikely to have affected the outcome in a reaction time experiment.

If you can assume that an intelligent reader will infer something, do not include it in your description. For instance, when participants are humans it is usually not necessary to comment that they were of normal intelligence. Similarly, if the participants were students in the same institution as the investigator (whose affiliation appears on the title page) there is no need to comment that they were drawn from this institution.

### Selection and allocation

As is frequently the case, when participants are selected and allocated to groups on the basis of some characteristic, the methods of selection and allocation to groups, and the criteria adopted for doing so, must be explained. For example, if participants were selected and allocated to groups on the basis of intelligence, details of the test and testing procedure used, and of the level(s) of intelligence adopted for selection and allocation to groups, must be given.

### Losing participants

Sometimes investigators lose participants, but usually this is not due to carelessness. More commonly, participants are lost as a result of illness or simply withdrawing. If any participants were lost from your experiment you should give brief details.

## Language

When describing participants, the use of language can become extremely pedantic, and you might need to seek advice. As a general guide, do not use terms that have any possible derogatory connotations, or that could be considered to be dehumanizing. When referring to individuals who are intellectually handicapped, for instance, it is preferable to give an operational definition of a more neutral term that can subsequently be used. For example, you might include in your description of the participants:

> Individuals who scored less than 70 on the Wechsler Adult Intelligence Scale were allocated to the low-intelligence group, and those who scored above 120 were allocated to the high-intelligence group.

Thereafter, you could describe the groups of participants as the low- and high-intelligence groups.

## Confidentiality

Confidentiality in regard to participants and respondents must be maintained. This means that a research report must never include participants' or respondents' names, or any information that could identify them. Similarly, institutions such as a school or hospital from which participants or respondents are obtained, must not be identified without the express approval of that institution.

## Respondents

In research involving the use of questionnaires or interviews, those who participate are referred to as "respondents". The description of respondents should be similar to that of participants. In addition, the proportion of those approached who participated in the study should be given as a percentage. This could be reported as, for example, "Of those approached, 54% completed the questionnaire," or simply, "The response rate was 54%."

## Subjects

When animals are used in experiments they should be described as subjects. Details of number, age, and sex should be given. In addition, details of the species and strain, physiological condition, and the handling of the animals need to be included. The method of allocation to experimental and control groups must also be described.

## Apparatus

Under this heading you describe any apparatus you used in your experiment. Only what could be described as "major" items, such as computers or tape recorders, need be included. Pieces of furniture, or minor items (such as note paper and pencils, or a stop watch) usually would not be mentioned. The use of such items should be evident from the description of the procedure followed – as in, for example, "Participants were required to take notes," or "A stop watch was used to time problem completion."

Special items of equipment, or items that have been modified in some way, will have to be described in some detail. This is particularly so for any specially constructed apparatus.

### Illustrations

Purpose.
Designing
figures.
Drawing
figures,
chap. 19

In some cases the reader will need to be able to form a mental image of apparatus so as to fully understand how it was used. If a verbal description becomes too complex and confusing, or inadequate, it might be necessary to provide an illustration. Any such illustration should be as simple as possible.

### Function of apparatus

Ultimately, the reader needs to know what the apparatus described was used for, and how it was used. When describing apparatus, therefore, it is a good idea to give a very brief indication of its use or purpose. For instance, you might point out that a lamp was used to present a visual stimulus, or that a switch was used by participants to make a response. The terminology used to describe apparatus can be helpful in this respect. For example, rather than stating only that the apparatus included a "switch", it might be better to describe it as a "response switch". Simply adding a word or two in this way can make the apparatus section much easier to follow and to understand.

### Computer software

Other than to describe its function, it is not usually necessary to provide any details of computer software that has been specially written for an experiment. Where appropriate, you should acknowledge the authorship of such software in a footnote.

## Materials

The principles applicable to writing an Apparatus section are equally applicable to a Materials section. What is required is a clear, concise, and simple description of the materials used in your research.

If you used a published test you need only refer to it by name and author.

For example, you could write something like, "The Advanced Colour Odour Test (Bright & Nasal, 2001)". Similarly, if you used some scale or other instrument previously developed and used by another investigator, you could refer to it in the same manner. For instance, you could write something like, "The party enjoyment scale developed by Gudentime (2000)". In both instances, of course, complete publishing details would be included in the reference list.

There should be no need to give a reason for using a particular instrument that is commonly used, such as a specific intelligence test. If there is some special reason for using a test, such as its particular appropriateness, this should have been discussed in the Introduction. Typically, this will be done when deriving an operational definition of the variable being measured.

Other materials, such as word lists or nonsense syllables, need to be described, as does how they were prepared. As an example, you might explain that you used three lists of two-syllable nouns that were randomly selected from some specified dictionary. Similarly, you might explain that you created a list of 10 three-letter nonsense syllables, each of which comprised a consonant, a vowel, and a consonant, and that these were constructed using randomly selected letters.

If you used an instrument, such as a scale that you devised specifically for the purpose of your research, you would need to discuss it in some depth. In particular, you would need to describe how you developed it, and how you assessed its validity and reliability.

Similarly, if you used a questionnaire in a study you should briefly explain what it was designed to achieve, and how it was constructed. For example, you might explain that you devised a questionnaire to assess students' enjoyment of a psychology course on research methods. In this case, you would need to describe the questionnaire in some detail (e.g., that it was composed of 10 questions, and how these were devised), what type of scale was used (e.g., Likert scale), what the scores indicated (e.g., Strongly agree, Agree, etc.), and, if an overall score was used, how this was calculated.

If the questionnaire is relatively short, it should be attached as an appendix to your report. This is not practicable for long questionnaires. In this case, you should describe the questionnaire more fully, and include several example questions. When this is done, a footnote to the effect that the complete questionnaire is available on request is usually included in the research report.

## Procedure

The Procedure section of a research report should be a simple, concise account of what you did and how you did it. Briefly describe the sequence of events and what was done at each step. However, you should assume that the reader is an experienced researcher, and so you do not need to recount every minute detail.

An experiment will normally involve two or more experimental conditions, and these need to be carefully described. Basically, what you need to explain is what was manipulated and how the participants were required to respond. Sometimes an experimental task can be quite complex, and so is difficult to explain concisely. This can be particularly so when the required response involves interacting with apparatus. In such instances, it is a good idea to describe the task(s), together with the apparatus, under a separate subheading. Sometimes it may be necessary to provide an illustration to help the reader to understand the task. Any such illustration should be as simple as possible.

When several complicated tasks are involved, the Procedure section can easily become long, complex, and confusing. You must avoid this. One strategy that can be helpful is to give a summary of the common aspects of all tasks and then to explain each task individually in relation to this. Although relatively simple, the following example illustrates the principle involved:

> For all experimental tasks, a warning tone was presented followed by the stimulus light, to which the children were required to respond by pressing the response switch as quickly as possible. In the fixed foreperiod condition the warning tone was always presented 3 seconds before the stimulus. In the variable foreperiod condition the interval between the warning tone and presentation of the stimulus varied randomly between 1 and 3 seconds. For all conditions the stimulus was a flash of white light of a duration of 50 ms.

Having given this general description, all that is needed is to explain the specific task required in a particular condition. For example, you could write something like:

> The children were required to perform two tasks, involving either a simple or a complex response, with either a fixed or a variable foreperiod. For the simple response task they were required only to press the response switch. For the complex response task they were required to touch first the red target, then the blue target, and then to press the response switch.

Note that the fixed and variable foreperiods, and the stimulus duration, have already been described, and so there is no need to repeat this description for each condition.

### Instructions

Reproducing instructions that were given to participants is usually not necessary. Rather, instructions should be paraphrased. If you have clearly described the experimental task, all you need to do is to explain that the participant was instructed to perform this task, sometimes with an additional instruction such as "as quickly as possible" or "as accurately as possible". Verbatim instructions are rarely reported. The only likely exception is when a between-group difference in instructions is a variable that is being manipulated. In this case it is important for the reader to understand how the manipulation was achieved. Short instructions may be given verbatim in the procedure section, but long instructions should be included as an appendix.

### Practice trials

In most experiments participants are given practice trials to ensure that they understand the task they are required to perform, or perhaps to allow them to achieve some level of performance. You should give details of practice, including the number of trials given. For instance, you might explain that, "Ten practice trials were given immediately before test trials."

### Counterbalancing

Where multiple experimental conditions and groups are involved, some form of counterbalancing will be employed. You should briefly describe how this was done. For example, you could explain that, "One group was tested in the simple followed by the choice condition, and the other group was tested in the opposite order."

### Scoring

In some instances, the method of scoring used in a study needs to be explained. For instance, you might have used independent raters to score responses. This is often done when responses are in the form of writing, drawings, or some overt behaviour such as smiling. How scores were determined in such circumstances should be carefully explained. Whether the method of scoring is included in the Procedure or the Results section is a matter of judgement. Sometimes it makes more sense to include it in one section, and sometimes it is more appropriate in the other.

### Ethics

Unless you are specifically required to do so, or there is some obvious reason, there is no need to describe how you complied with ethical requirements in your research. For example, there is no need to comment that all participants signed a consent form.

## ► Results

Presenting the results of a simple experiment is quite straightforward, but when the research is complex, care is required. The sequence and presentation of the results will already have been planned. However, care is needed when writing this section. *Results must be presented as simply, concisely, and clearly as possible.*

Reporting statistics can be quite complex, and requires careful attention to detail. Therefore, the reporting of statistics is discussed in detail separately in chapter 17. Put briefly, however, the Results section should present a concise summary of the results of your experiment, usually including descriptive and inferential statistics. In particular, the Results section reports the outcome of testing your hypothesis when one is involved.

A point to note is that sources should not be cited in the Results section unless there is some particular reason for doing so. This could arise if, for example, some unusual statistical technique were employed.

## Purpose

There is no need to explain why you calculated inferential statistics, or tested an hypothesis: The reason will be obvious. On the other hand, when multiple hypotheses or complex analyses are involved, it is helpful to the reader to make some comment. For example, you could begin a paragraph by writing something like, "To test the hypothesis that . . .", or "To investigate the relationship of . . .". This is not intended as an explanation, but merely as a guide to the reader.

In other instances, you will need to explain why you did what you did. For example, if you used a data transformation procedure, or some unusual approach to an analysis, you would have to explain why you did so.

## Introducing analyses

For simple analyses, involving commonly used statistical tests, there is usually no need to give the name of the test used. Most readers will be familiar with, for instance, the Student's $t$ test, and the inclusion of $t$ when reporting statistics indicates that this test was used. There is, then, little value in introducing the analysis by writing, for example:

> The data were analysed using a Student's $t$ test.

Rather, when you report the outcome of the test you only need to write, for example:

> There was a significant difference between mean scores in the stressed and unstressed conditions, $t(21) = 7.92$, $p < .01$.

When the analysis is more complicated, for instance involving a complex factorial design, it is often helpful to the reader to introduce it with an explanatory sentence. For example, you could write something like:

> The participants' mean scores were analysed using a 2 × 2 × 2 (Group × Age ×

> Complexity) mixed design analysis of variance, with repeated measures on the last two factors.

or

> The data were analysed using a 2 (Fatigue: high vs. low) × 2 (Stress: high vs. low) × 2 (Task Difficulty: simple vs. complex) repeated measures analysis of variance.

Such an introduction gives the reader necessary preliminary information in a simple and readily understandable form. For instance, in the examples given above, before considering the results, the reader knows that an analysis of variance was used; that it involved repeated measures; the number of factors included; and the number of levels in each factor. This helps the reader to understand the subsequently presented statistics, which can then be reported as, for example:

> The mean number of correct responses in the complex condition (27.3) was greater than that for the simple condition (12.7) and this difference was significant, $F(1, 22) = 24.32$, $p = .02$, $\varpi^2 = .34$ ($MSE = 76.42$).

## Commenting on results

An important point to understand is that in this section of your report you do not comment on any interpretation or implications of the findings. It is, however, acceptable to make comments such as: "The mean score for problem solving time was markedly longer for the Fatigue group," or "The correlation of A with B was substantial." These are observations, not interpretations. Similarly, it is acceptable to make comments like, "As was expected, there was a considerable difference in mean performance accuracy between the fatigued and non-fatigued groups." Again, such comments are observations.

The acceptability of commenting in the Results section on whether or not hypotheses were supported seems to be a matter of opinion. One school of thought is that it is not, and that such comments belong in the Discussion. However, simply commenting that an hypothesis has been supported, or has not, is only an observation, and so is acceptable. On the other hand, this same comment will have to be made again in the Discussion section, and so is redundant. Such comments, therefore, are best avoided.

## Statistical packages

Typically, data are analysed using some proprietary statistical package. Unless there is some particular reason for doing so, there is no need to give the name of the software used. Presuming that it is well designed, any statistical package should calculate statistics as accurately as any other. If this were not so, then using such software would pose a serious problem.

## ▶ Discussion

A literature
review,
chap. 11
The Discussion should flow on smoothly from the Introduction, which ends with the hypothesis to be tested. It follows that the Discussion must begin with some comment on whether or not this hypothesis was supported.

Returning to the example of the mental arithmetic experiment, you might write something like, "The hypothesis that the number of correct responses in a test of mental arithmetic will be greater after training in a rehearsal strategy than before such training, was supported." You could follow this with additional comments. For instance, you might want to remark that the improvement was observed in *all of the children* in the sample, or that there was a *marked* increase in mental arithmetic ability. In addition, you should comment on any other interesting findings or observations.

In the case of an experiment involving multiple hypotheses, obviously the Discussion should not begin with a list of the outcomes of testing the hypotheses involved. Rather, they should be discussed separately, preferably in the order in which they were given in the Introduction, and included in the Results section. This will have been considered when planning the research report.

### Outcome of testing hypotheses

A point that should be understood is that an hypothesis is a tentative prediction. It is based on an "If A, then B" form of reasoning. It follows that if the hypothesis is supported by the findings the results of the research provide *support* for this reasoning. An important point to understand is that supporting an hypothesis never "proves" anything: It merely provides support. There is always the possibility that the results of research can be attributed to chance or, for example, to the effect of some unknown variable, or a flaw in the research design.

The results of any research, therefore, can only *support*, or *fail to support* an hypothesis. Therefore, you should *never* use the words *prove* or *disprove* when writing a research report. On the other hand, depending on the circumstances, it might be appropriate to comment that the results, for example, *demonstrate*, *show*, *suggest*, or *indicate* something.

## Statistics

Because they have already been reported in the Results section, statistics are not given again when findings are referred to in the Discussion. An exception to this is where you might want to emphasize something. For instance, you might want to point out that a difference between means was very large, or that a correlation was only moderate. In such cases, it is appropriate to reproduce the relevant descriptive statistics. You could, for example, write something like:

> The mean score for the simple response condition (157 ms) and that for the complex response condition (274 ms) were substantially different.

On the other hand, the values of inferential statistics should never be repeated in the Discussion. An interested reader can find these details in the Results section. All that is needed is to comment that the finding was significant (or not), as in, for example:

> There was a significant difference between scores in the simple and complex conditions.

The word *significant* should only be used in a research report when referring to the outcome of a statistical test. When an hypothesis is not supported (e.g., no significant difference was found), the term to be used is *non-significant*, or you could comment that there was no significant difference (or relationship). You might, for example, write:

> There was a non-significant difference between scores in the simple and complex tasks.

or

> The difference between scores in the simple and complex tasks was not significant.

A mistake that students occasionally make is to refer to a difference as being *insignificant*. This is not, of course, the same as *non-significant*.

## Theoretical context

Once you have presented the outcome of testing your hypotheses, the next step is to link your findings back to your *theoretical hypothesis*. This requires relating the results of your experiment to the ideas, theories, and research findings of previous investigators that you examined in the Introduction, and which led to your investigation. In particular, you should comment on any similarities, or differences, between your findings and those of earlier investigators. For instance, in the example mental arithmetic experiment, presumably you would have found that training the children to rehearse material was successful. Although this would not be the major finding of your experiment, you should comment on the similarity of this outcome with the earlier findings mentioned in your Introduction.

It is important that you discuss your findings within a theoretical framework. In the Introduction you will have developed your hypothesis on the basis of not only the findings of earlier studies; but, more importantly, the theoretical context of those studies. It follows, then, that you must explain how your results fit with the existing theory or theories to which you have referred, and interpret your results in relation to that theory or those theories. In the example mental arithmetic experiment, for instance, you would refer to short-term memory, which is a theoretical construct, and the use of rehearsal as an aid to the retention of material in short-term memory, which again is theoretical.

## Alternative explanations

**Critical thinking**, chap. 1 and chap. 5

It is possible that the outcome of an experiment could be attributed to some factor other than the variable(s) manipulated by the experimenter (i.e., the independent variable or variables). You should always consider this possibility, and acknowledge any likely alternative explanation of your results. You must analytically and critically consider your own research as you would that of others.

## Negative results

Sometimes results are not as expected; that is, an hypothesis is not supported (often referred to as a negative result). If this happens, acknowledge that it has, and do not try to explain it away. You should, however, critically examine your experiment and acknowledge any important limitations or weaknesses that could lead you to qualify your results. In particular, you should consider effect strength and the power of your experiment.

A point that is often overlooked, or not recognized, is that negative results can be useful. For example, they can bring into question the validity of previous findings, or theories, on the basis of which an hypothesis was derived.

## Acknowledging weaknesses

While acknowledging any weakness in your experiment, do not write a lengthy, in-depth criticism of it. If you were submitting a manuscript for publication and you included a lengthy list of weaknesses in your research, the editor would wonder why you had bothered to submit it. Obviously, you should have detected and overcome these weaknesses before you carried out your research. In any event, if the research were so badly flawed it would not be publishable.

Of course, experiments conducted by undergraduate students as part of their studies are not carried out under ideal conditions. Consequently, there are likely to be numerous potential flaws and weaknesses associated with them. All that you need to do is to show that you are able to recognize some. For instance, in the example mental arithmetic experiment you could comment that the research design would have been improved by the inclusion of a control group.

## New material

You should not introduce new material in the Discussion section of your report. Obviously, if you are aware of relevant findings, ideas, or theories, you should have considered these and included them in the Introduction. It is not appropriate, therefore, to introduce new material at this point.

On the other hand, it is possible that you observed something unexpected in the results that was not directly relevant to your experiment, but was nonetheless interesting. In such a situation you could justifiably introduce new material that is relevant to this.

## Contribution to knowledge

Research is carried out with the aim of advancing knowledge. Therefore, you should illustrate how your findings contribute to knowledge in the area.

Undergraduate students often experience difficulty with doing this. For teaching purposes, experiments carried out in class by students are commonly a replication of some previous experiment, and frequently a simplified version of that earlier experiment. From a student's perspective, then, it can be difficult to see how the results of such an experiment can advance knowledge. Although this is not an unreasonable point of view, you should try to demonstrate that your findings do contribute. For example, your experiment might have extended previous findings by introducing a new variable, or by manipulating a previously used variable in a different manner. If nothing else, replicating an earlier experiment adds support to that earlier finding and its theoretical underpinning.

A mistake that students sometimes make is to comment that previous findings support their current research. This is illogical. Rather, the student's new results obviously add support to the earlier finding.

On the other hand, not infrequently the results of experiments carried out by students do not support an hypothesis that has been supported in previously published research. Typically, this results from inherent and unavoidable weaknesses in teaching experiments. In this case, it is difficult, if not impossible, to demonstrate how the finding contributes to knowledge. However, it is acceptable to make comments such as, "It is surprising that . . .", "This finding would seem to suggest that . . . , but if this were so . . .".

## Conclusion

**Conclusion**, chap. 9

In closing the Discussion section, and your report, you must summarize its contents, just as you would do in the Conclusion section of any paper. This does not, of course, mean that you duplicate the abstract. Here you must summarize the key points from the Introduction and the Discussion. You cannot simply make a comment such as, "The results of this experiment clearly show . . .". It is unreasonable to expect the reader to remember everything included in the report at this point. In addition, you must very briefly summarize the important aspects of your findings.

Emphasize the wider theoretical or practical implications of the research reported. In particular, comment on the validity of your conclusions and any theoretical consequences. Finally, you should briefly comment on directions for future research suggested by your findings. Do not, however, make obvious suggestions that could apply to virtually any experiment, such as using a larger sample or a wider range of participants.

## Value judgements

**Values**, chap. 2

Another point is that in your Conclusion you should not make any comments or suggestions that involve value judgements based on personal moral or ethical values. For instance, in the example mental arithmetic experiment you would not recommend that the government *should* introduce a programme of teaching children to rehearse material in short-term memory so as to improve their performance in mental arithmetic. On the other hand, you could quite reasonably comment that such training *could* result in improved performance. Although this might seem to be a subtle difference, it is nonetheless real.

## ▶ Appendices

Sometimes, although rarely, it is appropriate to include appendices in a research report. When this is done they must, of course, be referred to in the text. Material included in an appendix is *not essential*, but rather is additional material to which the reader might like to refer. It is, therefore, acceptable merely to refer the reader to an appendix. You could, for example, write:

Examples of typical responses are provided in Appendix D.

Sometimes, for teaching purposes, students are required to attach as "appendices" to their research reports their statistical calculations, raw data, or perhaps some other material. *These are not appendices in the correct sense of the word.* They should not, therefore, be referred to in the research report. Neither should they be headed as appendices. In effect, when writing the research report, students should disregard any such documents.

## ► Tense

As far as is possible, the *Introduction and Discussion are written in the present tense*, but the *Abstract, Method, and Results sections are written in the past tense*. The guiding principle is to use the present tense when referring to current and continuing opinions or conclusions, but the past tense when referring to earlier findings, opinions, or conclusions. Logically, then, the content of the Method and Results sections is written in the past tense because you are reporting what you did and what you found, in the same way as you would refer to what some previous investigator did and found. Similarly, the past tense is used in the Discussion when referring to the method employed in the research being reported, or to the results obtained.

**Tense,**
chap. 3

   The Introduction of a research report is a literature review, which concludes by proposing a research design. At this point, whether or not that research has been, or will be, carried out is immaterial. It is, therefore, tentative in nature. An Introduction is not a research proposal, explaining some research that will be carried out at some time in the future. Therefore, *it is neither appropriate nor logical to write in the future tense* as in, for example, "This procedure *will be* used in this experiment," or "This definition *will be* used in this study."

   On the other hand, the use of the present tense can be equally problematic. Students sometimes inappropriately use the present tense in the Introduction when referring to the experiment being reported. For example, a student might write something like, "Because this is the most suitable definition it *is used* in the present study," or "This approach *is adopted* in this experiment." Again, this is neither appropriate nor logical.

   An exception to the above principle is that hypotheses are written using the future tense. Hypotheses obviously are written in the future tense because they are, at the time of developing them, predicted future outcomes.

## ► First person personal pronouns

**Pronoun agreement**, chap. 21

The use of first person personal pronouns in scientific writing is discussed in chapter 2, and it is suggested in that chapter that personal pronouns may be used in the Method and Results sections of a research report. However, students often experience difficulty with the use of these pronouns, especially when they are involved in experiments conducted as a group. Usually, although they might have worked as a group, students are expected to write a research report as though they had carried out the research as individuals.

The easiest way in which to avoid these potential problems is simply not to use first person personal pronouns anywhere in a research report. In any event, do not use first person personal pronouns (e.g., *I* or *we*, *me*, or *our*) in an abstract.

## ► Editing drafts

chap. 10

chap. 2

Writing a research report involves the writing and editing of several drafts, as for any other paper. Of course, *a research report must be written in a scholarly manner*, following the accepted conventions of grammar, spelling, and punctuation, and the required editorial style. In addition, it must be written in a scientific style.

When editing drafts of a research report, particular attention should be given to the connection between its various parts. *A research report should read as an integrated whole*. In particular, it is important to ensure that the Discussion follows logically and smoothly from the Introduction. It should be possible to read only the Introduction and Discussion sections of a research report and for these to make sense without reading the Method and Results sections.

**Reference**, chap. 18

chap. 19

Another aspect to check carefully is that any figures or tables included in a research report are appropriately referred to in the text, and are suitably placed. In addition, you should check that they conform to the style requirements of the APA Manual.

# 17 Reporting Statistics

There is some debate in psychology on the appropriate use and reporting of statistical analyses. This is recognized in the APA Manual, which allows for some discretion in the matter. The recommendations given here are somewhat of a simplification, and cover only common applications. In some instances it might be advisable to consult the APA Manual, and/or other sources. For most purposes, however, this chapter provides the necessary advice and guidance.

## ▶ Basic requirements

The reader must be given sufficient information to understand the analyses reported. What is required will vary with the circumstances; but, as a general rule, you must give the sample size, where applicable, the number in each cell, the name of the statistical technique used, and appropriate descriptive and inferential statistics.

When writing the results section you should assume that the reader is familiar with statistical techniques. Under normal circumstances, therefore, you should not cite a statistics text. On the other hand, if you used some unusual statistical technique you would probably be advised to cite a source, but this is uncommon. Similarly, you should not give formulae for statistics that are commonly used, but you might need to do so in unusual circumstances.

## ▶ Statistical assumptions

The appropriateness of statistical techniques often involves assumptions. A particular example is that the appropriateness of parametric analyses is based on the assumption of a normal, or close to normal, distribution of the data involved. Before analysing data, such assumptions will have been considered, and might have been tested using appropriate techniques.

If the necessary assumptions have been met, there is no need to report any testing involved. For example, if the analysis used is based on the assumption of normality of the distribution, and the data were normally distributed, there would be no need to report that the data were tested for this and found to be normally distributed. Unless there is an obvious reason to question the normality of the distribution, the reader will assume that this requirement has been met.

On the other hand, preliminary analysis of the data might reveal some problem. For example, if the data were not normally distributed it might have been necessary to use some data transformation, or to use a non-parametric analysis. In this case, the outcome of the preliminary analysis would need to be reported to explain why the data transformation was used or non-parametric techniques were adopted.

## ▶ Descriptive statistics

Descriptive statistics summarize the data, and *must always be given*. These statistics include means, measures of variability such as standard deviation, and correlation coefficients. Most commonly, you will report means together with either standard deviations (*SD*) or mean square error (*MSE*). As an example, the means and standard deviations in a simple experiment could be reported as:

> The mean solution time for the simple task was 45.3 s (*SD* = 4.37), and that for the complex task was 87.6 s (*SD* = 6.83).

or

> The mean error scores (with standard deviations in parentheses) for Groups 1 to 3 were 7.12 (1.41), 6.95 (1.78), and 5.42 (0.57).

### Direction and magnitude

The reader must know the magnitude and direction of any differences observed. Reporting descriptive statistics, as in the examples given above, provides this information. On the other hand, sometimes a comment is made in the text to emphasize the magnitude of the difference. You might, for example, make a comment such as "The mean score in the complex condition was *markedly* longer than that in the simple condition."

A mistake that students often make is to comment that a statistic was significant when they mean that it was, for example, large or important. When discussing statistics, the word *significant* is used only to refer to *statistical significance*.

### Effect size

Effect size (or strength of effect) refers to the *size* or *strength* of the effect observed in an experiment. For example, manipulating anxiety might have had a very marked effect on task performance, or it might have had only a moderate, or even a small effect. Effect size is relevant because *it is possible for a finding to be statistically significant, but for the effect size to be small*, which might question the importance of the finding. It is, therefore, necessary for the reader to be able to make some assessment of the observed effect size.

The descriptive statistics presented in the Results section of a research report will give an indication of the effect size. For instance, in a reaction time experiment, the means reported might have been 758 ms for the complex condition, and 107 ms for the simple condition. In the same experiment, mean error scores might have been 18.1 for the complex condition, and 0.7 for the simple condition. Clearly, these are substantial differences, indicating a comparably substantial effect size.

On the other hand, effect size can be reported using descriptive statistics designed for this purpose. Suitable statistics include *omega-squared* ($\varpi^2$) or *Cohen's measure of effect size* (*d*). You could report effect size using one of these statistics, as in, for example:

> Although there was a significant difference between the cued and non-cued conditions, the effect was small, $\varpi^2 = .15$.

In the APA Manual, the comment made is that "it is *almost always necessary* [italics added] to include some index of effect size or strength of relationship in your Results section" (p. 25). However, it would seem that when the effect size indicated by the descriptive statistics reported is large, or even moderate, there should be no need to calculate specific effect size statistics. Moreover, these statistics provide only an approximate measure, in the same way as do correlations. Judgements of the measured effect size, therefore, are subject to individual views.

## Non-parametric statistics

Obviously, non-parametric statistics are used when the distribution of the data is not normal. In this case, mean scores are meaningless. Rather, either median or mode scores should be given. Similarly, standard deviation is a meaningless statistic, and so the range of scores should be given.

## ▶ Inferential statistics

Descriptive statistics are used not only to summarize data, but also as estimates of population parameters. In contrast, *inferential statistics provide an indication of the confidence that can be placed in a statistic as an estimate of a given parameter*. Usually, then, you will have to report inferential statistics in the Results section.

There are some rare instances in which inferential statistics are not appropriate. For instance, an investigator might be interested in the outcome of a study only in relation to some particular organization, and not in generalizing the findings further. The staff of the organization, therefore, is the *population* of interest. In this example, if all of the staff of an organization were asked in a questionnaire for their opinion on some matter, because *all* of the staff were asked, this would constitute a *census*, not a survey. The data collected in summary form in this instance would constitute *parameters*, not statistics. There is, then, no logic in using inferential statistics.

In most research, however, *statistics are used as estimates of population parameters*, and so the calculation of inferential statistics is required. Moreover, research is commonly designed to test hypotheses. In such instances the calculation of inferential statistics is needed to test these hypotheses. It is, therefore, necessary to report the values of inferential statistics.

## Probability

When an acceptable level of falsely rejecting the null hypothesis (i.e., the probability of a Type I error, or the alpha level) is set *before* analysing the data, this criterion is described as the *a priori* probability. That is, a finding will be accepted as statistically significant only if the probability of that outcome is less than the a priori probability. Usually, this is set at .05, although sometimes a level of .01 is used.

By comparison, the *a posteriori* probability is the calculated probability of a difference as large or larger than, or a finding as extreme as, that observed occurring by chance if the null hypothesis were true. This probability is calculated *after* (or *post*) the event. When data are analysed using electronic calculators or computers, the a posteriori probability calculated is usually given as an exact value (e.g., $p = .0352$).

One problem that sometimes arises is that a calculator or computer might calculate the a posteriori probability to only three decimal places. This can result in the probability being calculated as .000. Obviously, this is impossible, because there can never be a zero probability of anything happening by chance in psychological research. Conversely put, there can never be 100% certainty. Nonetheless, when reporting the a posteriori probability in such an instance, all that can be done is to report it as $p = .00$. (Inferential statistics are reported to two decimal places.) On the other hand, it is correct to report this finding as being significant at, for instance, the .05 level (i.e., $p < .05$).

## Reporting probabilities[9]

The APA Manual recommends that the exact a posteriori probability calcu-lated should always be reported.[10] This may be done either in the text or in a table.

Obviously, you will have set an a priori probability before analysing your data. One option, then, is to make an introductory statement to the effect that you have set this criterion before presenting the results of your analy-ses. You could, for example, write something like,

> For all statistical tests, an alpha level of .05 was used.

or

> The data were analysed using a $t$ test, with an alpha level of .05.

If you have stated the alpha level adopted at the beginning of the Results section, you can then simply report the exact a posteriori probability as, for example:

> The main effect of fatigue was significant, $F(2, 30) = 8.75$, $p = .04$.

Alternatively, for each instance of reporting the results of a test, you could include "$p < .05$" or "$p > .05$" (as appropriate) to show that you have adopted this level. If you adopt this approach, you will still have to report the exact a posteriori probabilities calculated. In this case, you would report your results as, for example:

> There was a main effect of Fatigue, $F(2, 30) = 8.75$, $p = .04$, which was signif-icant at the .05 level.

## Correlations

The descriptive statistic that is used when reporting a relationship between two variables is a correlation coefficient. When such a statistic is used to estimate a population parameter, the reader must be given an indication of the likelihood of the statistic accurately representing the parameter of inter-est. In this case, the a posteriori probability of finding a correlation of this magnitude by chance alone must be reported. If you have commented at the

---

[9] There is some debate on the appropriate interpretation and reporting of probability statistics, but this is beyond the scope of this book. You should be aware that you might encounter some differing opin-ions. The best advice that can be offered is to follow the recommendations given here unless you are instructed not to do so.

[10] If inferential statistics are calculated manually, the $p$ value will be determined using a table of critical values, and it will be impossible to report exact a posteriori probabilities.

beginning of the Results section that you have adopted the .05 level for all analyses, this correlation could be simply reported as:

> There was a significant correlation of intelligence with accuracy ($r = .87$, $p = .03$).

Alternatively, if you have not made an initial statement about the alpha level adopted, the correlation could be reported in the form of, for example:

> The correlation of intelligence with accuracy was $r = .87$, $p = .03$, which was significant at the .05 level.

Another possibility arises when a number of correlations are involved, and the exact posteriori probability values are reported in a table together with the correlation coefficients. In this case, it would be appropriate to report the correlations in the text, as in, for example:

> There was a significant correlation of study time with examination marks, $r = .71$, $p < .05$.

When reporting correlation statistics, students often confuse the *magnitude* or *strength* of the correlation with its *statistical significance*. The magnitude or strength of the correlation is given by $r$. In the above correlation this is .71, which represents a substantial relationship. By comparison, the a posteriori probability of obtaining a correlation of this magnitude by chance alone is given by the $p$ value, which in this case is less than .05.

*Note*: Correlations are often referred to in the form of, "There was a correlation between A and B," and the APA Manual uses this terminology. Although it is perhaps a pedantic point to make, referring to a correlation *between* A and B is incorrect. The correlation of A is *with* B. This means that as A increases (or decreases) B increases (or decreases); that is, the two vary systematically *with* one another. Correctly expressed, therefore, this should be referred to as, "There was a correlation of A with B."

## Confidence intervals

It is sometimes necessary to make an estimate of some population parameter while not comparing it with any other. For example, it might be necessary to estimate the mean time that is required to respond to some stimulus, such as a traffic signal. This is referred to as a *point estimate*, because the number involved represents a point on some continuum. Obviously, any such estimate is subject to error. It is important, therefore, to provide the reader of a research report involving such estimates with an indication of their accuracy. *Confidence intervals* are used for this purpose. When reporting a point estimate of a population parameter, then, it is necessary to report the sample mean observed, and the upper and lower intervals of the confidence limits selected. Usually, these limits will represent the 95%, or sometimes the 99%, confidence interval. Such a point estimate should be reported as, for example:

> The mean response time was 750 ms +/– 123 ms (95% confidence interval).


## Comparisons

When reporting the results of comparisons, the size and direction of any difference must be reported using descriptive statistics such as means together with an appropriate measure of variability. In addition, the results of the inferential statistic calculated must be reported, and a measure of the effect size might be included. This can be achieved, for example, by reporting results in the following form:

> Problem-solving time for the stressed condition ($M = 79.4$ s, $SD = 9.27$) was significantly longer than that for the non-stressed condition ($M = 32.3$ s, $SD = 6.01$), $t(16) = 7.93$, $p = .03$ (one-tailed), $d = .36$.

In this example, mean problem-solving time for both conditions is given. This allows the reader to see the direction of the difference, and easily to calculate its magnitude. Also, a measure of variability (standard deviation) is given for both group means, as are the name ($t$) and value of the inferential statistic, the a posteriori probability calculated ($p$), and a measure of effect size $d$ (Cohen's measure of effect size). Another point is that the analysis is described as *one-tailed*. Whether the test was one-tailed or two-tailed should be indicated.

Another example, using statistics from an analysis of variance, is:

> Mean error in the vision-precluded condition (35.7 mm) was significantly greater than that in the vision-available condition (16.4 mm), $F(1, 127) = 9.86$, $p = .03$, $\omega^2 = .47$ ($MSE = 6.32$).

Again, the mean values for both groups are given for the same reasons as in the first example. The abbreviation $M$ is not used because the text makes the statistic given clear. As in the first example, a measure of variability ($MSE$), the inferential statistic calculated ($F$) and its value, the a posteriori probability ($p$), and a measure of effect size (omega-squared) are given.

Other examples of reporting the results of an analysis of variance are:

> Mean error was significantly greater in the kinaesthetic (17.1 mm) than in the visual (9.4 mm) modality, $F(1, 22) = 24.32$, $p = .03$, $\omega^2 = .44$ ($MSE = 76.42$).

> There was a significant Length × Modality interaction, $F(1, 22) = 164.68$, $p < .05$, $d = .05$.

This analysis revealed that both the main effects of age, $F(2, 33) = 7.85$, p < .01, $\varpi^2 = .37$ ($MSE = 14.76$), and length, $F(1, 132) = 29.22$, $p < .01$, $\varpi^2 = .42$, ($MSE = 13.02$), were significant.

## ▶ Non-parametric statistics

When reporting non-parametric statistics, such as chi-squared, information such as the number in each cell or category and sample sizes should be given. You could, for example, report a chi-square ($\chi^2$) statistic as,

$\chi^2$ (4, $N = 50$) = 5.36, $p < .05$.

In this example, the name of the test is indicated ($\chi^2$), and the degrees of freedom (4), sample size (50), and the $p$ value are given.

## ▶ Comments on significance

Sometimes, but rarely, an author might comment that, for example, "The difference between scores was *highly* significant." Such a comment is meaningless. Before carrying out any research, the investigator decides on the acceptable level of statistical significance. By convention this is the .05 level, but this is purely arbitrary: In some instances either a lower or a higher level of significance might be appropriate. Whatever the level selected, the result of calculating inferential statistics is that either the difference, or relationship, involved is significant or it is not: It cannot be *highly* significant.

On the other hand, although again rarely, an author will make a comment on findings like, "The difference between scores was *marginally* significant." Such a comment is intended to introduce a note of caution. What the author is implying is that, bearing in mind the possibility of random error, if the research were replicated this finding might not be found to be significant. This is an acceptable comment.

The advice given above might seem to be contradictory, but it is not. Random error can quite easily result in a finding being significant when the difference or relationship involved is not significant (i.e., a Type II error). By comparison, random error is very unlikely to result in finding a very large difference, or relationship, which in turn will produce a very low probability of having occurred by chance (i.e., a "high" level of significance). It follows, then, that a note of caution is warranted in the former case, while in the latter a difference or relationship that is clearly significant is simply that.

## ▶ Negative results

Sometimes an hypothesis is not supported by the results of an experiment or study. This could be attributed to any one or more of a number of reasons. For example, there might have been some flaw in reasoning when developing the hypothesis, or some flaw in the research design.

In the event that a negative outcome is attributable to such flaws, it is most likely that the research would not be reported. On the other hand, in research reports written by students for teaching purposes, appropriate comments would be made in the Discussion section.

One possible cause that should be considered, and commented on in the Discussion section of a research report, is that the effect size was too small or the sample too small. The power of an experiment or study to detect a difference or relationship, presuming that one exists, is beyond the scope of this book. However, when reporting negative findings power should be considered. Closely related to this is the effect size. When reporting negative findings, therefore, effect size should be calculated and reported.

A common weakness in students' research reports is merely to comment that the failure to support some hypothesis can be attributed to the small sample size used. Significant differences or relationships are often found using only quite small samples. It is, therefore, quite probable that the failure to support the hypothesis can be attributed to some other factor(s). To argue that failing to support an hypothesis is attributable to the sample size requires the calculation of the strength of effect, and it would be necessary to illustrate that a sample size of $x$ would be needed to produce a significant result.

## ▶ Precision

*Inferential statistics are always reported to two decimal places.* As a general rule, descriptive statistics, such as means and measures of variability, are also reported to two decimal places. You should *avoid false precision*. For example, correlations, proportions, and measures of effect size are only approximate. They should not, therefore, be reported to more than two decimal places. Correlations, for instance, should be reported as, for example, "$r = .56$". Similarly, percentages are usually reported to the nearest whole number (e.g., 85%).

For other descriptive statistics, judgement is required. For example, when reporting reaction time scores in milliseconds it would be pointless to use any greater precision than 1 millisecond. Similarly, although two decimal places are normally used when reporting mean square error, it would be pointless to report a large mean square error to two decimal places. In such cases the statistic may be reported only to the nearest whole number.

When you have decided what level of precision to use for descriptive statistics for a given unit of measure, *you must be consistent within a paper*. Do not, for instance, report some means to two decimal places and others to one. You may, however, use different levels of precision for different units of measure. For example, you might report mean reaction time scores to the nearest millisecond, but mean error scores to one decimal place.

## ▶ Leading zero

If the value of a statistic is less than one, but could be more than one, a leading zero is used. For instance, when reporting error scores the mean could be more than one, and so mean scores would be reported as, for example, "The mean error score in the flexible condition was 0.4." Similarly, a leading zero is used when reporting a non-significant inferential statistic. For example, when reporting a non-significant $F$ value, as in "The main effect of stress was not significant, $F(1, 33) = 0.64$", a leading zero is required, because the $F$ value can be greater than one.

On the other hand, when the value of the statistic cannot be more than one the leading zero is omitted. Therefore, for example, when reporting correlations, proportions, or probability values (e.g., $p = .04$), a leading zero is not used.

## ▶ Recommendations

The results of simple analyses can be presented in text with relative ease. By comparison, for more complex analyses it is probably better to present the detailed results in a table as, for instance, is normally used for analysis of variance. When results are presented in tabular form, it is only necessary in the text to refer to the table. For example, you could comment that:

> Table 1 shows that there was a significant main effect of fatigue, with those in the fatigued condition solving the problems more slowly ($M = 27.3$ s, $SD = 7.1$) than those in the non-fatigued condition ($M = 15.2$ s, $SD = 5.9$).

Reporting results in this way makes the text easier to follow, and presenting all statistics together in one location makes them readily available for examination.

In the above example inferential statistics are not included in the text because they are presented in a table. On the other hand, the relevant descriptive statistics are given in the text. It would be possible to present the mean scores and standard deviations also in a table, in addition to the analysis of variance table. If this were done, there would be no need to give the mean and standard deviation statistics in the text. However, the reader would then have to refer to two tables. It is, therefore, advisable to present only the inferential statistics in an analysis of variance table, and to give descriptive statistics in the text, as has been done in the example given.

A point to note is that detailed statistics that are given in a table should not be reproduced in the text. Doing so would be redundant.

Another option is to present results in the form of a figure. However, only approximate values can be read from a figure. Therefore, it remains necessary to report the values of statistics. A basic principle is that data should not be presented in both a figure and a table, because to do so would be redundant. On the other hand, there is nothing wrong with presenting results in the form of a figure, and giving statistics, such as means and standard deviations, in the text.

A point that should be considered is that a figure has visual impact, and often a relationship that is readily evident in a figure is not so in either a table or text. For example, a three-way interaction is best illustrated by a figure. In such a situation there is nothing wrong with presenting results in the form of a figure, to illustrate the results visually, and in the form of an analysis of variance table.

In summary, if the analyses are straightforward, for example involving two or three $t$ tests or correlations, the results should simply be reported in the text. On the other hand, if the analyses are complex, as for example in a multifactorial design, it is often best to present the results in the form of a table, and/or a figure, and to refer the reader to the table and/or figure. What is the most suitable method of presentation will, of course, depend on the circumstances.

# 18 Using Figures and Tables

Illustrations such as graphs, diagrams, charts, line drawings, maps, and photographs are referred to as *figures*. Sometimes, a figure can be used to illustrate an idea. For instance, a figure in the form of a block diagram can be used to illustrate an information-processing model. Alternatively, a *table*, in the form of columns and rows, can be used to present an idea. For example, a stage theory of development can be presented in the form of a table. Most commonly, however, figures and tables are used to present information in the form of data. In this case, the figure or table is used to present information in support of some idea.

Figures can often convey information more efficiently and clearly than a lengthy and complex written description. For example, a figure can be used to illustrate a complex relationship more simply and clearly than will a written description. Similarly, tables are useful for presenting information in an easily readable form. They also have the advantage that either written or numerical information, or both, can be included.

Although valuable, figures and tables provide only an aid to the presentation of information or the expression of ideas; *they cannot completely replace written text*. A reader cannot be expected to understand what you are trying to convey solely on the basis of figures or tables. On the other hand, although perhaps with difficulty, a reader should be able to understand the information and ideas that you are presenting without referring to any figures or tables included in your paper. Your aim should be that your written text, together with any figures and/or tables that you have included, will provide an easily understandable communication of the necessary information or ideas. Put another way, a figure or a table should supplement the text.

## ► Reference

To facilitate reference, figures and tables are numbered consecutively, but separately, using Arabic numerals. Therefore, the first figure in a paper will be "Figure 1" and the first table will be "Table 1". Notice that, when referring to a specific figure or table by number, a capital (upper-case) letter is used.

When preparing a paper for publication, the author does not know exactly where figures and tables will be placed in the printed article or book.

Consequently, references such as "the following figure", "The table above", or "the table on page X" are not used.

In students' papers, if the figure or table appears on the same page as the text referring to it, it is acceptable to refer to it by writing "the figure above", or "the table below". However, during editing, text can be moved, resulting in the relationship between text and figure or table changing. A similar problem can result if page numbers are used for reference. As a general principle, then, it is better to *use the commonly accepted practice and to refer to figures or tables only by number*.

## ► Figures and tables in an appendix

If multiple figures or tables are included in an appendix, each is numbered with an upper case letter and an Arabic numeral. For example, Figure A1 would be the first figure in Appendix A. Similarly, Figure B2 would be the second figure in Appendix B. In this case, the figure or table could be referred to in the text as, for example,

> Figure 2 in Appendix B shows . . .

or

> Table B2 shows . . .

For the first reference in the text it is advisable to use the format of the first example, so that the reader knows that you are referring to an appendix. For any subsequent reference to any such figure or table, the format of the second example can then be used.

## ► When to use

Deciding when to use figures and/or tables is a matter of judgement, but they *should be kept to a minimum*. Frequent reference to numerous figures and/or tables is disruptive, and is more likely to hinder, rather than facilitate, the communication of information or ideas. The principle to follow is that, *if you can convey the information or an idea clearly and concisely in writing, do not use a figure or a table*. Put another way, if the information or idea can be described simply and clearly in writing, then that is all that is required. For instance, a small number of scores can quite effectively be reported and compared in writing. You could, for example, write something like,

> Mean reaction time scores increased with age, from 225 ms for the young group to 243 ms for the middle-aged group, and 320 ms for the old group.

Similarly, if an idea can easily and clearly be presented in writing, then that is all that is required. For example, you could write something like,

> Two processes are involved. The first involves perception of the stimulus, and the second a response choice.

In the above examples, the information or idea could be presented in either a figure or a table, but to do so would be unnecessary.

Following the same logic, there is no need to provide illustrations of items of apparatus with which it is reasonable to assume the reader will be familiar. For example, if you used a personal computer in an experiment you can assume that the reader has seen one before, and there is nothing to be gained from providing an illustration of one

On the other hand, a figure or table can clarify a description that would otherwise be lengthy and difficult to follow. For example, a simple diagram can be helpful when describing the layout of items of equipment used in an experiment, and a flow chart can be useful when describing a model.

## A figure or a table

When reporting data, *the same information should not be given in both a figure and a table*; to do so would be redundant. Therefore, a choice has to be made between the two forms of presentation.

A figure has visual impact and so is particularly helpful when illustrating differences between, or relationships among, variables. Tables do not have the same visual impact, but they are particularly useful for presenting a summary of large data sets. Another advantage of tables is that precise values of data are presented. By comparison, only approximate values can be read from a graph. The choice between a figure and a table, therefore, depends on which form of presentation you think will better illustrate what you want to show.

## What is shown

Figures and tables should include sufficient information to be understood without reference to the text, but they must always be referred to in the text. Although they can be a useful aid to the communication of information and ideas, *you must make clear in the text what you intend a figure or a table to show*. Sometimes a simple reference to a figure or a table is sufficient. For instance, when describing apparatus, you might write something like,

> The stimulus lights and response switches were positioned as shown in Figure 1.

In the above example the reason for providing a diagram of the layout of apparatus should be obvious. Similarly, the purpose of a table providing details of participants should be readily evident. For instance, when describing participants you might write something like,

> Details of the participants are given in Table 1.

As another example, when discussing a theory it might be appropriate to write,

> A summary of the stages of Piaget's theory of development is given in Table 3.

By comparison, when presenting data, the point that you want to illustrate may not be immediately apparent. For example, the following sentence is inadequate.

> Mean reaction time scores are shown in Figure 1.

This sentence only tells the reader where to look for the information. *You must make clear what you are illustrating.* For example, you might write something like,

> Figure 1 shows that reaction time increased with the number of possible responses.

The point might seem to be obvious; nonetheless, you must tell the reader what you intend the figure to show. Often, what you want to illustrate is not immediately obvious, and will require some explanation. As an example, you might write something like,

> Figure 2 shows that, although accuracy was markedly improved by practice in the complex condition, there was little effect in the simple condition.

or

> A comparison of Figures 3 and 4 shows that the error patterns differed markedly.

## ▶ Figures

What is being illustrated will dictate the nature of the figure involved. In some instances, a photograph or a map might be appropriate. For example, a photograph might be useful in a report of an experiment on eyewitness recall, or a map in a report of a survey. In undergraduate papers, however, such instances are not common. On the other hand, a figure could well be used to aid in the description of a model, apparatus, or procedure. For example, a diagram similar to Figure 1 could be used to illustrate a series of processes involved in movement control, or a line drawing similar to

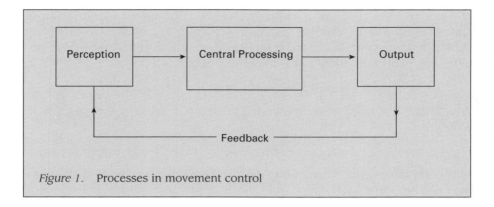

*Figure 1.* Processes in movement control

Figure 2 could be used to illustrate a maze used in an experiment. Notice that, although the maze illustrated in Figure 2 is quite simple, a verbal description could easily become rather complex and difficult to understand.

Sometimes, a chart or a line drawing will be the appropriate form of illustration. Most commonly, however, figures are used to present data. In this case, you will have to choose between one of several forms of presentation. Those that you will be likely to use are *line graphs*, *bar graphs*, *histograms*, and *scatter graphs.*

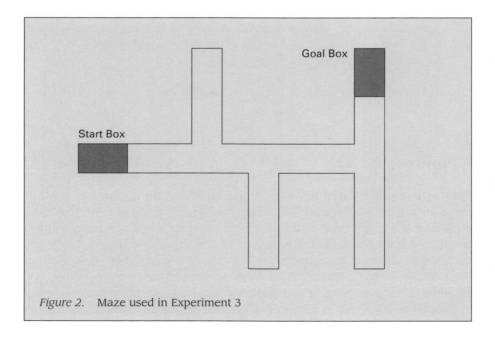

*Figure 2.* Maze used in Experiment 3

## Line graphs

Line graphs are useful for illustrating frequency distributions (which are often referred to as frequency polygons), relationships, trends, differences, and interactions. Graphs of this type should only be used when both the independent and dependent variables are *continuous* (i.e., in either interval or ratio scale). An example of a simple line graph is given in Figure 3.

Although line graphs should be used only when both variables are continuous, they are often used to illustrate differences and interactions when the independent variable is *categorical* (i.e., in either nominal or ordinal scale). An example of a line graph illustrating an interaction in which both independent variables are categorical, is given in Figure 4. In this figure, *Level of Stress* is shown on the *x* axis, but *Problem Complexity* could have been shown on this axis. Which variable is shown on the *x* axis depends on what makes most sense in terms of what you are illustrating.

Graphs of this type can be particularly useful when illustrating a three-way interaction. An example is given in Figure 5. This figure shows two graphs, drawn side by side, which have a common *y* axis.

Both graphs show solution time for two levels of *complexity* (*simple* and *complex*), plotted against two levels of *fatigue* (*low* and *high*), which are shown on the *x* axis. The graph on the left shows the relationship between these variables for a *low level of stress*, while the graph on the right shows the same relationship for a *high level of stress.* Again, which variables are shown on the *x* axis depends on what makes most sense in terms of what you are illustrating.

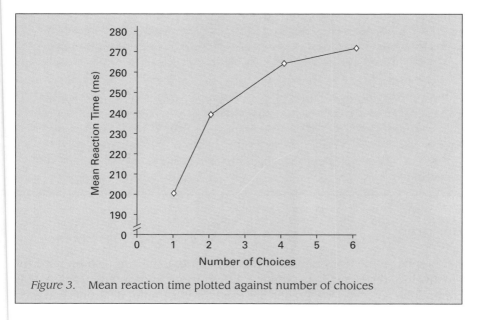

*Figure 3.*    Mean reaction time plotted against number of choices

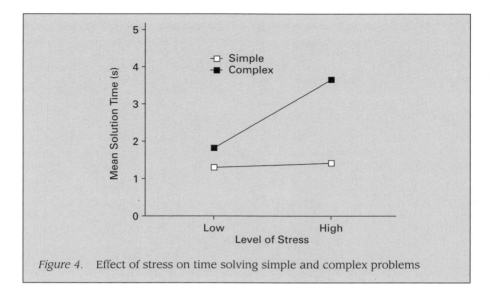

*Figure 4.*   Effect of stress on time solving simple and complex problems

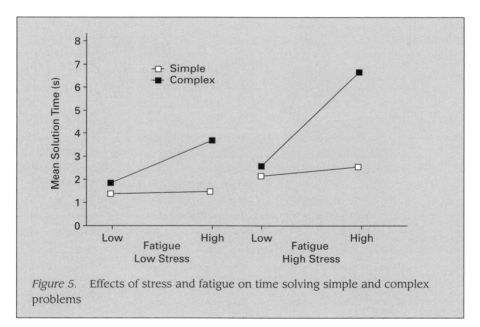

*Figure 5.*   Effects of stress and fatigue on time solving simple and complex problems

## Bar graphs

Bar graphs (sometimes referred to as column graphs) can also be used for illustrating relationships, trends, differences, and interactions. Most commonly, however, bar graphs are used for illustrating differences; trends

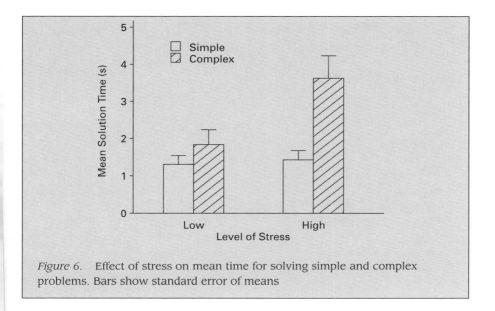

*Figure 6.*    Effect of stress on mean time for solving simple and complex problems. Bars show standard error of means

and relationships are usually better illustrated by, and interactions are more apparent in, a line graph. *Bar graphs are customarily used when the dependent variable is continuous, but the independent variable is categorical.*

Figure 6, in which both independent variables are categorical, is an example of a bar graph. This figure shows the same interaction as illustrated in Figure 4. A comparison of Figures 4 and 6 shows that the interaction is more obviously apparent in the line graph.

## Histograms

Histograms are a type of bar graph. The difference is that, in a histogram, *both the dependent and independent variables must be in either interval or ratio scale.* Therefore, because the data are continuous, each bar begins and ends, on the *x* axis, at the real limits of an interval, and so bars must touch each other. Graphs of this type are customarily used to illustrate frequency distributions. An example of a histogram is given in Figure 7.

## Scatter graphs

Scatter graphs (often referred to as scatter plots) can be used to illustrate relationships among variables, and they have the advantage of giving an indication of both the nature and strength of a relationship. However, relationships are usually more clearly illustrated by a line graph. In a scatter plot,

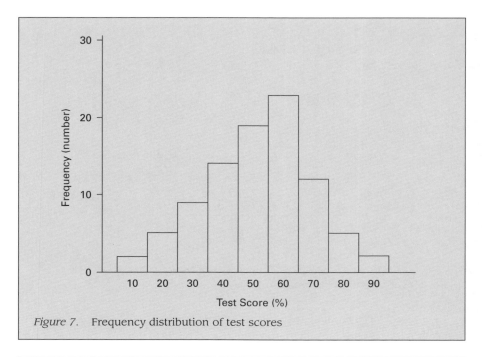

*Figure 7.*   Frequency distribution of test scores

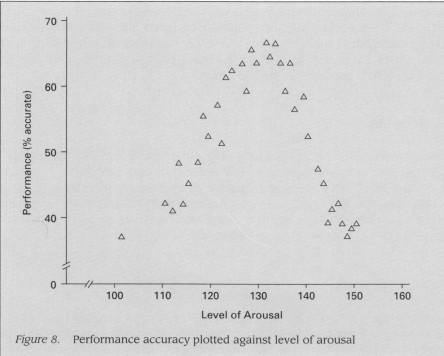

*Figure 8.*   Performance accuracy plotted against level of arousal

*both the dependent and independent variables must be in either interval or ratio scale.* An example of a scatter graph is given in Figure 8.

## ▶ Tables

Information can often be conveniently and efficiently presented in the form of a table, so saving words. For instance, rather than writing a lengthy description, the characteristics of participants in an experiment can be given in the form of a table. Similarly, a table can be used to present a theory, such as one involving stages of development. Most commonly, however, tables are used to report numerical data. In particular, a table is useful for the presentation of a large data set in an easily readable form. Such a table could be used to present material that is not necessary for an understanding of the paper involved, but might be of some interest to the reader. In this case, the table would be included as an appendix.

More commonly, tables are used to present numerical data in the body of a research report. For example, the results of a survey could well be reported in tabular form. Similarly, a number of correlations, or the results of an analysis of variance, could be reported in this manner.

On the other hand, rather than simply presenting information, a table can be used to illustrate something. A table could, for instance, be used to illustrate some difference in scores, or a trend or pattern in data. When this is done, the table must be carefully designed so that the point being illustrated is readily evident.

### Reference in text

When used in a paper, *tables must be referred to in the text.* The reason for inclusion of the table must be made clear.

If the table is used only to provide information that might be of interest, but is not necessary for an understanding of the text, and so is included as an appendix, only a simple reference is required. For example, you could write something like,

> Examples of comments made in response to Question 3 are given in Appendix A.

or

> Mean scores on all of the sub-tests are shown in Appendix B.

Although it is rare, there are some instances in which the reason for including a table in the text is immediately apparent. For example, the reason for inclusion of details of participants in an experiment in a research report will be obvious. In this case it is also acceptable to write a comment such as,

> Details of the participants are provided in Table 1.

However, if a table is used to *illustrate* something, this must be made explicit in the text. You cannot rely on the point being obvious to the reader. In this case, you could, for example, write something like,

> Table 2 shows that, for all participants, the scores in Condition 1 were high, but in Condition 2 were low.

or

> Table 3 shows that in all conditions the correlations were substantial.

Notice that, in instances such as this, there is no need to refer to every individual item in the table. Rather, the point being made is that there is some trend or pattern, and this is what is being illustrated.

## ► Acknowledgement

Although rarely, sometimes a figure or a table taken from a published source is included in a paper. If this is done, care must be taken. Figures and tables cannot be reproduced from another source, in whole or in part, without the copyright holder's permission. However, in student papers (which are not published) permission is not usually required. Nonetheless, you must acknowledge the source of any figure or table that you reproduce. For student purposes, the easiest way of doing this is to add an acknowledgement, as a note in the figure caption, or at the bottom of a table, as in the following examples for a journal article and a book:

> From "Students' Mental Meandering," by W. H. Y. Worry, 1992, *Journal of Student Problems, 16*, p. 99.

> From *A Study of Academic Woes* (p. 21), by I. Wonder, 1994, Istanbul: Gonmad Press.

## ► Placement

When submitting papers for publication, authors have little or no control over the placement of figures or tables. By comparison, when writing papers in the course of their studies, students do control this placment. The following advice is offered to guide students.

A figure or a table should be placed in a paper as soon as is convenient following the first reference to it. If it is relatively small (not more than about half of a page) it may be included on a page together with text. In this case, the figure or table should be placed immediately after the paragraph in which first reference is made to it. If the figure or table is large, it should be presented on a separate page. In this case, the page involved should be inserted into the paper as the next page following the first reference to it in the text. When this is done, the page on which the figure or table appears is numbered as the next consecutive page.

Sometimes, although it is small enough to be included with the text, a figure or table will not fit onto the page after first reference is made to it. Clearly, this will happen when the first reference to it appears too far down the page to allow it to fit onto the remainder of the page. When this happens, the figure or table may be placed on the immediately following page. If the following page begins with a new paragraph, the figure or table should appear at the top of the page before that paragraph. Otherwise, it should appear after the first ending of a paragraph on that page. Alternatively, the figure or table may be presented on a separate page as described above.

A table can never be split over two pages. No table should ever include so much data that it cannot fit onto a single page.

# 19 Preparing Figures and Tables

Although figures can be used to illustrate, for example, some piece of apparatus, and tables can be used to present textual material, most commonly they are used to present data in numerical form. The emphasis in this chapter, therefore, is on the design and preparation of such figures and tables. However, the principles involved apply equally to other figures and tables.

## ▶ Size

The size of a figure or table, and hence content, is obviously limited by the size of the page. A figure or a table should be centrally positioned on the page, with margins at the top, bottom, and both sides, of at least 35 mm. If a full page is not needed, any space not used is left at the bottom. Figures and tables may be presented in landscape orientation, but this is inconvenient for the reader and should be avoided if possible.

A simple figure need not be large, but a complex one will need to be large enough to show the necessary detail without becoming cluttered. As a guide, a clear figure will usually occupy about half, or more, of the space available between the top and bottom margins on a page. Similarly, a simple table need not be large, but a large data set will require a sizeable table. However, a table should never exceed a single page in a paper. On the other hand, a small typeface cannot be used to achieve this. Doing so can make the table difficult or perhaps impossible to read.

If a figure or table is included on a page together with text, it should be centrally placed on the page, with margins of at least 35 mm on the left- and right-hand sides. Quadruple spacing should be left above and below the figure or table to clearly separate it from the text.

## ▶ Purpose

Figures that are used to present data are intended to illustrate differences or relationships, and tables are often used for this purpose. Therefore, *the difference or relationship being illustrated must be clearly apparent.* If a table is used to present a summary of a large volume of data, it *must be easy to understand.* Moreover, a figure or a table should be able to be understood without reference to the text. Therefore, if a figure or a table is effectively to communicate the information or idea that is intended, it must be carefully designed.

## ▶ Statistical package figures and tables

Some statistical packages produce figures or tables. However, these are intended only to present a summary of the analysis involved. Statistical packages cannot interpret the meaning of the outcome of an analysis: This can only be done by the researcher involved. Only the researcher, then, can decide on what needs to be illustrated, and how best to do so. Moreover, figures and tables produced by statistical packages are sometimes of rather poor visual quality. In addition, there can be problems in areas such as scale, symbols used, labelling of axes on figures, and the form of presentation of data in tables. Finally, such figures and tables often do not comply with the APA Manual style requirements. Therefore, *figures and tables produced by statistical packages are often not suitable for use in papers.*

It is, then, often not satisfactory simply to photocopy such a figure or table and to include it in a paper. On the other hand, in some instances, a figure or table produced by a statistical package can be modified to illustrate clearly what an author wants to convey, and to comply with the APA style requirements. In such instances the figure or table can be modified and then photocopied. Any such modifications must, of course, be of a high standard.

## ▶ Designing figures

In newspapers and magazines, three-dimensional graphs, symbolic devices, and colour are often used in figures for visual effect; but these can produce visual distortions and so should not be used. By comparison, with very rare exception, figures in scientific journals are published in black and white, and three-dimensional figures are not used.

*A figure must always be as simple as possible.* Important information will not stand out in a figure that is cluttered by too many features. Therefore, only necessary details should be included.

### What is shown

The purpose for inclusion of a figure in a paper will always be explained in the text when the reader is referred to it. This could, for example, take the form of:

> Figure 3 shows that reaction time increased steadily over the four experimental conditions.

However, the reader must be able to understand the figure without reference to the text. Therefore, a figure must include sufficient detail to allow this. The basic information required is provided in a *figure caption*. In the case of line drawings, charts, maps, or photographs, other detail may be included in the form of labels. For a graph, additional detail is presented using symbols together with an explanatory legend. Sometimes explanatory notes are also included.

### Captions

A figure caption should clearly describe the contents of the figure in a short *sentence or phrase*, which should be as concise as possible, and should not include redundancies such as "Figure showing . . .". Any further information needed to clarify the figure, such as explanation of non-standard abbreviations, or symbols not included in the legend, may be added following the figure description. If error bars, or confidence limits, are shown in the figure, the measure of variability used should be explained. (For an example, see Figure 9.) When sample sizes differ, it is often helpful to give the number in each group.

Capital (upper-case) letters are used only for the first word in the caption, and any proper nouns. The word *Figure* and the figure number are typed in italics (and the figure number is followed by a full stop), but the figure caption is typed in the same typeface as the text of the paper. In student papers the caption should appear directly under the figure. All lines of text in a figure caption are aligned with the left margin of the page (see Figure 9).

### Labels

In charts and line drawings it is usually necessary to label components. This might require the use of arrows or lines to connect features to the necessary labels. In particular, this might be required if a photograph were used. Where possible, however, this should be avoided: Lines or arrows clutter a figure. In most illustrations, features of a drawing can be simply labelled on it. (For examples, see Figures 1 and 2 in chapter 18.) In both line and bar graphs, the axes of the graph must be labelled. (See Figure 6 in chapter 18, and Figure 10.)

### Legend

In the case of line graphs, a legend, which provides a key to the symbols used as plot points to identify curves, should be placed within the bound-

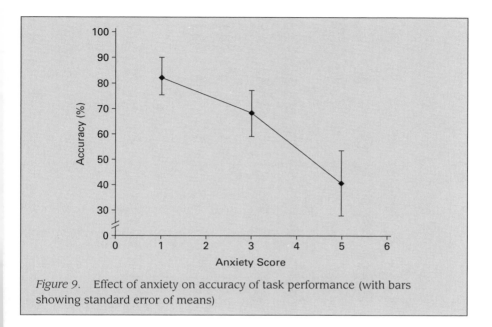

*Figure 9.* Effect of anxiety on accuracy of task performance (with bars showing standard error of means)

aries of the figure. (For an example, see Figure 10.) Similarly, a legend providing a key to the hatchings, symbols, or shading used to distinguish bars, should be provided in bar graphs. (For an example, see Figure 6 in chapter 18.)

## ▶ Line graphs

Line graphs should be as simple as possible. In particular, too many curves will result in a cluttered figure that cannot readily be understood. Therefore, the number of curves shown should be kept to a minimum – preferably no more than four.

## Axes

In a graph, the vertical axis is referred to as the *ordinate*, or *y* axis, and the horizontal axis is referred to as the *abscissa*, or *x* axis. (See Figure 10.) By convention, the dependent variable is shown on the *y* axis and the independent variable is shown on the *x* axis. (The *x* axis is drawn a*cross* the figure.) Both axes must be clearly labelled parallel to the axis, with the variable name and unit of measurement. Abbreviations may be used when labelling axes, but any non-standard abbreviations must be explained in the figure caption.

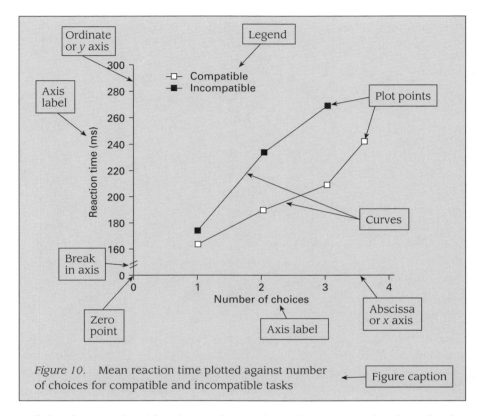

*Figure 10.*    Mean reaction time plotted against number of choices for compatible and incompatible tasks

If the data are in either interval or ratio scale, numerical values for the variable are shown next to grid marks on the axis, and the zero point is always included. To include the zero point, it may be necessary to break the axis. This is done by inserting two short parallel lines in the axis, close to the zero point. (For an example, see Figure 10.) When the independent variable is in either an ordinal or a nominal scale, appropriate labels are similarly shown on the *x* axis, but a zero point is not shown. (For an example, see Figure 6 in chapter 18.)

## Scale

A suitable scale should be selected for the *x* axis so that, when it is drawn, curves occupy all, or most, of the width of the figure. Sometimes, when the lowest value on the *x* axis begins considerably above zero, this requires breaking the axis. (For an example, see Figure 8 in chapter 18.) In this case, of course, the curve will not meet the *y* axis. Also, when the independent variable is categorical, because a zero point is not shown on the *x* axis, curves will not meet the *y* axis. (For an example, see Figure 4 in chapter 18.)

Choosing the scale for the *y* axis can be a little more difficult. When multiple curves are drawn on a figure they can be difficult to distinguish from one another. Where possible, therefore, the scale on the *y* axis should be large enough to result in a clear separation between curves. This will sometimes necessitate breaking the *y* axis (see Figure 9).

On both axes, the scale used must be selected with care: Use of an inappropriate scale can result in visual distortion and so a misleading figure. For example, the relationship between two variables can be visually exaggerated. To avoid such distortions, the scales chosen for a graph should result in a figure in which the height is about three quarters of the width.

## Plot points

So that the curves shown on a line graph can readily be identified, they must have some distinguishing characteristic. One option is to use dotted, dashed, and solid lines. However, because dotted and dashed lines are difficult to draw neatly and consistently, in hand-drawn graphs they should not be used, and most graphing programmes use only solid lines. Therefore, plot points (in the form of simple geometric shapes such as squares, circles, or triangles) are used to distinguish curves, and the meaning of these symbols is explained in the legend. (For an example, see Figure 10.)

## Variability

Variability of data is sometimes shown on the curves in line graphs in the form of small "bars", which usually represent the standard error of the mean. When these are included in a figure, they should be explained in the figure caption, as in Figure 9.

## ► Bar graphs

Bar graphs, like line graphs, should be as simple as possible. In particular, too many bars will result in a cluttered figure that cannot readily be understood. Therefore, the number of bars shown should be kept to a minimum – preferably no more than six.

## Bars

In bar graphs the *x* axis represents either a nominal or an ordinal scale. Consequently, there is no numerical relationship between the width of bars.

Therefore, *all bars must be of the same width*. Also, because the scale on the *x* axis is not continuous, *bars should not touch one another*. However, where logically they should be grouped on some basis, bars in a group may touch. (For an example, see Figure 6 in chapter 18.)

Graphs are read from left to right. Therefore, when the independent variable is measured in an ordinal scale, the position of bars on the *x* axis will be determined by their values. By comparison, when the independent variable is in a nominal scale, the position of bars is not determined by their values. However, it is likely that the nature of the data reported will suggest some order.

## Variability

Since bar graphs are commonly used to illustrate differences, measures of variability in the data are often included. To show variability, small error bars (in the form of a "T") are added to the top of each bar. These small bars usually represent the standard error of the mean. Commonly, the standard error is shown in only one direction (towards the top of the graph), but it can also be shown in both directions. When these are included in a figure, they should be explained in the figure caption. (For an example, see Figure 6 in chapter 18.)

## Hatching

In bar graphs, hatching (in the form of vertical, horizontal, or diagonal lines) is commonly used to distinguish bars. Less often, other geometric symbols such as crosses or plus signs, and sometimes different shadings, are used for this purpose. (See Figure 6 in chapter 18.)

## ▶ Histograms

Histograms are used to illustrate frequency distributions, and so *both the dependent and independent variables must be in either interval or ratio scale*. The bars in a histogram are centred over the midpoint of the class interval. Moreover, because the data are continuous, each bar begins, and ends, on the *x* axis, at the real limits of an interval. Therefore, *bars must be of the same width and touch each other*. There is, of course, no point in using hatchings in the bars. (For an example, see Figure 7 in chapter 18.)

## Class interval

In a histogram, it is the pattern revealed (i.e., the shape of the curve joining the tops of the bars) that is of interest. The pattern (or lack of one) illustrated depends to a very large extent on the size of the class interval used. It is, therefore, important to use a suitable interval, and this can only be determined by trial and error. A suitable interval can usually he derived by dividing the range of scores into about 10 to 20 intervals

## ▶ Drawing figures

The main advantage of a figure is visual impact, and this is enhanced by a crisp, clear image, with sharp contrast. Therefore, figures should always be drawn in black ink on white paper.

Figures included in student papers need not be of professional quality, but they must be of as good a quality as possible. In particular, they must be neat and tidy, and reflect some care. Rough, scrappy figures are not acceptable.

### Hand-drawn figures

A graph can usually be drawn by hand with relative ease. This can subsequently be traced onto plain white paper, and photocopied. However, care is needed to produce a figure of good quality. Other figures, such as line drawings, can be more difficult. Most people have little artistic ability, and so their ability to draw figures is limited, but it should be possible to draw simple line drawings that would be satisfactory for student papers. On the other hand, in the case of papers submitted for publication, or perhaps a thesis, it is a good idea to enlist the aid of someone who has some artistic ability.

### Computer graphics

Two types of graphics programs can be of help in the preparation of figures. For convenience, these can be referred to as drawing and graphing programs. Drawing programs can be used for the preparation of charts, diagrams, and simple line drawings, but they require some mastery, and usually a little artistic ability. By comparison, graphing programs are easier to use, although a familiarity with the options available and commands used is needed.

Graphing programs make drawing graphs easy, but those readily available tend to have some limitations when they are applied to drawing graphs for papers in psychology. In particular, graphing programs typically will not allow for the drawing of a line graph illustrating an interaction, as is, for example, shown in Figures 4 and 5 in chapter 18. There are often other problems. For instance, some programs do not include facilities for breaking axes or drawing error bars. Others, although they will readily draw bar graphs, will not produce a histogram. Finally, sometimes they will not label axes as required.

Some problems can be overcome with the judicious use of correcting fluid and a black pen, and subsequent photocopying. Similarly, labels can be typed or printed and added. Other problems can sometimes be overcome by using the commands available to "trick" the program into doing what is wanted.

No matter how good the drawing or graphing program, the quality of the illustration produced is largely determined by the printer or plotter on which it is drawn. Figures produced by a laser printer are usually of very good quality, and a plotter produces excellent results.

## Photocopying

Photocopying is very useful when drawing figures by hand. In particular, the caption, axes labels and values, and legend can be added by typing or printing them, and affixing them to the figure before making a photocopy. Another advantage is that a figure larger than needed can be drawn, making drawing easier. The figure can then be reduced to an appropriate size when photocopying. Moreover, this reduction in size often hides imperfections, such as a little "unsteadiness" in lines.

There are similar advantages for line drawings. Again, details such as the caption or labels can be added by typing or printing them, and affixing them to the figure before making a photocopy. In addition, the size of the figure can be adjusted.

## Integrated software

Some software allows for the integration of text and graphics. If such software is used, figures can be included with text on a page. However, the figure must not occupy more than about half of a page, and *text must not "flow around" a figure* (as is often seen in magazines). Care is needed when using such software. For example, care is needed to ensure that a figure is not split over two pages. Moreover, pagination can be a problem. It is usually much easier to simply produce a figure on a separate page and to insert it into a paper. Figures must be presented on separate pages in a manuscript submitted for publication.

## ▶ Preparing a table

Preparing a table is usually quite straightforward. Tables can be typed using a typewriter or a word processing program. A point to note is that it is usually unwise to use a table preparation option in a word processing program. Typically, this option will not allow for preparation of a table in the style required by the APA Manual. Lines can be drawn on a table using the line-drawing facility of a word processing program. Alternatively, the table can be typed without lines. These can be inserted using a ruler and black pen, and the table can then be photocopied.

## ▶ Statistical package tables

Often, statistical computer packages produce tables of data. Such tables cannot be simply copied and inserted into a paper.[11] One reason is that the software involved will commonly use abbreviations that are not readily understood. In addition, such tables are unlikely to comply with the APA Manual style requirements.

More importantly, as for figures, tables produced by statistical packages are intended only to present a summary of the analyses. Again, statistical packages cannot interpret the meaning of the outcome of an analysis: This can only be done by the researcher involved. Only the researcher, then, can decide on what needs to be illustrated, and how best to do so.

## ▶ Designing a table

Although tables can be used to present written information, or qualitative data in the form of words, typically they are used to present numerical data. Sometimes a table is used simply to present a large data set in an easily readable form, but most commonly a table is used to summarize data or to illustrate some pattern. What is being presented or illustrated must be made readily evident.

Important information will not stand out in a table that includes too much data. Therefore, *tables must always be as simple as possible*. No unnecessary detail should be included.

### What is shown

The purpose for inclusion of a table in a paper will always be explained in the text when the reader is referred to it. However, the reader must be able

---

[11] For teaching purposes, students might be required to attach such a computer-printed table to their research reports as an "appendix". In this case the attached table is not a true appendix and should not be referred to in the report. Moreover, it does not obviate the necessity to include an appropriate table in a paper when one is clearly needed.

to understand the table without reference to the text. Therefore, a table must include sufficient detail to allow for this. The basic information required is provided in a *table title*. Additional detail is presented using *column* and *row labels*, and sometimes *notes*.

## Title

A table title should clearly describe its contents in a short *sentence or phrase*. This should be as concise as possible and should not include redundancies such as "Table showing . . .". The title of a table always appears above the table, and is typed in italics. The word *Table* and the table number are typed in normal characters, above the table title, and the table number is not followed by a full stop. Both the word *Table* and all lines of text in the table title are aligned with the left margin of the page. (For an example, see Table 2.)

## Lines

Horizontal lines are customarily used to separate headings from the body of the table, and to indicate columns grouped under a *spanner heading* (see Tables 2 and 3). Vertical lines are not used in a table. Spaces left between columns should be large enough to clearly separate columns of data, but should not be so large as to make it difficult to visually align rows. For large tables it is often a good idea to group the data in sets (of say 5 or 10) and to leave a horizontal space between groups. This can make a table easier to read.

## Layout

Information in a table is presented in columns and rows. Usually, levels of the independent variable are given in the left-hand column (the *stub*), and the data for the dependent variables are listed in columns in the body of the table. Subheadings may be shown in the stub by indenting, and columns in the body of the table can be grouped under a spanner heading. For example, in Table 2, *Male* and *Female* are subheadings in the stub, and the columns *Without cue* and *With cue* are grouped under the spanner heading *Mean no. of words recalled.*

As far as possible, information should be entered into a table so as to make any relationship or pattern obvious. For example, you might want to show that as one set of scores increased in value another set decreased. In this case the first set of scores should be presented in either ascending or

Table number

TABLE 2
*Recall of a Word List by Children and Adults, With and Without Cues*

Table title

| | Mean no. of words recalled | |
|---|---|---|
| Group[a] | Without cue | With cue |
| Children | | |
| Male | 4.1 | 6.8 |
| Female | 3.9 | 7.1 |
| Adults | | |
| Male | 4.6 | 7.3 |
| Female | 4.8 | 6.9 |

Stub head

Stubs

Column spanner

Column heads

*Note*: There were 12 words in the list.
[a] There were 7 subjects in each group.

Notes

TABLE 3
*Time Needed to Solve Simple and Complex Problems*

| | | Mean time(s) | |
|---|---|---|---|
| Age (years) | n[a] | Simple | Complex |
| 21–30 | 17 | 18.3 (4.32) | 21.3 (5.01)[b] |
| 31–40 | 16 | 14.6 (2.97) | 19.7 (3.97) |
| 41–50 | 18 | 12.1 (3.56) | 17.2 (4.24) |

*Notes*: [a] Number in each group. [b] The score for one subject in this group was 42 seconds. Figures in parentheses are standard deviations.

descending order. The other set should then, at least approximately, be in the opposite order. Alternatively, you might want to point out some pattern of differences between scores. For instance, you might want to illustrate that the differences between one set of pairs of scores were statistically significant, while those between another set were not. In this case you should group the two sets of scores so that this pattern is obvious. When data are presented in this way a space should be left between groups of scores so that they are visually separate. Also, subheadings can be used to label groups of scores.

## Notes

Notes can be used to provide further information and to clarify the contents of a table. Any such notes are positioned under the table, as in Tables 2 and 3. A note can either provide general information or be specific. Within a table, a specific note is indicated by a lower-case letter in superscript. (For examples, see Tables 2 and 3.)

## Abbreviations

Standard abbreviations and symbols may be used in the title or body of a table. Non-standard abbreviations may also be used, but they must be explained, either in the table title or in a note.

## Probability levels

Probability levels can be shown on a table using symbols that are explained in a note, as in Table 4. The convention is that an increasing number of asterisks indicates a lower probability (e.g., $*$ $p < .05$, $**$ $p < .01$, $***$ $p < .001$, and $****$ $p < .0001$). If there is a need to distinguish between two- and one-tailed probabilities, an asterisk is used for two-tailed, and some other symbol for one-tailed probabilities.

TABLE 4
*Intercorrelations of Test Scores*

| Test | 1 | 2 | 3 | 4 |
|---|---|---|---|---|
| 1. Motor Ability | – | .04* | .56** | .32* |
| 2. IQ | | – | −.03 | .43* |
| 3. Accuracy | | | – | .31* |
| 4. Reaction Time | | | | – |

*$p < .05$ **$p < .01$

## Problem

There is, however, a problem with reporting a priori probabilities using this technique. The *APA Manual* recommends that the exact a posteriori probability calculated should always be reported. Therefore, if the a priori probability is reported in a table using asterisks (or other symbols), exact a posteriori probabilities will need to be reported in the text. Including exact a posteriori probabilities in a table would clutter it. By comparison, using asterisks to indicate probabilities is much simpler and clearer.

How probabilities are reported in a table, therefore, involves judgement. (Noticeably, in the example correlation table given in the APA Manual probabilities are not included, while in the example regression table they are indicated using asterisks.) In the case of a small set of data, it would seem to be preferable to report exact a posteriori probabilities in the table. By comparison, in a large table, it would seem to be preferable to use asterisks to indicate a priori probabilities. This would prevent the table from being cluttered and would clearly indicate any pattern or trend involved. In this case, it would be cumbersome to report a large number of exact a posteriori probabilities in the text. As an alternative, it would seem to be preferable to include these in an appendix.

## Detail

Unnecessary detail, which distracts the reader's attention, should not be included in a table. For example, when reporting group data, if there is an equal number of participants in each group, it would be superfluous to include a column showing the number in each group. This information can easily be given in a note, as in Table 2, or, if the number of participants is obvious, omitted. Similarly, the number of decimal places used when reporting data should be kept to a minimum. When decimal places are included in tables, the number of decimal places must be consistent within a column. Also, decimal points must be vertically aligned.

Precision, leading zero, chap. 17

## Empty cells

When a cell is empty because it is not applicable, leave it blank. When data are missing, insert a dash and explain the use of the dash in a note under the table.

## ► Common tables

The format of a table will depend on its content and the nature of the information to be presented. There can, therefore, be a large number of possible designs for tables. However, correlation matrices and analysis of variance tables are common, and their designs are relatively fixed.

## Correlation matrices

In a table showing a correlation matrix, each intercorrelation is shown only once, which results in data appearing in a triangular form. Also, correlations of an item with itself are not included, but are shown as a dash. (For an example of a table of intercorrelations, see Table 4.) There is no need to explain the meaning of these dashes.

For purposes of illustration, the a priori probability values are shown in this table using asterisks. However, exact a posteriori values could be shown instead. See the earlier discussion of probability levels.

## Analysis of variance tables

When the results of an analysis of variance are shown in tabular form, the source, degrees of freedom, and $F$ ratios are shown in the columns. Mean square errors are shown enclosed in parentheses, and exact a posteriori probability levels are shown. Strength of effect statistics are also often included. It is, of course, important to ensure that factors are clearly labelled and that the meaning of any abbreviations included is clear. There can be variations in the presentation of an analysis of variance table, but a typical example is given in Table 5.

TABLE 5
*Analysis of Variance for Movement Time*

| Source | $df$ | $F$ | $\eta$ | $p$ |
|---|---|---|---|---|
| Between subjects | | | | |
| Motor ability (M) | 1 | 4.98 | .17 | .027 |
| Between-group error | 22 | (3782.05) | | |
| Within subjects | | | | |
| Stimulus modality (S) | 1 | 45.20 | .63 | .008 |
| M × S | 1 | 0.52 | .04 | .396 |
| Within-group error | 22 | (2943.06) | | |

*Note*: Values enclosed within parentheses are mean square errors.

# Part 6
# Qualitative Research

# 20 Qualitative Research Reports

To a very large extent, the advice and guidance given in Part 5 of this book are applicable to research of any form. This chapter offers additional advice and guidance that is relevant to the preparation, planning, and writing of a qualitative research report. It is, however, important to understand that, because the nature of qualitative research varies widely, the content and structure of the resultant research report similarly varies. It is, therefore, only possible to provide general guidelines that can be modified to suit a particular set of circumstances. In addition, qualitative research can present a number of potential problems of a practical and ethical nature. Again, it is impossible to cater for every eventuality. This chapter has been written on the basis that the research involved will be in the form of a "teaching study" designed for students. It is, therefore, written on the assumption that any potential problems, in particular of an ethical nature, will have been catered for.

## ▶ Qualitative research

Part 5 of this book is based on quantitative research, which remains the predominant form of research in psychology. A detailed comparison of quantitative and qualitative research is beyond the scope of this book, but a brief overview is warranted.

Quantitative research is referred to as such because the variables involved are quantified using numerical units. In contrast, the data in qualitative research are words, phrases, or sentences; although numerical data can also be used to supplement or complement the qualitative data involved.

Apart from the difference in data, the most notable difference between quantitative and qualitative research is the setting. Quantitative research is most commonly carried out in a laboratory, or in some other setting in which extraneous, and possibly confounding, variables can be excluded or controlled. In contrast, qualitative research is carried out in natural settings. For example, in participant observation research the investigator becomes part of the group under investigation. Qualitative research, therefore, has often been described as "field research".

Another difference between these approaches is the testing of hypotheses. In chapter 14 it is pointed out that not all research is designed to test hypotheses, although in quantitative research this is most commonly the case. By comparison, although qualitative research can be used to test hypotheses, usually it is not.

Perhaps the most important difference between the two approaches is that quantitative research is based on some theoretical grounding, while qualitative research most commonly is not. Typically, in qualitative research, theory is developed from the data collected. Therefore, *a distinguishing feature is that quantitative research is most commonly used to test predictions derived from some theory, or to investigate an application of a theory, while qualitative research is most commonly used to develop theory.*

## ▶ Scientific method

Like any other research, qualitative research follows the scientific method. It does not, however, follow the six steps of the scientific method in the discrete manner that is shown in Table 1 of chapter 14.

As pointed out in chapter 14, the first two steps of the scientific method (Identifying the research problem, and Reviewing the literature) are interrelated. In qualitative research the third and fourth steps (Designing the research, and Carrying out the designed research) often are also interrelated. This arises because the method used is sometimes modified during the conduct of the research. Similarly, these two steps may be interrelated with the fifth step (Analysing the results). This arises because in qualitative research, data analysis is frequently carried out concurrently with the research. As a result, for instance, an unexpected theme that warrants investigation might be detected, and this might necessitate a change in research design. Finally, because analysis and interpretation of the data are often concurrent processes, the fifth and six steps (Analysing the results, and Interpreting the findings) may be interrelated. Therefore, all of the steps of the scientific method may be interrelated.

## ▶ Overview of a research report

At a conceptual level, the overview of a research report given in chapter 14 is equally applicable to a qualitative research report. Any research report must present the research problem, how it was investigated, and the outcome of that investigation.

A particular point to note is that it was suggested in chapter 15 that a research report can be thought of as a story; that is, it tells the reader what the research problem was, what was done, and what the outcome means.

This analogy is particularly relevant to a qualitative research report, which typically involves recounting personal observations and the interpretation of those observations. Like any story, there must be some structure, and this is provided by the steps of the scientific method. With minor changes to subheadings, the format of an experimental research report given in chapter 14 could be used for a qualitative research report. This could result, for example, in the format shown in Box 4.

**Box 4**   Possible format of a qualitative research report

Title
Abstract
Introduction
Method

*Sample*
*Materials*
*Procedure*

Results
Discussion
References
Appendices (if any)

While this format might suit some qualitative research reports, often it will not. Also, it is often more appropriate to use different headings. For instance, rather than "Method", it might be more appropriate to use "Research Design and Method", or perhaps simply "Research Design", as a heading.

An alternative possible structure of a qualitative research report is given in Box 5. This example illustrates how the structure and headings of a qualita-

**Box 5**   An alternative possible format of a qualitative research report

Title
Abstract
Introduction
Setting
Characteristics of the Group
Research Design and Method
Findings
Discussion
References
Appendices (if any)

*Note*: Suitable subheadings may be used under the section headings.

tive research report might differ from those of a quantitative research report.

Because of its variable nature, however, the formats suggested here might well not be suitable for a particular report. For example, it might be more appropriate to combine the Findings and Discussion sections. Another possibility is that the findings might be partly interpreted in the Findings section, and more fully discussed in the Discussion section. In this case the heading "Findings and Preliminary Analysis", for example, could be used.

## ▶ Preparation of a qualitative research report

The advice and guidance on the preparation for a research report offered in chapter 15 are generally applicable to a qualitative research report. A particular exception, however, is that hypotheses are usually not involved in qualitative research, and so the material included on hypotheses may typically be disregarded. Similarly, when numerical data are not involved (as is often the case) the advice given on statistical analyses may be disregarded.

Perhaps the most important part of preparation for a qualitative research report is the interpretation of the data collected. This involves a synthesis and analysis of the data to provide a solution to the research problem or an answer to the research question under investigation. In particular, interpretation of the findings will require careful consideration of the ideas, concepts, and constructs involved, and of any relationships between these.

In addition, consideration will have to be given to deciding how best the outcome of the research can be summarized and presented. The outcome of the research must be presented so that it is easily understood. This might involve, for example, the design and preparation of tables, or figures illustrating relationships between ideas or constructs.

chap. 18
chap. 19

## ▶ Planning a qualitative research report

At a conceptual level, the discussion of the planning of a research report given in chapter 15 is equally applicable to a qualitative research report. Usually, however, there will be no theoretical basis to the research and no hypotheses will be involved.

A particular point is that when "telling the story" in an experimental research report not all of the events involved are reported. For example, problems discovered in a pilot study that resulted in some modification to the research design are normally not included. In contrast, because the method followed in qualitative research is often modified during the course of the research, the details of any change and the reason for it must be included.

Planning a qualitative research report requires a careful consideration of the content and how best to present it. This involves planning the sequence, and choosing suitable headings and subheadings that will help to guide the reader.

It is impossible to give a structure that would suit any particular qualitative research report. All that can be done is to provide an example that can be used as a guide, and that can be modified to suit the particular piece of research. The structure given below provides such an example.

**Introduction**
1. Introduce the research problem.
2. Derive a research question.
3. Outline a research approach to investigate this question.

**Setting**
4. Describe the setting in which the research was carried out.

**Sample**
5. Describe the people under investigation.

**Method**
6. Describe the method followed in the study.

**Findings**
7. Describe the findings of the study.

**Discussion**
8. Describe the outcome of the research.
9. Discuss how the findings relate to the research problem.
10. Discuss any other implications of the findings.
11. Indicate any flaws or weaknesses, or possible alternative explanations.
12. Suggest the next step required to investigate the research problem.

## Introduction and Discussion

As in an experimental research report, in a qualitative research report the Introduction and Discussion are the most important sections. Together, these present the research problem and question, and an interpretation of the findings – including any implications.

**Introduction**
The Introduction of a qualitative research report, like that of any research report, is a literature review that identifies the problem to be investigated,

A literature review, chap. 11

summarizes the current state of knowledge in the area, and leads logically to the investigation being reported. It does, however, typically differ from the Introduction to a quantitative research report in that there is no theoretical basis for the research and that no hypotheses are involved. On the other hand, albeit not in the form of an hypothesis, often some prediction with regard to the outcome of the research can be made. For example, this might take the form of reasoning, such as, if people have some particular attitude, they would be expected to behave in a certain way.

It is important, when planning the Introduction, to understand that qualitative research is not based on idle curiosity. There must be some specific research problem, and this must be clearly identified. Moreover, at least the initial approach to the investigation of this research problem must be outlined.

### Discussion

The Discussion section of a qualitative research report will begin with a brief summary of the outcome of the investigation, which must involve a synthesis and interpretation of the findings. This will involve a careful analysis of any observed relationships among and between the variables involved.

In this section of the report, the outcome of the investigation must be related to the research problem. Ideas and concepts that are developed must be clearly explained and supported, as must observed relationships among and between them. Moreover, how these ideas, concepts, and relationships relate to the research problem must be made clear.

As in any research report, how the outcome of the investigation contributes to the body of knowledge in the area must be made clear. In particular, the theoretical relationships identified should lead to one or more predictions that can be tested in subsequent research.

### Setting

Often it is necessary to describe the setting in which the research was carried out. For example, the research might have involved studying the behaviour of some particular group in a small town. A description of the town could, then, be necessary. This could, for instance, involve details of the population, geographical location, and other relevant features.

### Sample

In a quantitative research report the participants involved are described under the subheading *Participants* in the Method section. By comparison, in a qualitative research report it is often preferable to describe the people under investigation in a separate section of the report. For this purpose, *Sample* might be a suitable heading, but other headings that are considered to be more appropriate may be used. In any event, those involved in the research must be described. During this description, they might be referred to as participants, but often this term is not entirely appropriate; other terms, such as the "group members", or "townspeople", might be more suitable. If some particular group (such as a club or association) is involved, it must be described. Such a description would include the composition of the group, and details such as, for example, membership requirements, style of dress, or other relevant characteristics.

## Method

Obviously, how the research problem or question was investigated must be described. Although the heading "Method" has been used in the example structure given, some other heading might be more appropriate in particular circumstances.

Typically, in a qualitative research report this involves a more complex description than is involved in a quantitative research report. As has already been pointed out, changes in the method used might well occur during the course of the research. Any such changes, and the reasons for them, must be described. Moreover, analysis of the data collected is often an ongoing process. Therefore, some data analysis might well be included in the Method section. This section, then, is likely to be more than a simple description.

## Findings

Although data analysis may be an ongoing process, and some analysis might well have been included in the Method section, it is usually desirable, if not necessary, to present a summary of the findings of the research in a separate section of the research report.

A particular problem with the reporting of results or findings is the volume involved. Qualitative research produces a very large volume of data, typically in the form of field notes or transcriptions of interviews. Reducing this to a meaningful summary is extremely difficult. How this is done will vary with the circumstances.

In some instances, findings are reported in normal prose, with the inclusion of appropriate examples, such as quotations taken from interviews. In other instances, data may be presented in tabular form showing, for example, categories of ideas. In yet other instances, reporting the findings might necessitate the inclusion of photographs or maps to illustrate some point, or a figure to show how some ideas are related. Rarely will numerical data be included, but it is sometimes appropriate to include numerical data to supplement or complement the qualitative data being reported.

## Appendices

Because of the very large volume of data involved in qualitative research, and the difficulty of summarizing it, appendices can provide a useful means of including some data in the report. For instance, examples in the form of quotations could be included in an appendix. However, this does not mean that a qualitative research report should include numerous and voluminous appendices. Rather, appendices should be kept as brief as possible, and limited in number.

## Length

Another point to be considered when planning the content of a qualitative research report is its length. Because of the need to describe in detail any changes in the method used that arise during the course of the research, and the reasons for them, and to develop new ideas or concepts, a qualitative research report is often longer than is a quantitative research report. On the other hand, like any other paper, a qualitative research report should be written as concisely as possible. In particular, when a word limit is set the report must be written within this limit.

It is, of course, impossible to give any useful guidelines for the length of the parts of the report. However, as a consequence of the flexible nature of the research involved, it is possible that not all of the sources that ultimately prove to be relevant are included in the Introduction. Because of this, and the absence of a theoretical discussion, the Introduction of a qualitative research report is often shorter than that commonly found in an experimental research report. On the other hand, it is possible that some sources not included in the Introduction subsequently prove to be of value, and so are introduced in the Discussion section. In addition, it is in this section that new ideas, concepts, and relationships between the variables involved are developed and identified. This section of a qualitative research report, therefore, is likely to be longer than that in an experimental research report.

## Ethics

Ethics is a particular consideration in a qualitative research report. In an experimental research report there is usually no need to describe how the investigator complied with ethical requirements. Typically, this is straightforward, and it can be assumed that the research was approved by an ethics committee before it began. It can, therefore, usually be assumed that the investigator has complied with ethical requirements. By comparison, in qualitative research, compliance with ethical requirements is not so straight-forward. In particular, deception is often involved. For example, an investigator who is carrying out a participant observational study will not be in a position to reveal to members of the group involved that he or she is carry-ing out research: Obviously, doing so would be likely to affect the outcome. Moreover, because of the flexible nature of the research and possible changes to the method initially adopted, it cannot be assumed that the research was approved in its entirety by an ethics committee before it began.

When reporting qualitative research, therefore, how ethical considerations were catered for must be described. Sometimes, it might be appropriate to include this description in the Method section of the report. Alternatively, ethical considerations might be discussed in the Sample section (if one is used). In yet other instances, it might be necessary to include details of ethical considerations under a separate heading.

## Confidentiality

An important aspect of ethics that must be carefully considered when reporting the outcome of qualitative research is confidentiality. Obviously, as in any research report, the identities of the individuals involved must not be revealed. In qualitative research this often also applies to the identities of groups. Members of a group might not be entirely pleased if the name of the group were published in a research report. Often, this problem can be over-come by use of alphabetical characters or fictitious initials when referring to individuals, or a pseudonym when referring to a group.

Another point that requires careful consideration is that individuals have a right to privacy. For instance, in an interview an individual might reveal something that he or she would not want to become public knowledge. In this case, that information must not be revealed. For example, it would not be acceptable to include in a research report a quotation from the individual who revealed this information. This might apply equally to some information that is confidential to a particular group. Before writing a qualitative research report, therefore, careful consideration must be given to what information is included in it.

## ▶ Writing a qualitative research report

Although a qualitative research report is a narrative, *it is not simply a story*. Rather, it is a description of some research problem, the steps taken to investigate it, the outcome of that investigation, and the conclusion reached. It is both an academic and a scientific document. Therefore, the principles of academic and scientific writing, which are discussed in chapters 1 and 2, apply. Similarly, the principles involved in writing an academic paper, which are discussed in chapter 9, are also applicable.

On the other hand, in some qualitative research, such as participant observation, the report should "bring to life" the lives, feelings, and view of the world of the people involved, in an interesting and engaging manner. This requires somewhat of a literary style. As a result, a qualitative research report is, in parts, sometimes a *little* less formal than is the normal quantitative research report.

Writing a qualitative research report, therefore, can be difficult. It must be intellectually rigorous, yet often at the same time interesting and engaging. This requires considerable writing skill.

## Ideas and concepts

**Information and ideas**, chap. 1

The basis of qualitative research is information in the form of words and language. However, it is the ideas and concepts involved that are important. It is, therefore, important for ideas, concepts, and relationships to be clearly and precisely presented. Moreover, observed or proposed relationships must be supported by evidence. This will require clear and logical reasoning.

## Subjectivity

**Objectivity**, chaps 2 and 12

By its nature, qualitative research often requires insight, and involves subjective judgement. This can present a problem, because in some circumstances the author will have to distinguish between his or her personal values and ethical principles and those of the people or group being investigated. Moreover, it might be necessary to make any conflict arising evident. This allows the reader to form a judgement on the possibility of subjective bias that might distort the investigator's interpretation of the data or findings. Therefore, *writing a qualitative research report often requires a delicate balance between scientific objectivity and subjectivity.*

## Value judgements

**Values**, chap. 2

Although subjectivity will necessarily be involved in interpreting some data and findings, this must be distinguished from value judgements based on the investigator's moral or ethical principles. This can be an important consideration in some qualitative research. For example, the research might involve people who have a sexual orientation that differs from that of the investigator and of which he or she strongly disapproves. It is not an investigator's role to make judgements on what is morally or ethically good or bad; or what, for example, legislators should or should not do.

## Style

The discussion of style provided in chapter 3 is equally applicable to the writing of a qualitative research report. However, in some parts of the report a slightly less formal style might sometimes be appropriate. In particular, it is sometimes appropriate to use first person personal pronouns. For example, an author might write, "It occurred to me that . . . Consequently I . . .". This might be necessary, for example, in the Method section, when the author is explaining why some change in method was adopted. In addition, obviously, when quoting someone who is involved in the research, it is necessary to reproduce that person's words exactly, including, for example, colloquialisms. On the other hand, a qualitative research report must be written in a formal academic style and in a scholarly manner.

**First person personal pronouns,** chap. 2

**Pronoun agreement,** chap. 21

# Part 7
# Resource Material

# 21  Grammar

Grammar can be thought of as the set of rules that govern the use of a language. Most people are not familiar with some of the finer points, but an understanding and application of basic grammatical concepts is essential if an author is to communicate effectively in writing. However, everyone has to check some points from time to time. This chapter provides a source that can be used for this purpose.

## ▶ A clause

A group of words that includes a verb and a subject, sometimes including adjectives or adverbs, is referred to as a *clause*. A clause that makes sense on its own, and constitutes a sentence, is a *main clause*: One that does not is described as a *subordinate clause*.

## ▶ A sentence

A sentence is a group of words that makes sense and communicates a complete thought. That is, it must be able to be understood without referring to the context in which it is written. Of course, a sentence must start with a capital (upper-case) letter, and end with a stop (a full stop, question mark, or exclamation mark). However, although the following groups of words (which were taken from students' papers) start with a capital letter and end with a full stop, they do not include a verb and do not make sense. Therefore, they do not form sentences and do not communicate any meaning.

Not randomly selected.

A need such as hunger or sport or load learning.

Parental respect with scales of acceptance and minimum amount of rejection, ambiguity, and disgust.

To make sense, a sentence must have a *subject* and a *verb*. The following two words, for example, make sense and form a sentence.

Rats        drink.
(subject)  (verb)

Two-word sentences, however, are very rare, and the vast majority have a *subject*, a *verb*, and an *object*, as in the following example.

The rats    pressed    the bar.
(subject)  (verb)      (object)

This sentence could be expanded by adding an *adjective* and an *adverb*.

The   *young*         rats  *frequently*    pressed the bar.
       (adjective)          (adverb)

It could be further expanded by adding more information in the form of a non-defining (or non-restrictive) clause.

The young rats, *which had been specially selected*, frequently pressed the bar.
                                (non-defining clause)

Notice that the addition of the adjective, adverb, and non-defining clause adds further information, but does not change the essential meaning of the sentence.

Simple sentences should be easy to write, but some students find difficulty in doing so, as is illustrated by the following examples taken from student papers.

Understanding the values of society and regulating behaviour.

Seated in pairs, all in the same room.

30 university students (half male and half female).

These examples are really sentence *fragments* and not sentences. Notice that the last example does not begin with a capital letter. Sentences must not begin with Arabic numerals. Moreover, the students referred to were, apparently, rather unusual.


## Verbs

A verb is central to the meaning of a sentence. Moreover, the verb must be in the appropriate tense. There seems to be a tendency for those who write scripts for news broadcasts on television not to understand this, as is illustrated by the following example.

Teenage girls the biggest users.

The intended meaning of this group of words might have been,

Teenage girls *are* the biggest users.

However, the intended meaning could equally have been, for example, *are not*, or *were*, or *are becoming* "the biggest users".

## Participles

Participles of verbs are used to form compound tenses. The present participle is used to form the present continuous tense, and the past participle is used to from the past perfect tense. For example, *testing* is the present participle of the verb *test*, and *tested* is the past participle, and so,

> She is *testing* the participants.

is the present continuous, and

> She has *tested* the participants.

is the past perfect.

Some who write scripts for broadcast news reports seem not to understand sentence structure; in particular the forming of tense using participles. The following example, which was taken from a television news broadcast, is typical.

> A final decision expected later this year.

Presumably, the intention was to mean that a decision *is* expected later this year. In this case, the sentence should have been written as:

> A final decision *is* expected later this year.

However, it might have been intended to mean, for example, that a decision *is not expected*, or *might be expected*.

Such poor models influence students, and a resulting example taken from a student's paper is:

> Making it difficult for the researcher to draw a conclusion at times.

Presumably the student meant that something *is*, or perhaps *was*, "making it difficult". Note that the "sentence" does not include a subject.

## Meaning

A sentence must, of course, accurately communicate some information or idea. Even if a sentence is correct, and makes sense, it might not convey what is intended. For instance, presumably in error, one student wrote:

> Twenty-four rats conducted the experiment.

The following are additional examples taken from students' papers. In each case the meaning of the sentence is not clear.

> This situation, however, does have latent benefits that unemployed do not get the opportunity which provides support for their situation.

> Environmental factors in IQ can also be determined by environmental influence.

## Length

The problem is exacerbated when the sentence is long (and includes grammatical errors), as in the following example from a student's paper.

> This finding suggests that could be possible that Kohlberg, and other believe to be abstract principles and values, like that of placing life above property, may be seen as a normal way of thought socialized by the family in the same way that perceived existing laws and rules of society are socialized in a different family.

Problems often arise with long sentences. It is, therefore, usually preferable to write short sentences. On the other hand, the meaning of short sentences can be unclear. For example, the meaning of the following sentence, which was taken from a television broadcast, is not clear.

> I have no doubt in my mind that is it not unsafe.

## Single idea

As has been pointed out, a sentence must include only one idea. The following sentence, apart from other problems, includes two separate ideas, and its meaning is not clear.

> Although as a general rule, the larger the sample the more precise the estimate of a characteristic in a given population, questionnaires even if distributed using a stratified random sampling procedure, may still suffer several fundamental problems.

## Run-on and fused sentences

A *run-on* or *fused* sentence is two, or more, sentences that are separated by a comma or commas. The following is an example of a run-on sentence:

> The mean scores for both conditions were compared, a significant difference between means was found.

When sentences are written in this way, but the comma is omitted, the result is usually referred to as a fused sentence.

Both run-on and fused sentences can be rectified in several ways. The two most simple are to rewrite the run-on sentence as separate sentences, or to use a conjunction to join the sentences. For example, the run-on sentence above could be rewritten as two separate sentences.

> The mean scores for both conditions were compared. A significant difference between means was found.

Alternatively, the sentences could be joined using a conjunction:

> The mean scores for both conditions were compared, and a significant difference between means was found.


## Conjunctions

*Conjunctions* are words that are used to join parts of a sentence, or two words. These include, *and*, *but*, *or*, *yet*, and *nor*. For instance, *and* is used for this purpose in the above example.

Both *and* and *but* may be used to begin a sentence. However, this should be done sparingly. Usually, it is preferable to use these words to begin a sentence only for the purpose of emphasis. For instance, *but* is used for this purpose in the second sentence in the following:

> Women have often been thought not to be capable of this task. *But*, women clearly are capable of such tasks.


## Subject–verb agreement

Another common problem is lack of agreement in number between subject and verb. A singular subject takes a singular verb, and a plural subject takes a plural verb. As an example, it would be incorrect to write:

> The computers *is* on the bench.

Obviously, because the subject of the sentence (The computers) is plural, the verb also should be plural. Therefore, the sentence should be written as:

> The computers *are* on the bench.

Sometimes students become confused when the subject and verb are separated by a clause, as in the following example.

> This argument, which is found in a number of papers, *are* not logical.

Because the subject of the sentence is *This argument*, which is singular, the singular verb *is*, and not the plural *are*, should be used. The sentence, therefore, should be written as:

> This argument, which is found in a number of papers, *is* not logical.

Confusion also sometimes arises when two singular subjects are connected by *and*, as in:

> The experimental rat *and* the control rat *was* tested in the simple response condition.

Here, the subject of the sentence is *The experimental rat and the control rat*; that is, *two* rats, and so the plural *were* should be used, as in:

> The experimental rat and the control rat *were* tested in the simple response condition.

By comparison, if two or more singular verbs are connected by *or*, *nor*, or *but*, a singular verb must be used. For example it is correct to write:

> Neither the experimental rat nor the control rat *was* tested in this condition.

The failure of subject and verb to agree in number can also occur as a result of lack of knowledge of singular and plural forms of words. Usually this occurs with words of Latin or Greek origin, such as stratum, criterion, or phenomenon. The most frequent error of this type occurs with the word *data*, which is plural (the singular is *datum*). It is, therefore, incorrect to write;

> The data *was* analysed using a one-way analysis of variance.

This should, of course, be written as:

> The data *were* analysed using a one-way analysis of variance.

## ▶ Comparisons

Comparisons often present difficulties. For instance, the preposition following *different* can be either *from* or *to*, although the preferred form is *different from*. In particular, the preposition following *compare* often causes problems.

Compared *with* is used to draw attention to dissimilarities:

> Compared with those of other students, this was a very good paper.

Compared *to* is used to draw attention to similarities, in the same sense as *similar to*:

> This research can readily be compared to similar earlier work.

## Comparative

When the comparison is between *two*, an adjective is used to denote a higher (or lower) degree:

A was *larger* than B.

The score for A was *smaller* than that for B.

### Errors

It is, of course, incorrect to use a double comparative, as in "more larger". Words such as *more*, *larger*, and *bigger* are comparative adjectives used when comparing two items, and mean greater in quantity or number. Therefore, to claim that something is "more larger" effectively means that it is "greater greater" in quantity or number.

On the other hand, words such as *much* (meaning a great deal) are not comparative adjectives. Therefore, it is correct to comment, for example, that something is "much larger". It is also correct to use an adverb as in, for instance, commenting that something is "considerably larger".

## Superlative

The superlative is used to indicate the highest degree of some attribute when comparing three or more instances:

The *largest* of the three scores

The *smallest* of the three scores for the group

### Errors

It is obviously incorrect to comment that something is the "most largest". Something can only be the largest, and cannot be more so.

## ▶ Pronouns

Difficulty is often experienced with the use of pronouns. The following notes cover the most commonly experienced problems.

### *That* and *which*

The use of the relative pronouns *that* and *which* often causes confusion. There are two general rules that determine the use of these pronouns.

In a *defining clause* (i.e., one that is essential to the meaning of the sentence; also known as a restrictive clause), either pronoun can be used. An example is:

The switch *that* operated the light was painted green.

In the above sentence, *which* could be used in place of *that*. Usually, however, in this situation *that* is used in preference to *which*.

By comparison, in a *non-defining clause* (i.e., one that adds further information, but is not essential to the meaning of the sentence – also known as a non-restrictive clause), *which* must be used. In the following sentence, the clause, *which was similar to the others*, provides additional information that is not necessary to its meaning.

The third rat, *which was similar to the others,* was deleted from the experiment.

Without this clause, the sentence would read:

The third rat was deleted from the experiment.

Therefore, because the clause *which was similar to the others* is a non-defining or non-restrictive clause, *which* must be used. An important feature of the non-defining clause is that it is enclosed within commas.

A common mistake is the unnecessary use of *that* following a comparison. in the following sentence, for example, *that* is unnecessary, and should be omitted.

The quicker *that* the participants responded, the more trials were completed.

## ▶ Pronoun agreement

Pronouns are words used to replace nouns. These include personal (e.g., *him* or *her*), possessive (e.g., *his*, *hers*, *its*, or *their*), indefinite (e.g., *one*, *each*, or *both*), demonstrative (e.g., *this*, *that*, or *those*), and interrogative (e.g., *who*, *which*, or *what*) pronouns. There are several conventions governing the use of pronouns.

## Number

A pronoun must agree in number with the noun that it replaces. For example, it would be incorrect to write:

The *rat* was trained to press the bar with *their* nose.

The noun replaced (*rat*) is singular, but the pronoun *their* is plural; instead, the sentence should be written using the singular pronoun *its*, as:

The *rat* was trained to press the bar with *its* nose.

## Gender

A pronoun must also agree in gender (i.e., masculine, feminine, or neuter) with the noun it replaces. For example, it would be incorrect to write:

> The *computer* controlled *her* printer.

The noun *computer* is neuter, but the pronoun *her* is feminine. Therefore, the sentence should be written using the neuter pronoun *its*, as:

> The *computer* controlled *its* printer.

### They *and* their

Both *they* and *their* are plural pronouns: Neither, therefore, can be used to replace a singular noun. It would, be incorrect to write:

> *Each* respondent was asked to enter *their* ratings on a scale of 1–10.

In this sentence, *Each* is singular, and so the plural pronoun *their* does not agree in number with the noun that it replaces. The sentence, therefore, should be written as:

> Each respondent was asked to enter *his or her* ratings on a scale of 1–10.

Alternatively, the problem can be simply overcome by writing the sentence in the plural, as:

> The *respondents* were asked to enter *their* ratings on a scale of 1–10.

In this sentence both the noun (*respondents*) and the pronoun (*their*) are plural.

#### Exceptional use of they and their

In some exceptional situations *they* and *their* can be used when it would seem that a singular pronoun should be used. For example, an unnamed author could be male or female, or could be an association (e.g., a group or an institution). That is, the author(s) could be of masculine, feminine, or neuter gender; and could be singular or plural. Because of this uncertainty, it would be correct to write, for example:

> *Each* of the authors suggested that *their* views had been misrepresented.

In this sentence, *Each* is singular, but it could refer to a single author (either masculine or feminine), to an association (neuter singular), or to a group of authors (possibly both masculine and feminine, or neuter plural). There is, therefore, no option but to use *their* as the pronoun.

Another example of appropriate use of *they* or *their* as a substitute for a singular noun arises with the use of *none* (i.e., no one), which is singular. For example, it would be correct to write,

> *None* of the investigators was confident of *their* findings.

In this case there are no investigators, because *"None"* was confident. Therefore, the question of gender and plurality is not relevant. Again, there is no option but to use *their* as the pronoun. Similarly, it would be correct to write:

> *None* of the investigators reported that *they* were confident of *their* findings.

There are, therefore, situations in which use of the plural pronoun *they* or *their* is appropriate although it would appear that a singular pronoun should be used. However, *this does not mean* that the plural pronouns *they* and *their* can always be used as singular pronouns.

## His *or* her

The only problem with the use of *his or her* (and *he or she*, *him or her*) arises if it is frequently repeated, which can become cumbersome. The construction *he/she* is effectively the same as *he or she*, and would be read as such when reading aloud; the construction *s/he* is rather awkward, and cannot be pronounced when reading aloud. Neither of these constructions, therefore, solves the problem. Similarly, the alternate use of *he* and *she* throughout the text of a paper becomes confusing, and this approach should not be used.

Some authorities suggest that the use of *they* and *their* as singular pronouns to avoid the use of *he or she*, and *his or her*, has become accepted practice. However, this usage can present problems. (See also the discussion under "Gender" in chapter 2.)

## Who, whom, *and* that

The pronouns *who* and *whom* are used to refer to people, and the pronoun *that* is used to refer to other living things or inanimate objects:

> the man *who* never was

> the woman to *whom* the test was given

> the rat *that* was tested

> the computer *that* was used

A common error is to use *that* when referring to people. For example, it would be incorrect to write:

> the man *that* never was

or

> the participants *that* were tested

On the other hand, it would be correct to write:

the subjects *that* were tested

Following the APA Manual recommendation, people in an experiment are referred to as *participants*, but animals are referred to as *subjects*.

## *Who* and *whom*

The use of these pronouns often causes problems. *Who* is the subject case and *whom* is the object case. When the subject of the sentence is replaced by a pronoun, *who* should be used.

the participant *who* was tested last . . .

When the object of the sentence is replaced by a pronoun, *whom* should be used.

**Pronoun agreement**, chap. 21

the participants to *whom* the questionnaire was given . . .

## *Which* and *what*

Both *which* and *what* may be used as interrogative adjectives. When the choice is from a restricted number, *which* is used, as in, for example:

*Which* of the subjects did not respond to the blue stimulus?

By comparison, *what* is used in reference to an indefinite number, as in, for example:

*What* argument could be advanced?

A particular error, which betrays lack of familiarity with the English language, is the misuse of *what* as in, for example:

This group was more accurate than *what* the other group was.

or

The subject scored better than *what* was required.

In both of the above sentences the inclusion of *what* is not only superfluous, it is incorrect.

## ▶ **Voice**

When the active voice is used, the subject of the sentence performs the action. By comparison, when the passive voice is used, the subject receives the action. The following sentence is written in the active voice:

The rats operated the switches.

This sentence could be rewritten in the passive voice as:

The switches were operated by the rats.

Notice that the subject of the sentence in the active voice is "The rats", whereas when the sentence is written in the passive voice the subject is "The switches". Generally, writing in the active voice is more direct and emphatic. Consequently, the active voice is preferred. There is, however, nothing grammatically wrong with use of the passive voice.

# 22 Punctuation

Punctuation is important because it helps to make the author's meaning clear. Even a relatively simple sentence can convey an unintended meaning if appropriate punctuation is not used. As an illustration, consider the following two sentences:

> This child was not included in the sample, because his intelligence was well above average.

> This child was not included in the sample because his intelligence was well above average.

The first sentence means that the child *was not* included in the sample, and the reason for his exclusion was, "because his intelligence was well above average". By comparison, the second sentence means that the child *was* included in the sample, and that his inclusion was *not* because his intelligence was well above average. The only difference between the two sentences, which have quite different meanings, is the inclusion of a comma before *because* in the first, and the omission of this comma in the second. As another example, consider the following two sentences:

> The student, who had fallen asleep, was left in the room.

> The student who had fallen asleep was left in the room.

The first sentence means that a student was left in the room, and that that student had fallen asleep. By comparison, the second sentence means that a specific student, namely the one who had fallen asleep, was left in the room. Again, the only difference between these sentences is the use of punctuation – two commas in the first, and none in the second.

These examples show that even a small difference in punctuation can result in a very different meaning. Obviously, then, it is important to use correct punctuation.

## ▶ Computer syntax

Although some symbols used in computer syntax appear to be punctuation marks, they are not. In particular, the *slash* does not indicate an alternative and the symbol ":" is not a colon. In the absence of other terms, however, they are referred to as such. Similarly, the *dot* is not a full stop.

## ▶ Checking punctuation

As a rough check, punctuation errors can sometimes be found by reading a paper aloud, but this will not detect all mistakes and can even be misleading. To some extent the use of punctuation is determined by personal taste, but there are some conventions that should be followed.

## Comma

Commas are used:

- To enclose a non-defining, or non-restrictive clause (i.e., one that is not essential to the meaning of the sentence):

    Participant 3, who had become ill, withdrew from the study.

This sentence means that Participant 3 withdrew from the study. The clause, "who had become ill", provides additional, but not essential, information.

*Note*: A defining, or restrictive clause (i.e., one that *is* essential to the meaning of the sentence) is *not* enclosed in commas.

    The child who had the lowest score was deleted from the study.

In this sentence, the clause "who had the lowest score" is essential to identify which of the children was deleted from the study.

- to enclose words interrupting a main clause:

    All of the scores, therefore, were included in the analysis.

- after an introductory word, adjectival clause, or phrase that precedes the main clause:

    Obviously, the only possible score was zero.

    On the other hand, higher scores are sometimes possible.

- between adjectives preceding and qualifying a noun:

    A large, white rat was in the cage.

- before a conjunction joining main clauses:

    The trials were completed, and the apparatus was disconnected.

*Note*: In the opinion of some authorities, the use of a comma before the conjunction joining main clauses is optional, and some suggest that it should be omitted when the clauses are relatively short.

- To introduce a short quotation included in text:

    Blair (2003) claimed that, "The evidence is not in question." (p. 9).

- To introduce statistics:

    There was a significant between-group difference, $F(1, 33) = 7.95$, $p = .04$ ($MSE = 25.23$).

- To enclose statistical details that are included in a sentence in the same manner as a non-defining clause:

    There was a significant complexity by fatigue interaction, $F(1\ 136) = 97.3$, $p = .03$ ($MSE = 0.43$), $p < .05$, and Figure 1 shows that the effect of complexity was greater in the fatigue condition.

- To avoid the use of parentheses within parentheses.

    (See Blik, 2003, for a discussion.)

- Following the abbreviations *i.e.* and *e.g.*

    (e.g., Bush, 2003)
    (i.e., the complex task)

- To separate the author and year when citing sources:

    (Blair, 2003)

- To separate the date and page, chapter, or paragraph number from the year when citing sources:

    (Seagoon, 1994, p. 25)
    Eccles (1995, p. 25)
    (Bluebottle, 1990, chap. 4)
    Moriarty (1993, para. 7)

- To separate groups of three digits in numbers exceeding 999:

    1,000
    3,235,659

*Note*: Exceptions to this rule include years, page numbers, frequencies, and numbers to the right of a decimal point:

    1942
    page 1013
    1000 Hz
    3.6587

*Note*: Commas must not be used to separate numbers when entering data into a computer.

- To separate items in a series of *three or more* items:

    Each subject was tested in the two-choice, four-choice, and six-choice tasks.

    the young, middle-aged, and older groups

    Jones, Smith, and Brown (1993)
    (Jones, Smith, & Brown, 1993)

*Note*: It is more common practice in some countries not to use a comma before the conjunction *and* where it separates the last two items in a series. The APA Publication Manual, however, uses a comma in this position as shown in the above examples. The important factor to consider is clarity of meaning. Consider the following sentence:

    Black and white and red and green stimuli were used.

For comparison, this sentence could have been written as:

    Black and white, and red and green stimuli were used. (i.e., two stimuli)

    Black, and white, and red and green stimuli were used. (i.e., three stimuli)

    Black, and white, and red, and green stimuli were used. (i.e., four stimuli)

The example above is contrived, but it makes the point. Perhaps a more realistic example is:

    Record the person's name and date of birth as accurately as possible.

This sentence means that *both* the person's name and date of birth should be recorded as accurately as possible. By comparison, consider the following sentence:

    Give the person's name, and date of birth as accurately as possible.

This sentence means that *only* the date of birth should be recorded as accurately as possible. Presumably the person's name can be accurately recorded. Again, the inclusion of a comma before *and* alters the meaning of the sentence.

## Semicolon

Semicolons are used

- To separate series in which the items are separated by commas:

The three conditions were administered in the order 1, 2, 3; or 3, 2, 1.

(Como, 1956; Foster & Allen, 1992; Sinatra, Davis, & Lawford, 1960)

• To separate clauses or phrases which already contain commas:

A paper must be objective, accurate, and concise; but grammar, punctuation, and spelling are also important.

• To join two main clauses:

The children in the first group were 8-year-olds; those in the second group were 10-year-olds.

• Before, and with a comma after, a conjunctive phrase connecting main clauses:

Only 20 students volunteered; as a result, there were only 10 students in each of the two groups.

This applies to other conjunctive phrases such as, *for example*, *in other words*, *in addition*, *that is*.

• Before, and with a comma after, adverbial conjunctions connecting main clauses:

Each condition involved 50 minutes of testing; consequently, the two conditions were administered on separate days.

This applies to other adverbial conjunctions such as *moreover*, *however*, *therefore*, and *nevertheless*.

## Colon

Colons are used:

• To introduce a list, or series of words, phrases, or sub-paragraphs, when these are introduced by a complete sentence.

There were three levels of stress in the experiment: low, moderate, and high.

When the introduction is not a complete sentence a colon is not used.

The three levels of stress were low, moderate, and high.

• To introduce a quotation, when the introduction is a complete sentence.

Renton (1990) commented on the use of punctuation:

Punctuation mistakes arise from both carelessness and ignorance. The former include the use of opening brackets or quotation marks which are not followed by closing brackets or quotation marks. The latter frequently involve the insertion of commas in inappropriate places as well as the failure to use commas where they are really required. (p. 36)

- To indicate a ratio:

    1:3

- To separate amplifying phrases, or subtitles, from the main title of a book or an article:

    Vampires and other Denizens of the Night: A review of the literature

- To separate the place (city) of publication and the publisher in publication details:

    Nightsburg: Transylvania University Press.

The colon can also be used to form a link between two main clauses. Usually this is done when the second clause explains, enlarges on, or summarizes the first:

    The experimental tasks were of two levels of difficulty: simple and complex.

If the amplifying clause is a complete sentence, it should begin with a capital letter.

    The participants were of widely differing ages: This may account for the marked variability in reaction time scores.

*Note*: According to some authorities, the clause following a colon need not begin with a capital letter, even if it is a complete sentence. The APA Publication Manual, however, suggests that it should.

## Hyphen (or en-dash)

A hyphen is used in forming compound words and in the addition of prefixes to words.

### Compound words
A hyphen is used:

- To join words to form a compound word:

    two-choice
    forced-choice
    mother-in-law

*Note*: Care is needed when forming compound words in this way. For example, the following are both correct, but have different meanings:

> an on-line source
> a source available on line

*Note*: In the APA Manual the spelling "online" (with no hyphen) is used for both meanings.

- With numbers, to form a compound "word":

> 2-year-old
> 23-year-old

*Note*: When compound words are formed using hyphens, and they have a common base, in a list the common base may be omitted until the final compound word, but the hyphen is retained.

> the low-, moderate-, and high-difficulty tasks
> the 15-, 20-, and 25-year-old groups

- When writing numbers between 21 and 99 in words:

> twenty-two
> ninety-seven
> one hundred and fifty-one

## Prefixed words

A hyphen is sometimes used in prefixed words.

> anti-gravity
> ante-room
> damp-proof

*Note*: There is a distinction between the use of the hyphen or en-dash when forming compound words. For example, "Irish-American relations" refers to relatives who originated from Ireland but are now resident in America. By comparison, "Irish–American" relations refers to the political, or perhaps cultural, relationships between Ireland and America.

## Dash (or em-dash)

Dashes are, and should be, infrequently used: Usually some other punctuation mark is more appropriate. The most common use of the dash is to separate words that are not essential to its meaning from the rest of a sentence:

> The casual approach – as it was described – resulted in poor class discipline.

Used in this way, dashes provide an alternative to parentheses. The difference, although small, is that dashes tend to emphasize, whereas parentheses tend to de-emphasize.

*Note*: When used in this way, a dash has a space before and after it to distinguish it from the use of the dash in forming compound words.

Another use for the dash is to link a brief comment to the end of a sentence, usually as emphasis:

Students enjoy writing essays – especially in psychology.

*Note*: A dash is typed either as an em-dash or as two single hyphens with no space between them.


## Parentheses

Parentheses (or "round" brackets) are most commonly used to enclose words without which the sentence would still be complete, but which provide additional information, explanation, or definition:

Because of the ceiling effect (all participants achieved nearly perfect scores) there was very little variability in the data.

Similarly, a complete sentence in a paragraph, which provides additional information, may be enclosed within parentheses.

Other common uses of parentheses are

- To enclose all or part of a reference:

  Smith (1988)
  (Smith & Brown, 1991)
  (Smith & Brown, 1991, p. 35)

- To enclose references to material within a paper:

  (see Figure 4)
  (see Table 3)

- When introducing an abbreviation:

  choice reaction time (CRT)

- To enclose the page number when directly quoting:

  Windsor (1986) commented that, "The . . ." (p. 13).

- To set off letters used to identify a series:

  The assessment items were (a) two short essays, (b) one long essay, and (c) an examination.

*Note*: Parentheses should *not* be used within parentheses in text.

## Brackets

Brackets ("square" brackets) are used:

- To enclose words inserted into a quotation:

    The meen [*sic*] score for the older group [adults] was higher than that for the children.

- To set off material within other material that is already enclosed in parentheses:

    The intelligence of all participants was measured (using the Wechsler Intelligence Scale for Children [WISC]) to assess intellectual ability.

*Note*: The use of brackets within parentheses, when the material would normally be enclosed in parentheses, can often be avoided by using commas:

(See Reavley, 1995, for a discussion.)

There was a significant main effect of age, $F(1, 33) = 6.589$, $p < .05$, and of complexity, $F(1, 33) = 9.799$, $p < .05$.

## Apostrophe

An apostrophe is used in contractions to show the omission of letters, and in the possessive case to show possession.

### Contractions

The apostrophe is used to indicate the omission of a letter, or letters, in contractions:

    it's
    can't
    don't

A common mistake is to use *it's* as a possessive form, as in, "*It's* effect was . . .". This is obviously incorrect because *it's* is a contraction of *it is*.

*Note*: Contractions are not used in formal writing.

### Possessive case

An apostrophe is used in the possessive case to show ownership.

When the noun is singular, and does not end with *s*, the possessive is formed by adding '*s*:

> the rat's paws
> the participant's response

The same rule applies with the plural form of the noun when the noun does not end with *s*:

> the children's books
> the geese's wings

When the singular form of the noun ends with *s*, the possessive may also be formed by adding *'s*:

> the gas's odour
> the dress's hem

More commonly, this occurs with personal names:

> Jones's
> Charles's

An alternative view is that, when a singular noun ends with *s*, the possessive may be formed by adding an apostrophe only:

> gas'
> Jones'
> Charles'

Those who hold this view suggest that the choice should be made on the basis of which "sounds" better. Certainly, some words do result in unusual forms if *'s* is added, and in such cases it is probably better to add the apostrophe only:

> Donders' experiment
> Flanders' model

When the plural form of a noun ends with *s*, the possessive is formed by adding an apostrophe after the *s*:

> their parents' opinions
> the subjects' responses
> the participants' scores

To form a joint possessive, as in referring to a co-authored article, the *'s* or apostrophe alone (as appropriate) is added to only the last name:

> Smith and Brown's (1992) theory
> Alan and Flanders' (1941) article

Where separate articles are referred to, however, each name takes the possessive case:

> Green's (1941) and Brown's (1953) papers

The same rule applies to compound words:

> brother-in-law's books

The apostrophe (or 's) is also used with expressions of time that are regarded as possessive:

> 1 week's leave
> 1 minute's rest
> 3 days' delay
> 2 hours' wait

and with the possessive forms of pronouns

> everyone's
> anybody's
> everybody's
> one's

However, with the exception of *one's*, an apostrophe is not used with the possessive form of personal pronouns:

> his
> her
> its

When referring to individual participants, respondents, or subjects by number, 's may be added to the number to show possession:

> Participant 4's response
> Subject 3's first trial

## Plurals of letters

The apostrophe may also be used to prevent confusion when expressing the plurals of letters of the alphabet:

> the a's
> the s's

## Plurals of words

A *common error* among students is using an apostrophe to form the plural of a noun, as in, for example:

> The story's were well written.
> The country's differed in climate.

The plural of a noun *cannot* be formed by adding an apostrophe and an *s*.

## Quotation marks

Double quotation marks are used to enclose direct quotations that are included in the text. Long quotations, which are shown as a separate, indented block of text, are not enclosed within quotation marks.

Quotations within quotations, or other words enclosed within quotation marks by the original author, are enclosed within single quotation marks:

> Bloggs (1991) commented that, "The boy said he was 'confused' by the instructions." (p. 13).

*Note*: Although in the APA Publication Manual double and single quotation marks are used as in the above example, according to some authorities they should be used in the opposite manner (i.e., double within single). The use of double quotation marks reduces any possible confusion between quotation marks and apostrophes.

Quotation marks are also used to indicate

• The use of a slang or colloquial term:

> The child described his teacher as "way out" and his father as "not with it".

• An unusual use of a word:

> The Method and Results sections are "sandwiched" between the Introduction and Discussion.

• An invented term:

> the "high-risk" condition

*Note*: After its introduction, an invented term is subsequently used without being enclosed in quotation marks.

On the *rare* occasion when the title of an article, book, or chapter is included in text, it is enclosed within quotation marks:

> Nod's (1983) book, "A Study of Sleep" provides a discussion of . . . .

## Slash (solidus, virgule, or shill)

The slash is used to denote fractions and mathematical expressions.

> 1/3
> 4 m/s

Also, to avoid the awkward construction *and or or*, a slash is used to indicate the alternative:

and/or

The slash should not be used when it might result in confusion or ambiguity. For example, "abnormal/developmental" might be intended to mean "abnormal *or* developmental", "abnormal *and* developmental", or "abnormal-developmental" (i.e., pertaining to abnormal development).

*Note*: The constructions *he/she*, *she/he*, or *s/he* are not used. These would be read as *he or she*, or *she or he*, and so do not solve the perceived problem.

## Series (lists)

A series, or list, of simple items may be included in a sentence without labelling the individual items.

The stimuli used were blue, red, and white.

*Note*: Following the APA Manual style, the *and* before the final item of the list is preceded by a comma. This avoids any possible confusion or doubt.

When the items are more complex, they are usually labelled alphabetically, using lower-case letters.

There were two conditions in the experiment: (a) A visual stimulus requiring a simple response, and (b) a visual stimulus requiring a complex response.

*Note*: If the series is introduced with a complete sentence, the sentence ends with a colon, and the first item in the series takes a capital letter, as in the above example. If, by comparison, the introduction is not a complete sentence, a colon is not used and the first item does not take a capital letter.

The two conditions in the experiment were (a) a visual stimulus requiring a simple response, and (b) a visual stimulus requiring a complex response.

More complex items, which require lengthy descriptions, are listed as numbered paragraphs, using Arabic numerals:

Two scenarios were used in the experiment:
1. The first scenario involved only . . . .
2. The second scenario was more complex, requiring . . . .

# 23 Spelling and Capitalization

Sometimes errors in spelling can be amusing. There is, for example, the story of a parent who received a notice from a private school, advising that in future fees should be paid "anally". The parent, in reply, wrote to the school inquiring why the previous practice of "paying through the nose" could not be continued. In other instances errors can be confusing, and obscure an author's meaning.

It is true that spelling can sometimes be a problem. For example, there is a difference between *compliment* and *complement*, and *stationary* and *stationery*. There can also be confusion in some areas, as in the use of single or double *l* in words such as *skilful*, *finally*, *completely*, and *analytically*. However, there is no reason why spelling cannot be checked in a dictionary. Errors in spelling suggest carelessness, and lack of pride in a paper.

A detailed discussion of spelling is beyond the scope of this book. This chapter is intended only to draw attention to some of the more common problems experienced, and to provide guidance in these areas. When in doubt, an appropriate dictionary should be consulted.

## ▶ Alternative spellings

Some words have alternative spellings that are equally acceptable, (e.g., *adviser* or *advisor*, and *program* or *programme*). When there are alternative spellings, both are usually shown in dictionaries, with the preferred spelling being given first. A particular example occurs with the use of *z* or *s* in words such as *organize* or *organise*. Incidentally, there are those who think that the use of the *z* in such words is American spelling, but this is not so. Both the Oxford and Collins dictionaries – which are British – give *organize* as the preferred spelling, with *organise* as the alternative. On the other hand, the Australian Macquarie dictionary gives *organise* as the preferred spelling.

In such cases the choice of spelling is a matter of personal preference. However, some institutions and publishing houses specify the use of a particular form. Having decided to use a particular form of spelling (e.g., *recognize*, instead of *recognise*) you must be consistent, and use this form throughout a paper. *Lack of consistency indicates carelessness.*

## ▶ Differences

There are some variations in spelling between countries, but the main difference is between British or Standard English and American spelling. If you are writing for an American publication, you should use American spelling, and a dictionary such as Webster's. In other instances you should use what might be described as Standard or International English. The best advice in this case is to use a British dictionary, such as the Oxford or Collins.

The difference in American as compared with Standard English spelling is most evident in words ending in *re* or *er*, *our* or *or*, and *ce* or *se*:

| *British* | *American* |
|-----------|------------|
| theatre   | theater    |
| behaviour | behavior   |
| defence   | defense    |

and in words of Latin or Greek origin containing *ae* or *oe*:

| | |
|----------|---------|
| anaemia  | anemia  |
| toxaemia | toxemia |
| foetus   | fetus   |
| diarrhoea| diarrhea|

Another difference is that in British or Standard English *license* and *practise* are verbs, whereas *licence* and *practice* are nouns. In American English, *license* and *practice* are both verbs and nouns, although *advise* is a verb, but *advice* is a noun. Other differences are found in doubling of the final consonant before adding a suffix:

| | |
|-----------|-----------|
| equalled  | equaled   |
| signalling| signaling |
| kidnapper | kidnaper  |

On the other hand, some words that would be expected to differ in spelling do not. For example, the following words are spelt in the same way in both forms of English:

| | |
|----------|-----------|
| glamour  | aeon      |
| tremor   | aesthetic |
| appealed | enrolled  |

## ▶ Word choice

In some cases, what appears to be a spelling error is actually an error in word use. Similarities between words can cause confusion. Some examples are:

| | |
|---|---|
| affect | effect |
| oral | aural |
| alternate | alternative |
| compliment | complement |
| dependent | dependant |

## ▶ *A – an*

The indefinite article *a* is used before a noun or an adjective beginning with a consonant:

> a trial
> a condition
> a good response

However, when the consonant is not pronounced, *an* is used:

> an hour
> an honour
> an hors d'oeuvre

When the word begins with a vowel, *an* is used:

> an adjective
> an elephant
> an energetic person

Similarly, when preceding an abbreviation, either *a* or *an* is used depending on the pronunciation of the first letter of the abbreviation.

> a BA
> a DSO
> an MA
> an RFD

In other instances, the use of *a* or *an* can vary with the pronunciation of the word preceded. If the word is pronounced as though it begins with a consonant, *a* is used:

> a one-off event
> a unifying variable
> a European

Commonly, in the past, in some words beginning with *h*, the *h* was not sounded. For example, *hotel* was pronounced in the French manner (i.e., without sounding the *h*). Therefore, *an hotel* was used, but this is no longer common usage. Similarly, *a hospital*, *a habitual* response, and *a historical* event, are now the common usage. However, personal preference can influence choice of the use of *a* or *an* in these situations. Some authors, for example, would write *an historical* event or *an hypothesis*.

## ▶ Compound words

Compound words are formed by joining two or more words together. Sometimes this is done by simply joining the two words:

    blackboard
    backbencher
    commonwealth
    database

Other compound words are formed by joining words using a hyphen:

    deep-rooted
    all-or-none
    to-be-recalled
    state-of-the-art

In some instances either form is acceptable:

    backbencher
    back-bencher

When in doubt, the best advice is to check with a dictionary. However, when either form is acceptable care needs to be taken to ensure that the correct meaning is conveyed. For example, there is a difference between a *blackboard* and a *black board*. The former is for writing on with chalk, the latter is simply a board that is black.

There are some instances in which words should not be joined with a hyphen to form a compound word. In particular, a compound word cannot be formed when the first word is an adverb (characteristically ending with *ly*), as in:

    randomly assigned
    widely used
    relatively slow

In addition, compound words are not formed for common fractions:

    one quarter
    two thirds
    four fifths of five eighths of zero

However, compound "words" can be formed with numbers:

    2-year-old
    23-year-old

*Note*: When compound words are formed using hyphens, and they have a common base, in a list the common base may be omitted until the final compound word, but the hyphen is retained:

the low-, moderate-, and high-difficulty tasks
the 15-, 20-, and 25-year-old groups

## ► Prefixed words

In a manner similar to the formation of compound words, a hyphen is sometimes used in prefixed words. Often, the use of a hyphen in this way is optional, and either form is acceptable. A case in point is *e-mail*. Either *e-mail* or *email* is acceptable, although more commonly the latter is used.

In some cases, however, there can be a rather awkward clash of vowels or consonants, and it is preferable to use a hyphen:

re-emerge
anti-icing
damp-proof
micro-organism

Also, a hyphen should be used when there can be confusion between words:

| | |
|---|---|
| re-collect | to collect again |
| recollect | to remember |
| re-count | to count again |
| recount | to tell |

Although it is perhaps a pedantic point, there is a difference between *on line* and *on-line*. For example, "This document is available on line," tells the reader where the document can be located, in the same way as does, "This document is available in the library." By comparison, "an on-line journal" refers to a journal that is published on line.

## ► Plural nouns

Forming the plurals of nouns can sometimes present difficulties. The general rule, which is applicable to most nouns, is that the plural is formed simply by adding *s*:

| | |
|---|---|
| rat | rats |
| computer | computers |

*Note*: Care is needed when forming some plurals that are comprised of two parts. For example:

courts marshal
governors general
Forms B

There are, however, several rules that apply to words with specific endings. Nouns ending in *o, s, x, z, ch, sh,* or *ss,* have *es* added to form the plural:

| | |
|---|---|
| zero | zeroes |
| bus | buses |
| fox | foxes |
| buzz | buzzes |
| switch | switches |
| wish | wishes |
| kiss | kisses |

For nouns ending in *f* or *fe,* the *f* or *fe* often is replaced by *v.*

| | |
|---|---|
| shelf | shelves |
| knife | knives |

For most nouns ending in *y,* the *y* is replaced with *ies.*

| | |
|---|---|
| reality | realities |
| society | societies |

There are, however, a number of exceptions to these rules. These include, for example:

| | |
|---|---|
| child | children |
| foot | feet |
| die | dice |
| piano | pianos |
| belief | beliefs |
| play | plays |

Some nouns do not change in the plural. These include, for example:

aircraft
cannon
fish
sheep

Some nouns are used only in the plural. These include, for example:

corps
dregs
pants
scissors

Nouns of French, Greek, and Latin origin can cause difficulties. There can, for example, be confusion between Latin and Greek origins, especially for words ending in *us.* As an instance, platypus is of Greek, not Latin, origin.

The correct plural of "platypus", therefore, is *platypodes*, and not *platypi*. However, "platypodes" is never used. In the scientific literature "platypus" is commonly used as both singular and plural.

For some words the original plural form is retained in English, as in the Latin plurals *agenda* or *strata*. In other cases, the original plural is never used, as in the Greek plural *octopodes*, and the Anglicized version of the plural is always used for some nouns, as in *hippopotamuses*, or *geniuses*.

For some words, either the original plural or its Anglicized form may be acceptable. For example:

| | |
|---|---|
| bureaux | bureaus |
| formulae | formulas |
| indices | indexes |

Although in popular literature the Anglicized form is often used, *in scholarly or scientific writing the original French, Greek, or Latin form is preferred*. A selection of words that often cause problems is listed in Box 6.

*Note*: In the APA Publication Manual, *appendixes* is given as the plural of *appendix*, but *matrices* is given as the plural of *matrix*. Also, *schemas* is given as the plural of *schema*. The preferred plurals of these words are *appendices*, *matrices*, and *schemata*.

## An exception

There can be exceptions to some rules. An interesting example is the use of *datums* as a plural. When maps and charts are drawn, a base level (approximately sea level) is used from which heights and depths are measured. This base level is referred to as *a datum*. When referring to several maps or charts, then, each of which might be drawn on the basis of a different datum, the plural datums is correct. There is no option. Of course, in this sense, "datums" does not refer to data.

## ▶ Capital (upper-case) letters

The use of capital (or upper-case) letters can cause confusion. The following guidelines cover the majority of uses.

## Where capital letters are needed

Capital letters are used for:

**Box 6**   Singular and plural forms of words

| Singular | Plural |
|----------|--------|
| agendum | agenda |
| analysis | analyses |
| antenna | antennae |
| appendix | appendices |
| aquarium | aquaria |
| axis | axes |
| basis | bases |
| bureau | bureaux |
| cactus | cacti |
| crisis | crises |
| criterion | criteria |
| curriculum | curricula |
| datum | data |
| emphasis | emphases |
| formula | formulae |
| forum | fora |
| hypothesis | hypotheses |
| index | indices |
| locus | loci |
| matrix | matrices |
| medium | media |
| nucleus | nuclei |
| oasis | oases |
| parenthesis | parentheses |
| phenomenon | phenomena |
| plateau | plateaux |
| radius | radii |
| referendum | referenda |
| schema | schemata |
| stimulus | stimuli |
| stratum | strata |
| tableau | tableaux |

- The first word in a sentence, including complete sentences following a colon.

*Note*: A sentence must not begin with Arabic numerals: Words must be used:

> Seventy-six trombones led the big parade.

- Titles:

> Doctor Foster

General Percival
Viscount Slim

- Proper nouns (i.e., names of people or places):

  Pavlov      Koori
  London      Canberra

- Nouns used as proper nouns (i.e., in a specific sense):

  the University of Adelaide
  the Government of Australia
  the Results section
  the Queen
  the President
  the Prime Minister

If the noun is non-specific a capital is not used:

  the government of a country
  the president of a country
  a university

*An example*
The word *aborigine* means an original inhabitant. Because it is general in meaning, it does not take a capital. By comparison, in Australia *Aborigine* refers to an original inhabitant of Australia. Therefore, because it is specific in meaning, it does take a capital. Similarly, the word *aboriginal* is an adjective which is non-specific, and so does not take a capital. In Australia, *Aboriginal* is an adjective used when referring to the original inhabitants. Therefore it does take a capital. However, some original inhabitants prefer to be referred to using a tribal group identity such as *Koori*, among others.

- Specific geographical locations defined by political or cultural boundaries:

  Northern Ireland
  South Australia
  the English Channel

When the area is not specific, capital letters are not used:

  They travelled from southern to northern Australia.
  the northern part of America

- Nouns followed by numerals or letters:

  Day 1        Experiment 1
  Trial 2      Figure 2
  Condition 1  Table 3
  Item C       Factor A

*Note*: Exceptions to this, following the APA Manual, are:

1. when referring to parts of a book:

   chapter 3
   page 6

2. when referring to parts of a table:

   column 3
   row 4

- Trade names and names of tests:

  a Jaguar car
  the Wechsler Adult Intelligence Scale
  the Minnesota Multiphasic Personality Inventory

- Names of parts of a research report:

  the Method section
  the Results section
  the Discussion

- All main words in headings and subheadings (other than indented paragraph headings):

  Method
  Discussion
  Results
  Movement Time Analysis

- Major words and those of more than four letters in titles of books and articles included in the body of a paper. When a hyphenated compound word is included, the second word is not capitalized. The first word following a colon is capitalized.

  In their book, *Life-span Developmental Psychology: Current Issues*, the authors argue . . .

*Note*: In the reference list, only the first word of a book title, and the first word following a colon or dash, take capital letters.

- Major words in the title of a journal:

  Journal of Experimental Psychology

- Some abbreviations and acronyms:

  Dr      NATO
  IQ      ANOVA

- Major words in table titles
- The first word in a figure caption

- The first word in a list, or series of items, which is introduced by a complete sentence followed by a colon.
- Names of variables when appearing with a multiplication sign:

    Sex × Reaction Time interaction
    (Group × Task Difficulty) design

## Where capital letters are not used

Capital letters are not used:

- When referring to variables in the absence of a multiplication sign:

    the sex and reaction time variables

- When referring to effects:

    the group effect

- For names of conditions or groups in an experiment

    the experimental group
    the control group
    the stressed condition
    the simple response condition

- For words other than the first word in a title in a reference list, and words other than those following a colon or dash in a title:

    Life-span developmental psychology: A longitudinal study

- For the word following the hyphen in a compound word

    On-line sources are sometimes used.

- For names of theories or laws:

    Kohlberg's theory of moral development
    Erickson's theory of socioemotional stages
    the empirical law of effect
    the associative learning model

- In non-specific references to tests:

    an intelligence test
    a verbal recall test

- When referring to parts of a book:

    chapter 3, page 6

- When referring to parts of a table:

    column 3, row 4

# 24 Abbreviations and Numbers

Most people remember only common abbreviations, and there is some variation in their usage. For instance, sometimes punctuation is used in abbreviations – for example, B.A., Ph.D., i.e. – while sometimes it is not – for example, BA, PhD, ie. Similarly, there are variations in the manner in which numbers are given in text. When in doubt you should consult a dictionary or style manual. As in other matters, however, you must follow the style requirements of the publisher for whom you are writing, or the style adopted in your institution or organization. In any case, it is essential that you are consistent.

## ▶ Abbreviations

Abbreviations are useful for avoiding the repetition of long or cumbersome technical terms, but they should be used sparingly. A reader cannot be expected to remember a large number of non-standard abbreviations. Moreover, such abbreviations can be confusing. The meaning of the following sentence, for instance, may not immediately be evident:

> There were significant differences between SRT and CRT for the LH and RH responses in both the V and NV condition.

As a general principle, non-standard abbreviations should not be used unless they are easily understood and their use avoids cumbersome repetition of long, technical terms.

### Standard abbreviations

Standard abbreviations such as *e.g.*, *etc.*, or *kg*, which are found in dictionaries, can be used without explanation. Similarly, statistical abbreviations and symbols, such as *df*, *p*, *M*, or *SD*, are regarded as being standard and do not require explanation.

A selection of commonly used standard abbreviations is given in Appendix

D, and of commonly used statistical abbreviations and symbols in Appendix E.

## Non-standard abbreviations

The meaning of non-standard abbreviations must be explained in the text. This is achieved by giving the term in full when it is first used, followed immediately by the abbreviation enclosed in parentheses. For example, if the term *choice reaction time* were to be abbreviated as *CRT*, in the first instance this abbreviation would be explained as:

> choice reaction time (CRT)

Thereafter, the abbreviation may be used without further explanation. Although some non-standard abbreviations, such as STM or RT, are commonly used in psychology, they should still be explained in this manner. It is possible that the reader is not familiar with the abbreviation.

Often, abbreviations are used when referring to experimental conditions in research reports. For example, a *vision available* condition might be abbreviated as the VA condition, and a *vision precluded* condition as the VP condition. If you do this, try to choose abbreviations that are intuitively logical and easily remembered.

There are a small number of abbreviations that, although not standard, are sufficiently familiar to be used without explanation. These include, IQ, ESP, AIDS, and HIV.

## Plurals of abbreviations

The plural of an abbreviation can be formed by adding an *s*, with no apostrophe. For example, the plural of RT is RTs and of Vol. is Vols. An exception to this rule is that the plural of *p.* (for page) is *pp.* Also, this rule does not apply to standard Latin abbreviations such as *e.g.*, or to abbreviations for units of measurement, such as *mm* or *kg*.

## Punctuation in abbreviations

In some styles, such as that adopted by the military, no punctuation is used in abbreviations. More commonly, as a general rule, abbreviations that do not end with the final letter of the word abbreviated are followed by a full stop, while those that do end with the final letter of the word are not. Therefore, for example, the names of the Australian states Victoria and Queensland should be abbreviated respectively as *Vic.* (with a full stop) and

*Qld* (without a full stop). However, the APA Manual does not follow this rule and uses a full stop with abbreviations such as *Eds.* (editors) and *Vols.* (volumes). The APA Manual style is used in this book.

A full stop follows an initial that is an abbreviation of a person's given name (e.g., J. Bond), and reference abbreviations (e.g., Vol., ed., and p.). Full stops are also used in standard Latin abbreviations such as *e.g.*, or *i.e.* Note that *e.g.* is the abbreviation of two words (*exempli gratia*), as is *i.e.* (*id est*), and so both letters are followed by a full stop. By comparison, *cf.* is the abbreviation of one word (*confer*, meaning "compare"). An exception to this rule is that *etc.*, which is the abbreviation of two words (*et* and *cetera*), is treated as a single word followed by a full stop.

Abbreviations of units of measure, such as *mm*, *kg*, and *s*, are not followed by a full stop. Similarly, full stops are not used in capital letter abbreviations such as RT, IQ, NY, UK, or NSW; or in acronyms such as NATO or ANOVA.

## Et al.

The abbreviation *et al.* is comprised of the word *et* and the abbreviation *al.* The Latin word *et* means *and*, whereas *al.* is the abbreviation of *alii*, which means *others*. Consequently, *et* is not followed by a full stop, but *al.* is.

Although in some publications "et al." is shown in italics, following the APA Manual style it is not. This abbreviation is used in a reference list *only* when there are more than six authors, in which case the first six authors' names are given followed by "et al."

## Abbreviations in a sentence

A sentence may begin with a capitalized abbreviation or an acronym such as CRT or NATO, but this should be avoided if possible. Lower-case abbreviations such as *e.g.*, *i.e.*, or *cf.* must never be used to begin a sentence.

*The abbreviations i.e. and e.g. are used only when enclosed in parentheses.* For example, it is correct to write, "All participants (i.e., those in both groups) were tested," but it is *not* correct to write, "All participants, i.e., those in both groups, were tested."

Similarly, *the ampersand (&) is used only when enclosed in parentheses.* For example, write "Jones and Smith (1996)" as part of a sentence, but "(Jones & Smith, 1996)" when the reference is enclosed in parentheses. An exception to this rule is that, although not enclosed in parentheses, the ampersand is used between authors' names in a reference list.

## Prohibited abbreviations

*Experimenter*, *participant*, and *subject* must not be abbreviated as *E*, *P*, or *S*, and *Figure* must not be abbreviated as *Fig.*

## Colloquial abbreviations

Abbreviations such as *ad* for advertisement, or *uni* for university, which are sometimes used colloquially, are never used in formal writing.

## Symbols

Symbols, such as +, –, =, >, or → must never be used in written text as abbreviations, or in lieu of words. These symbols are, of course, appropriate when used in mathematical expressions, statistics, or formulae included in text.

## ▶ Numbers

The general rule is that numbers below 10 are expressed in words and numbers of 10 and above are expressed in figures. There are, however, some exceptions to this rule. Numbers below 10 are shown in Arabic numerals for:

- numbers in an abstract

- units of measurement:

    7 mm
    5 kg

- mathematical functions:

    multiplied by 7
    3 times as many

- ratios:

    1:3
    5:12

- times:

    2 h 21 min
    1:21 p.m.
    for 2 hours
    in 3 minutes

*Note*: In the APA Manual "hour" is abbreviated as *hr*, but the international system abbreviation is *h*.

- dates:

    6 June 1944

*Note*: In the APA Manual, dates are given using the American style, as in, June 6, 1944.

- ages:

    3 years old
    8-year-old children

- scores:

    a score of 3 on a 5-point scale

- sample sizes:

    5 participants
    30 subjects

- percentages:

    3%
    33%

- proportions:

    0.45 of the sample
    0.32 of the scores

- monetary amounts:

    $3
    4 cents
    7 pence

- references to pages or chapters:

    page 5
    chapter 2

- references to figures and tables:

    Table 3
    Figure 1
    column 3
    row 4

- location in a series:

Stage 2
Day 2
Trial 5
Level 3
Subject 7

## Plural of numbers as Arabic numerals

Plurals of numbers are given as:

the 1990s
the 10s

## Numbers as words

Words are used to express numbers:

* to begin a sentence (regardless of the number involved):

  Twenty-four individuals were interviewed.

* usually for *zero* and *one*, if easier to understand the numbers in the context:

  there was only one response
  one-line response
  zero-based measurement

* to express common fractions:

  three quarters
  one half
  one third of respondents
  four fifths of five eighths

* when reporting statistical tests:

  two-way interaction
  one-tailed test

* when describing an experiment:

  three sessions
  four trials
  two conditions
  six items
  three-dimensional figure

* to express ordinal numbers:

the third list
the second item

- with words that are not precise measurements:

two words
the only one

## Comparative numbers

Where numbers are presented in the same sentence or paragraph for purposes of comparison, if one or more of the numbers is 10 or above, all numbers are expressed in Arabic numerals, as in, for example:

in 3 of the 20 trials
on the 2nd of 20 trials

This rule is not applicable when there is no comparison, as in:

There were 15 trials in each of the three conditions.

## Compound words

If you use a compound word such as *two-choice* condition, two is a number less than 10, and in this case does not fall within one of the exemption categories. By comparison, in *2-year-old* children the number refers to the age of the children, and age is an exception to the rule of using words to express numbers of less than 10.

Some care is needed when writing sentences using such compound words. For example, the following are awkward and rather confusing constructions:

There were 42 2-year-old children.

or

There were two two-choice conditions.

In such instances, it is better to rewrite the sentence to avoid the problem, but an acceptable option is to use words for one of the numbers:

There were forty-two 2-year-old children.
There were 2 two-choice tasks.

## Plurals of numbers as words

The plurals of numbers expressed in words are formed by adding *s* or *es*:

fours
sixes

## Roman numerals

Roman numerals should only be used where it is conventional to do so (e.g., Type I error, or World War II) or, where appropriate, in publication details in a reference list (e.g., Vol. III).

# 25 Typing and Presentation

First impressions count, and you do not want a reader to approach your paper with a negative attitude. A paper that is neat and tidy, and that conforms to given presentation requirements, gives an impression of care and pride. In contrast, one that is not, and does not, suggests carelessness, and this is usually reflected in the content of the paper.

## ▶ Student papers vs. manuscripts

Papers submitted for publication (i.e., manuscripts) are what can be described as "working copies" on which, for example, editors insert typesetting instructions. By comparison, papers written by students are submitted in their *final form*. There are, therefore, some differences in presentation between papers submitted for publication and those that students write. The requirements given here are consistent with those given in the APA Manual, but with minor amendments to suit student papers.

Your department or institution will have its own specific requirements for the format and layout of written assignments. Obviously, you will need to comply with these. However, it is very likely that, with perhaps some minor differences, the requirements given in Appendix A will apply. The following notes are an elaboration on some of the requirements given in Appendix A, and provide additional information and advice.

## ▶ Format

There are some minor variations between the presentation formats for an essay or literature review and a research report. The general formats for these papers are shown in Box 7.

## ▶ Headings

In relatively short papers in the form of essays or literature reviews, headings should usually *not* be included. On the other hand, headings and subheadings are always used in research reports. The APA Manual provides

**Box 7**  General format for papers

| *Essay or literature review* | *Research report* | *Pages* |
|---|---|---|
| Title page | Title page | Separate page |
| Abstract (if required) | Abstract | Separate page |
| Essay or literature review | Report | Start on new page |
| Reference list | Reference list | Start on new page |
|  | Appendices (if any) | Separate pages |

*Note*: For a research report the Method, Results, and Discussion sections do *not* start on a new page.

for five levels of headings, the typing formats for which are illustrated in Appendix F. The headings and subheadings commonly used in a simple research report are illustrated in Appendix G, and those commonly used in a research report involving multiple experiments are illustrated in Appendix H. The use of headings in qualitative research reports is discussed in chapter 20.

## ▶ Title page

The requirements for layout of a title page will vary, and you will need to check your department's specific requirements. Those given here are based on the layout used for a paper submitted for publication, with amendments to suit student papers. An example format of a title page is shown in Appendix I.

## Title

The title is typed using upper- and lower-case letters, and is centred at the top of the page. Major words and those of more than four letters are capitalized.

## Certificate

If you are required to include a certificate to the effect that the paper is entirely your own work, you may not alter the wording of this certificate. In effect, you are certifying that you have not plagiarized any material included in your paper. If you are in doubt about the meaning of plagiarism you should read chapter 4. *The certificate is signed and dated in handwriting.*

## Contact address

This is provided to allow the academic involved to contact you easily. Usually it is required only for students who are studying by distance education or part time. The contact address may be an email address.

## Word count

The word count is the number of words in the paper, excluding the title page, abstract (if any), reference list, and appendices (if any). Figures and tables, obviously, are also excluded.

**Counting words**, chap. 10

## Spacing

The spacing used on a title page is not critical. Rather, the aim should be to present a pleasing appearance. It is, therefore, desirable to leave space between the elements. Space should be left at the bottom of the page for the marker's comments.

## Alignment

The title, author's name and affiliation (i.e., department and university) are centred, but the remaining elements on the page are aligned with the 35 mm left-hand margin.

## Running head

A running head is an abbreviated title. It is typed, all in upper-case letters, 35 mm from the top of the page, and flush with the 35 mm left-hand margin. A running head should not exceed 59 character spaces (including punctuation and spaces). Usually, a running head is not required for student papers.

Some departments require students to include their name at the top of each page of an assignment. In this case, the student's name should usually be typed in the location used for a running head – presuming that one is not required.

## ▶ Body of the paper

## Title

According to the APA Manual, the title of a paper is typed at the top of the first page of the Introduction. This is to allow for blind review when the title page is not given to referees. In student papers it is superfluous to do this. Therefore, the title should not be typed at the top of the first page of text.

## Right justification

Papers submitted for publication must not be right justified. Similarly, papers written by students should not be so.

## Paragraphs

As in most books, *the first line of each paragraph is indented by five to seven spaces* to show that a new paragraph has started. If this is not done it can be difficult to identify individual paragraphs in double-spaced text, especially when a paragraph begins at the top of a page.

An exception to this is that the first line of the abstract is not indented. In addition, there is no need to indent the first sentence in the Introduction, or the first sentence immediately following a heading or subheading. It is obvious that a new paragraph begins following a heading or subheading. (In papers submitted for publication, however, the first line of all paragraphs is indented.)

As in most books, *additional space is not left between paragraphs*. Doing so merely wastes space. The normal double spacing is maintained between paragraphs.

## Footnotes

Footnotes are indicated in the text by inserting an identifying number as a superscript, immediately after any punctuation mark present – with the exception of a dash, in which case it precedes the dash. In student papers, footnotes may be typed, following the identifying number, at the bottom of the relevant page. In papers submitted for publication, footnotes must be typed on separate pages.

## ► Reference list

The presentation of a reference list is described in chapter 8. The basic requirements are that it begins on a new page, under the centred heading "References", and that double spacing is used *only* between sources. In a manuscript, double spacing is used throughout, but in a student's paper this is not necessary.

## ▶ Appendices

Each appendix starts on a new page, but is not paginated. Appendices are headed with the word "Appendix" and an upper-case letter (A, B, C, etc.) in the order in which they are referred to in the text. An exception is that when there is only one appendix, the alphabetical character is unnecessary and so is omitted. The appendix heading (e.g., "Appendix A") is centred at the top of the page, and is typed in normal characters. The title of the appendix is centred below the heading, but is typed in italics using upper-case and lower-case letters. In a manuscript an appendix is typed using double spacing. In student papers, however, a long appendix may be typed using single spacing to allow it to fit on a single page.

## ▶ Typing

The basic requirement is that a paper must be typed on A4 paper using double spacing, and with 35 mm margins at the top and bottom, and on both sides. This is to allow space for comments to be made on the paper. Allowed exceptions to double spacing, for student papers, are given in Appendix A. The margin specification of 35 mm is nominal, and a few millimetres either way is not important.

### Pagination

With the exception of the title page, pages are paginated at the top right-hand corner, within the 35 mm margins.

### Spacing within text

The general rule is that a single space is left between words and following punctuation marks. Therefore, for example, a single space is left following a comma, a semicolon, and a colon.

According to the APA Manual, a single space is also left following the punctuation mark at the end of a sentence. However, *it is preferable to leave a double space at the end of a sentence because this makes reading easier.*

A single space is left before opening, and after closing parentheses or brackets, but no space is left between parentheses or brackets and the characters enclosed. Also, a single space is left before and after minus signs (e.g., a − b); and before, but not after a negative sign (e.g., −7). No space is left either before or after hyphens or dashes (e.g., 2-year-old). However, when dashes are used parenthetically, or when adding a comment to the end of a sentence, a space is left before and after the dash.

When citing statistics, a single space is left between numerical values and symbols, but no space is left between the symbols $F$ or $t$ and the opening parenthesis enclosing the degrees of freedom. Examples are:

2 mm

3 s

$3 \times 2 \times 2$

(a − b)

$F(2, 23) = 6.75, p = .03$

$t(13) = 1.06, p > .05$

## Typeface

A serif typeface is easier to read than is a sans serif typeface, and Times New Roman is commonly used. Therefore, a paper should be typed in 12 point Times New Roman typeface, but a sans serif typeface, such as **Arial**, may be used for labels on figures and tables. Text that should be in italics should be typed in italics, and not underlined. However, if you are using a typewriter, or your word processing program does not support the use of italics, underline the necessary text to show that it should be in italics. Text that should be in bold should be typed in bold.

The terms *typeface* and *font* are often confused, and sometimes they are used interchangeably. In word processing programs "font" is often used to mean "typeface". A typeface is a set of characters that have a common design. Examples of typeface are Courier and **Arial**. A font is a set of characters that have the same typeface, size, and spacing, among other attributes. Therefore, for example, **Arial 10 point** and **Arial 12 point** are different fonts.

Note that the space occupied by characters can vary. In Times New Roman, for example, in the word "with" the *i* occupies less space than the *w*. Fonts in which this occurs are referred to as *proportional*. By comparison, in Courier each character occupies the same space. This is referred to as a *fixed-pitch* font, or non-proportional. Typewriter fonts and some used in word processing programs are of this form.

Fonts or typefaces can also be either serif or sans serif (from the French *sans*, meaning "without"). Serifs are the finishing strokes at the top and bottom of characters. Courier and Times New Roman, for example, are serif, while **Arial** is sans serif. Both the readability and appearance of a paper can be enhanced by a wise choice of font or typeface. It is generally accepted that a serif typeface is easier to read. However, a sans serif typeface, such as **Arial**, is often a better choice for the headings in tables and for labels in figures.

What might be described as "fancy" typefaces, such as *Pepita* or *Mistral*, can be difficult to read, and should *never* be used in academic papers.

## Boldface

The APA Manual does not specify the typing of headings and subheadings in bold in manuscripts submitted for publication. However, in student papers – which are in their final form – titles, headings, subheadings, and the titles of appendices may be typed in bold.

## Underlining

Underling is used *only* to indicate that the words or letters underlined should be in italics. This is done when an italic font is not available.

## Italics

Italics are used for:

- titles of books, journals, and unpublished manuscripts and theses in a reference list;
- titles of tables, but not the labels;
- figure labels, but not the figure caption;
- volume numbers of journals (but not issue numbers) in a reference list;
- statistical symbols and abbreviations;
- subheadings;
- the word *Note*, when notes are shown under a table.

A further use of italics is to introduce a new technical or key term, as in, for example, "For the *forced-choice* task participants were required to . . .". Having been introduced in this way, the term is subsequently typed in normal characters. Also, words may be shown in italics to add emphasis.

## Greek letters

If the font is available for Greek letters they should be typed. If it is not, they may be handwritten.

## Hyphens

Words should not be hyphenated at the end of a line of text.

## Statistics

Descriptive statistics are usually given in two parts: as numbers and an abbreviation of the unit of measurement (e.g., 32 mm). The two parts should not be split at the end of a line. For instance, a line should not end with "32" and the next line start with "mm". Inferential statistics can be thought of as comprising three separate parts: (a) The statistical symbol and degrees of freedom [e.g., $F(2, 23)$], (b) the value of the statistic (e.g., 17.63), and (c) the probability (e.g., $p = .03$, or $p < .05$). These parts should not be split at the end of a line. For example, a line should not end with "$F(2,$ ", and the next line begin with "23)".

## ▶ General points

The following notes refer to general aspects of preparing a paper that are also important.

## Proof reading

You must always proof read the final version of your paper before submission. It is surprising how often flaws become evident at this point. Any such flaws must, of course, be attended to before you submit your paper. Do not make any such corrections in handwriting.

## Paper

Use white, standard A4 paper, and print or type on only one side of the paper.

## Print quality

Always make sure that the print on a paper produces a clear, sharp image with good contrast. If need be, you will have to replace the ink cartridge of your printer, or the ribbon of your typewriter.

## Copy

You must always keep a copy of your paper. Although it is unlikely, it is possible for a paper to be lost.

## Binding

The pages of a paper must be firmly bound together. This is usually achieved by stapling at the top left-hand corner. If the paper includes too many pages to allow for normal stapling, some other method must be used. A paper can be accidentally dropped, and if it falls apart the reader is likely to be somewhat annoyed, and one or more pages might be lost. Papers should *not* be enclosed in plastic sleeves, and *individual pages must never be so*.

## Decorations

Do not "decorate" your paper with "pretty drawings", "clip art" or any other such illustrations. A professionally presented paper does not include such "decorations". Also, do not draw lines around pages.

# 26  Marking Papers

Students typically do not understand the process involved in the marking of their papers. A comment often made is something like, "I put a lot of effort into writing this paper, but I was given a poor grade." The problem with this comment is that what one person thinks of as a lot, another does not. In any event, writing a paper is always time consuming and difficult. Students often do not fully appreciate this, and think that simply because they put time and effort into writing a paper, it should be given a good grade. *A paper is marked on the basis of what is presented, not how much time and effort was involved.*

Another common misperception is that if a large number of sources are referred to, a paper should be given a good grade. It is important to understand that *it is not the number of sources that are cited, but rather how sources are used in a paper that is important.* Merely referring only very briefly to a large number of sources is not indicative of analytical and critical thinking. Neither is it indicative of an understanding of the use of sources.

Finally, a not uncommon comment is something like, "It is the content of my paper that is important, not how it is written." This reveals the student's lack of appreciation of *the need for scholarly writing.* In addition, students often seem not to understand the meaning of "style": They confuse this with, for example, the need to cite sources, or to place citations appropriately.

The following notes are provided to help students to understand the considerations involved when marking a paper. However, academics differ somewhat in their approach, and the emphasis can vary with the specific purpose for which an assignment is set. The notes provided here, therefore, are only of a general nature.

## ▶ Criteria

When marking a paper, the critical question is, "Has the student satisfactorily completed the required task?" What is involved in this will, of course, vary with the nature of the paper. As an example, however, an essay must address the specific question set, and present a clear and reasonable thesis or conclusion that is developed by a well supported argument: One that does not would be expected to fail.

An important point to understand is that "satisfactory" is a relative term. When making this judgement, an academic will take into consideration the level of the subject or course involved. Obviously, better papers are expected at higher levels of study.

Secondary considerations are: "Is the paper written in a scholarly manner?" and "Has the student complied with the given requirements?" By comparison with the increased standard expected in other areas, that expected in the area of grammar, punctuation, and spelling; and on matters of requirements given (such as presentation), will be high from the outset.

## ▶ Grades

Grading a paper, in part, can be based on an objective assessment of whether or not the student has satisfactorily completed the required task. A point to understand is that *a paper that is satisfactory does not warrant a credit or distinction grade.* There must be aspects of it that are more than satisfactory to warrant a grade higher than a pass.

It is relatively easy to recognize a well structured paper, logical reasoning based on sound information and well supported assertions, and comments that indicate careful analytical and critical thinking. Nonetheless, evaluation of the quality of a student's argument, for example, will involve a subjective judgement. This cannot be avoided. However, those marking papers will have written many, read many, and graded many. They are, therefore, adequately equipped to make such judgements.

It is important to understand that a paper is marked as whole, not on the basis of it parts.[12] The well-known concept, "The whole is greater than the sum of the parts," is applicable. To illustrate this, you might like to think of judging the quality of a meal in a restaurant. Having finished the meal, you might judge it to have been of modest quality. Thinking about it, you might consider that the entrée (the introduction) was poor, the main course (body of the paper) was very good, and the dessert (conclusion) was somehow lacking. Taking this a step further, you might have considered that in the main course (body), the salad was good, although the tomatoes could have been of better quality, but the steak was excellent. That is, while you were able to make judgements of individual parts of the meal, your final judgement was one of an overall nature; in this case, that the meal was of modest quality.

Another consideration in this analogy is the restaurant. For example, if the restaurant were "mid-range" and the prices moderate, you might consider that the meal was quite good and "good value for money". By comparison, if the restaurant were of a higher standard and the prices comparably so, you might consider the meal, although exactly the same, to be of poor quality, and "not good value for money".

---

[12] An exception to this is that the parts of a research report are often marked separately.

This analogy illustrates two points. The first is that the quality of the meal was judged on an overall basis, just as is the quality of a student's paper. The second is that expectation (a modest vs. a high-quality restaurant) can affect judgement, just as the quality of a paper submitted by a student is judged on the level at which the student is studying.

Although flaws such as errors in grammar, punctuation, and style and presentation requirements are secondary, they can have an influence. Such flaws are detrimental to the communication of information and ideas, and are distracting. Moreover, they give the impression of lack of care or ability. To continue the analogy above, if the service in the restaurant were poor, the room cold, and the music too loud, although these do not directly affect the quality of the food, they do affect the overall judgement of one's enjoyment of the meal. It follows, then, that it is in a student's best interest to ensure that he or she avoids flaws that are likely to distract, confuse, or annoy the reader, or that suggest carelessness or lack of ability. *A paper that is not written and presented in a scholarly manner is very unlikely to be given a good grade.*

Of course, for the meal to be considered more than satisfactory, or quite good, there must have been something about it that made it "stand out". For instance, perhaps it was particularly well prepared and presented, and the chef added his own special sauce. Similarly, for a student's paper to be given a grade higher than a pass there must be something that makes it stand out. Apart from being well structured and written, it should include clear evidence of analytical and critical thought, and the student's own ideas (rather than a simple reproduction of the ideas of others).

A point not to be overlooked is that a meal finishes with dessert, and this creates the final impression. Therefore, a poor dessert can detract from an otherwise good meal. Similarly, a paper ends with a conclusion. This must summarize the author's argument and supporting evidence. In particular, it must clearly present the author's thesis or conclusion. In the same way that a poor dessert can detract from an otherwise good meal, *a poor conclusion can detract markedly from an otherwise good paper.*

As a final observation, the quality of a meal is not judged on the basis of the time and effort put into preparing it by the chef. From the diner's point of view, this is irrelevant. The same applies to papers written by students. From the marker's point of view, the time and effort involved in writing a paper are not relevant.

## ▶ The future

An important point for you to understand is that the papers that you write in your future career will be similarly graded. The only difference is that the paper will not be returned to you with a grade. On occasion, someone might remark that a paper that you wrote was particularly good, but this is not common. Rather, your ability to write a paper of good quality will be simply expected. On the other hand, if you write a poor paper, often no comment will be made. However, your inability to write a good paper will be noted, and this is likely to affect, for example, your chances of promotion. More importantly, as was pointed out in the beginning of this book, *how well you write can affect people's lives.*

# Appendix A
## Recommended presentation and style requirements for student papers

*(Incorporating recommended options in, or deviations from, the APA Manual)*

1 The title of the paper should not appear at the top of the first page.

2 A running head is not required.

3 All pages, other than the title page and appendices, should be paginated at the *top right-hand corner*, within the 35 mm top margin. If pagination cannot be readily included, pages on which figures or tables are presented separately may be not paginated. However, they are numbered in that they occupy a particular page in the paper.

4 Text should *not* be right justified.

5 When possible, the typeface used throughout a paper (including the title page), should be 12-point Times New Roman, with the exception that headings and labels in tables and figures may be in a sans serif typeface such as Arial.

6 Headings and major subheadings may be typed in boldface (e.g., **References**, **Method**, or ***Participants***).

7 When words should be italicized they should be typed in italics, and not underlined.

8 Double spacing should be used throughout a paper with the exception that single spacing should be used:

- within references in a reference list;
- for table titles and headings;
- for figure captions and labels;
- for long quotations;
- for footnotes; and
- in some instances, for appendices.

9 Quadruple spacing (i.e., double double-spacing) may be used before any main heading – but not subheading – and before and after any figure or table included in a page of text.

10 Additional space is not left between paragraphs (i.e., double spacing is maintained throughout the text).

11 The first line of each paragraph is indented by 5–7 spaces, with the

exception of the first line of text in a paper and the first sentence imme-diately following a heading or subheading.

12  A double space is left following the end of a sentence.

13  Figures and small tables occupying no more than half a page may be included on a page of text, but text may not "flow around" a figure.

14  Large figures and tables should be presented on separate pages, as soon as is convenient following the first reference to the table or figure in the text.

15  Large figures or tables may be printed "landscape".

16  Paper used should be standard A4 (210 × 297 mm).

17  Margins at the top and bottom, and on both sides of pages should be 35 mm.

# Appendix B
## Citing sources

### ▶ Examples of citing common sources

### Single author

Durant (1999) has argued. . . .

or

It has been argued that . . . (Durant, 1999).

*Note*: The reference is part of the sentence, and so the full stop follows the reference.

### Two authors

Abbott and Costello (2002) have suggested. . . .

or

It has been suggested that . . . (Abbott & Costello, 2002).

*Notes*:
1. The ampersand (&) is used *only* within parentheses.
2. For two authors there is no comma before the *and* or ampersand.

### More than two, but less than six, authors

**First reference in a paper**

Moore, Maguire, and Smyth (2004) proposed. . . .

or

It has been proposed that . . . (Moore, Maguire, & Smyth, 2004).

*Note*: When there are three or more authors there is a comma before the *and* or ampersand.

**For subsequent reference to the source in the same paper**

Moore et al. (2004) also proposed. . . .

or

It has also been proposed that . . . (Moore et al., 1992).

*Note*: When not enclosed in parentheses the "al." is followed only by a full stop, but when enclosed in parentheses it is followed by a full stop and a comma.

### Possessive case
When referring to a multiple-authored source in the possessive case it must be referred to as, for example:

The findings of the Moore et al. (1992) study. . . .

or

The Moore et al. (1992) findings. . . .

An apostrophe may *not* be added to form a possessive abbreviation, as in "et al.'s".

## Six or more authors

When there are six or more authors, the "et al." abbreviation is used for the first and all subsequent references.

## Page numbers

Page numbers are given when referring to books or long articles, as in, for example:

Alexander (1941, p. 25)
(Alexander, 1941, p. 25)
Slim (1944, pp. 31–34)
Ritchie and Wavell (1941, p. 67)
(Ritchie & Wavell, 1941, p. 67)

*Page numbers must always be given for quotations, regardless of source*, as in, for example:

Leahey (2000) points out that, "All sciences, including psychology, were originally part of philosophy." (p. 3).

or

It has been commented that, "All sciences, including psychology, were originally part of philosophy." (Leahey, 2000, p. 3).

*Note*: The page number always follows the material quoted.

## Chapter numbers

If an entire chapter is referred to, it may be cited as:

Leahey (2000, chap. 7)

## On-line sources

On-line sources that are not paginated may be referred to using either paragraph or section and paragraph number.

**Paragraph numbers**

Johnston (2003, para. 3)

**Section and paragraph number**

Simpson (2003, Method section, para. 5)

## Duplication of authors

When two or more references in the same paper reduce to the same form, a sufficient number of author's names must be included to avoid confusion. For example, the following two references would both reduce to Kirk et al. (2012), and so could not be distinguished from one another:

Kirk, Spock, McCoy, and Sulu (2012)

Kirk, Sulu, McCoy, and Spock (2012)

To avoid possible confusion, these references would be reduced to:

Kirk, Spock, et al. (2012)

Kirk, Sulu, et al. (2012)

However, if only three authors were involved, "et al." cannot be used. There would be only one author's name remaining after the first two, and *al.* means *others*, which is plural. For example, the following two references cannot be reduced to "Picard et al. (2007)" because of the resultant confusion, but neither can they be reduced to "Picard, Riker, et al. (2007)" or "Picard, Troi, et al. (2007)", because only one author's name has been omitted.

Picard, Riker, and Crusher (2007)

Picard, Troi, and Crusher (2007)

Therefore all three authors' names would have to be given throughout the paper.

## Same surname (or family name)

When two or more authors who have the same surname are cited, authors' initials are given to avoid confusion, even when the year of publication differs:

> T. R. Smyth (2002)
> P. V. Smyth (1995)
> T. R. Smyth and Darley (2001)
> P. V. Smyth and Darley (2003)
> Smyth and B. Darley (2002)
> Smyth and J. Darley (2004)

## Multiple publications by the same author in the same year

When two or more publications by the same author in the same year are cited, alphabetical characters are added to distinguish between them:

> Bond (2001a) found . . . , but Bond (2001b) comments. . . .

## Multiple publications by the same author

Multiple publications by the same author are shown in the same parentheses.

> Moneypenny (1998, 1999a, 1999b, 2001, in press) has found. . . .

## Multiple references

When reference is made to a number of different sources, they are listed in *alphabetical order* of the authors' surnames (first author where applicable), regardless of date:

> In a number of papers (Kirk, 1999; McCoy, 1997; Spock, 2001, 2001a; Spock & Kirk, 1995) it has been suggested that. . . .

*Note*: Sources published by different authors are separated by a semicolon. Sources published by the same author(s) are separated by a comma. For instance, in the above example, the two Spock publications are separated by a comma.

## Secondary references

When reference is made to material that has not been read, but that is cited in another source that has been read, the source that has been read is cited:

> Abbott and Costello (as cited in Howard, 2003) argued that. . . .

*Note*: In this example, Howard (2003) is the source of the material. Therefore, the date of the Howard, but *not* the Abbott and Costello, article is given. Also, the publication details of the Howard article *only* are included in the reference list.

## ▶ Examples of citing less common sources

## Articles accepted for publication but not yet published.

> Entwhistle (in press)

## Republished article

A classic article that has been republished is cited by giving the original and new years of publication:

> Donders (1869/1969)

## Organizations or groups

When reference is made to a source published by an organization or group, and there is no specific author, the source is referred to using the name of the organization or group and the date of publication.

**Short names**
If the name is short it is usually given in full throughout a paper:

> University of Canberra (2003)

**Long names**
If the name is long it may be abbreviated after the first citation.

*First reference*

> One explanation is . . . (Australian and Torres Strait Islander Commission [ATSIC], 2005).

*Subsequent references*

> It has been shown that ... (ATSIC, 2005).

## No author

If, as in rare instances, an article has no author's name, give the title of the article or chapter (enclosed in double quotation marks) followed by the date, as in:

> ("Clumsy Children", 2005)

*Note*: If the article has no title, give the first few words of the entry in the reference list and the year.

In the case of a periodical, book, or report, the title is typed in italics, as in:

> *Rites of Passage* (2002)

## Anonymous

A source is referred to as anonymous only if it is specifically indicated that it is to be attributed to an anonymous author.

> (Anonymous, 2007)

## No date

If an article is not dated, use the abbreviation "n.d.":

> Bludnott (n.d.)
> (Bludnott, n.d.)

## Legislation

When referring to an act of parliament, give the name of the act and its date.

> Mental Health Act (2009)

## Manuals

When citing a manual, at first citation give the name of the association (or agency, institution, etc.) and the name of the manual in full, together with an abbreviation, if appropriate.

American Psychiatric Association, Diagnostic and Statistical Manual of Mental Disorders, 4th ed. [DSM–IV] (1994)

Thereafter, an abbreviation may be used:

*DSM–IV* (1994)

*Note*: For this manual it would seem that the year of publication could be omitted after the first citation, because the edition number is given.


## Personal Communications

In some instances it may be necessary to refer to a personal communication in the form of, for example, a telephone conversation, a letter, or an email. To refer to a personal communication, give the person's name – including initials, and the date as accurately as possible.

(T. R. Smyth, personal communication, 22 January 2004)


## Newspaper article (no author)

Revolting students. (2013, 1 April). *Student News*, p. 13.

*Note*: In the APA Manual the date is shown in the American style, as "April 1".

# Appendix C
# Examples of presentation of publication details in a reference list

► **Common print sources**

Journal articles

### Single author

> Gordon, N. (1969). Helping the clumsy child in school. *Special Education, 55*
> (2),19–20.

*Note*: The title of the journal – not the title of the article – is typed in italics.
Also, the volume number, but not the issue number, is typed in italics. The
issue number (2 in this example) is included only if each issue of the
journal begins with page 1.

### Two or more authors

> Brenner, M. W., & Gillman, S. (1966). Visuomotor ability in schoolchildren.
> *Developmental Medicine and Child Neurology, 8*, 686–703.

> Gubbay, S. S., Ellis, E., Walton, J. N., & Court, S. D. M. (1965). Clumsy children:
> A study of apraxic and agnosic defects in 21 children. *Brain, 88*, 295–312.

*Note*: If there are two or more authors, there is a comma before the ampersand. There would seem to be no need to include a comma when only two
authors are involved (as is done when referring to a source in the text of
a paper). However, the APA Manual includes a comma in this case.

### More than six authors
If there are more than six authors, give the first six authors' names followed
by "et al."

### Seven authors
If there are seven authors it would be incorrect to use "et al." In this case all
seven authors names would be given.

### Same author in same year

> Gubbay, S. S. (1975a). Clumsy children in normal schools. *The Medical Journal
> of Australia, 1*, 233-236.

Gubbay, S. S. (1975b). *The clumsy child: A study of developmental apraxic and agnosic ataxia.* London: W. B. Saunders.

## In press

Stress, A. (in press). Overcoming the trauma of writing in psychology. *Journal of Student Rest and Recreation.*

*Note*: An "in press" article has been accepted for publication, but not yet published. Obviously, therefore, the volume and page numbers will not be available. It is possible to have more than one article in press. In this case "in press–a", "in press–b", etc., should be used.

## Books

### Single author

Ferguson, G. A. (1966). *Statistical analysis in psychology and education.* New York: McGraw Hill.

### Two or more authors

Fiske, S. T. & Taylor, S. E. (1991). *Social cognition.* New York: McGraw-Hill.

### Edition

Ryckman, R. M. (2000). *Theories of personality* (7th ed.). Belmont, CA: Wadsworth.

*Notes*:
1. The edition number is not shown in italics.
2. The city of publication is given first, followed by a colon, and then the publisher. In this example, the state in the United States of America (i.e., California) is shown in abbreviated form (i.e., CA).

## Chapter in an edited book

### Single editor

Connolly, K. *(1980).* Motor development and motor disability. In M. Rutter (Ed.), *Scientific foundations of developmental psychiatry* (pp. 138–153). London: William Heineman Medical Books.

### Multiple editors

Rutter, M., & Yule, W. (1970). Neurological aspects of intellectual retardation and reading retardation. In M. Rutter, J. Tizzard, & K. Whitmore (Eds.), *Education, health, and behaviour* (pp. 54 – 74*)*. London: Longman.

*Notes*:
1. The page numbers of the chapter must be included.
2. The editor's initials are given before the surname.

## ▶ Electronic sources

### Electronic version of a journal article

When a journal article is an exact duplicate of the printed version, give the publication details in the same way as for the printed version, with the inclusion of the words "Electronic version".

Holmes, S. (2007). Moriarity's guilt [Electronic version]. *Journal of Criminal Research, 77,* 42 – 44.

### On-line only journal

If the journal is *published only on line*, give the date of retrieval and the URL.

Watson, J. (1908). Holme's techniques. *Journal of Investigation Research, 83,* Article 1007. Retrieved 1 April, 2009, from http://galactica.edu/wat.html

*Note*: The URL should not be underlined.

### Other on-line only material

If other on-line only material is cited in a paper, include in the reference list sufficient detail to allow a reader to gain access to it. Include the author, the date of publication (if available), the title of the document, and the URL. It is critical that the URL be typed exactly as it appears.

If the document is likely to be changed in the future, include the date of retrieval. This indicates that the source was cited in the form in which it existed at that date.

There should be no need to include any other information, such as the database or "search engine" used to locate the source. All that is required is that a reader can use the necessary URL to locate the material.

The URL given should allow the reader to gain direct access to the document cited. It is not satisfactory to direct the reader to a site through which access may be gained.

## ▶ Less common sources

### Group author

When the author is not a person, but an association (e.g., a group, institution, government agency or department, or a corporation), give the name of the association as the author, followed by the date. In this situation the author is usually also the publisher, and there is no point in repeating the name of the association as the publisher. Therefore, the word "Author" is given in lieu of the name of the publisher.

> American Psychiatric Association. (1994). *Diagnostic and statistical manual of mental disorders* (4th ed.). Washington, DC: Author.

### No author

If the article or document has no author, give the name of the article as the author, followed by the year of publication

> British Medical Journal. (1962). *Clumsy children. 2*, 1665–1666.

### No publication date

If there is no publication date, follow the author's name with "n.d.".

> Jones, S. (n.d.) *Lost in time*. Nirvana: Lotus Eater Publishing

### Republished translation of an earlier work

> Donders, F. C. (1969). On the speed of mental processes. In W. G. Koster (Ed. & Trans.), *Attention and performance II*. Amsterdam: North Holland Publishing. (Reprinted from *ACTA Psychologica*, 1969, 30, 412–430.) (Original work published 1869.)

### Unpublished manuscripts

### Not submitted for publication

> Poppinoff, W. H. Y. (2007). *High population density and stress* . Unpublished manuscript, The University of Far Eastern Siberia, Coldingrad.

### Submitted for publication

> Attempt, A. N. (1994). *Overcoming submission anxiety*. Manuscript submitted for publication.

**Unpublished thesis**

> Kirk, J. T. (2020). *The effects of space travel on visual perception*. Unpublished master's thesis, Enterprise University, Galactica.

## Abstracts

> Williams, H. G., Woollacott, M. H., & Ivry, R. (1992). Timing and motor control in clumsy children. *Journal of Motor Behavior, 24* (2), 165–172. (Abstract obtained from *Psychological Abstracts*, 1993, 80, Abstract No. 989.)

## Magazine article

> Jones, T. H. (2002, 1 April). Students think editorial style is not warranted. *Student Review, 13*, 21–22.

## Daily newspaper article (author given)

> Kent, C. (2005, 1 April). Jumping tall buildings. *Gotham Chronicle*, pp. 7–9.

## Daily newspaper article (no author)

> Who is Superman? (2005, 2 April). *Gotham Chronicle*, pp. 3, 8–9.

## ▶ Notes

### Place of publication

Give the *city* as the place of publication. For material published in the United States of America, the city is followed by the Postal Service abbreviation for the state or territory:

> Hillsdale, NJ:

For locations other than the United Sates, the APA Manual requires the city to be followed by the state, territory, or province, and the country:

> Clayton, Vic., Australia:

The APA Manual gives a list of cities that are well known for publication, and for which these details need not be given. However, it would seem to be reasonable to disregard this requirement for well-known cities, as in:

Sydney: Earlbaum

## Multiple cities

Often, publishers give several cities (e.g., London, New York, Melbourne). In this case give the first-mentioned city only.

## No city

Sometimes, book publishers do not clearly give the city of publication. In this case the publisher's address will be given with the publication details (including the ISBN number, etc.). Use the city included in the publisher's address.

## Publisher

Do not include, in the name of the publisher, terms or abbreviations such as "Company", "Ltd", or "Inc".

# Appendix D
## Common standard abbreviations

### ▶ References

| | |
|---|---|
| chap. (chaps.) | chapter(s) |
| Ed. (Eds.) | editor(s) |
| ed. | edition |
| 2nd ed. | second edition |
| Rev. ed. | revised edition |
| MS (or ms) | manuscript |
| MSS (or mss) | manuscripts |
| No. (Nos.) | number(s) |
| n.d. | no date |
| p. (pp.) | page (pages) |
| Pt. | part |
| Suppl. | supplement |
| Trans. | translation |
| Vol. (Vols.) | volume(s) |

### ▶ Latin abbreviations

| | | |
|---|---|---|
| a.m. | *ante meridiem* | before noon |
| p.m. | *post meridiem* | after noon |
| cf. | *confer* | compare |
| e.g. | *exempli gratia* | for example |
| etc. | *et cetera* | and so forth |
| et al. | *et alii* | and others |
| et seq. | *et sequens* | and following |
| i.e. | *id est* | that is |
| N.B. | *nota bene* | note well |
| viz. | *videlicet* | namely |
| vs. | *versus* | versus, against |

# ▶ Measurements

| | |
|---|---|
| mm | millimetre(s) |
| m | metre(s) |
| km | kilometre(s) |
| | |
| ms | millisecond(s) |
| s | second(s) |
| min | minute(s) (*also* minimum) |
| h | hour(s) |
| | |
| g | gram(s) |
| kg | kilogram(s) |
| ml | millilitre(s) |
| L | litre(s) |
| | |
| $m^{-1}$ | one per metre (wave number) |
| $m^2$ | square metre(s) |
| m/s | metres per second |
| Hz | hertz |

*Notes*:
1. Centimetres are not used in the international system of measurement.
2. In the *APA Manual* hour is abbreviated as *hr*, but the international system abbreviation is *h*.
3. To prevent misreading, do not abbreviate day, week, month, and year.

# Appendix E
## Abbreviations commonly used in statistics

| | |
|---|---|
| $M$ | sample mean |
| $Mdn$ | sample median |
| $SD$ | sample standard deviation |
| $SS$ | sum of squares |
| $MS$ | mean square |
| $MSE$ | mean square error |
| $SE$ | standard error |
| $SEM$ | standard error of measurement |
| $ns$ | non-significant |
| $N$ | number in a sample |
| $n$ | number in a subset of a sample |
| $f$ | frequency |
| $f_e$ | expected frequency |
| $z$ | standard score |
| $p$ | probability |
| $df$ | degrees of freedom |
| $F$ | Fisher's $F$ ratio |
| $t$ | Student's $t$ |
| $U$ | Mann–Whitney $U$ |
| $r$ | Pearson's product moment correlation |
| $r^2$ | Pearson's product moment correlation, coefficient of determination |
| $r_s$ | Spearman's rank-order correlation |
| $r_{pb}$ | point biserial correlation |
| $pr$ | partial correlation |
| $sr$ | semipartial correlation |
| $R$ | multiple correlation |
| $R^2$ | multiple correlation squared |
| $d$ | Cohen's measure of effect size |
| $d'$ | measure of sensitivity |

*Note*: These abbreviations are typed in italics. If your typewriter or word processing program cannot produce italics, type the abbreviation in normal characters and underline it.

# Greek characters commonly used as statistical symbols

| | | |
|---|---|---|
| $\alpha$ | alpha | probability of a Type I error |
| $\beta$ | beta | probability of a Type II error |
| $\chi^2$ | chi-squared | value of chi-square test |
| $\eta^2$ | eta-squared | strength of relationship |
| $\mu$ | mu | population mean |
| $\omega^2$ | omega-squared | strength of relationship |
| $\sigma$ | sigma | population standard deviation |

*Note*: If your typewriter or word processing program cannot produce these symbols, they may be inserted by hand.

# Appendix F
## Typing format for headings and subheadings

| Typing format | Level |
|:---:|:---:|
| CENTRED UPPER CASE | 5 |
| Centred Upper Case and Lower Case | 1 |
| *Centred Upper Case and Lower Case* | 2 |
| *Flush Left Upper Case and Lower Case* | 3 |
| *Indented lower case.* | 4 |

*Note*: The Level 4 heading is a paragraph heading. It ends with a full stop, and the text of the paragraph begins two spaces after the full stop, on the same line.

# Appendix G
## Headings and subheadings for a simple research report

| Subheading | Heading | Level |
|---|---|---|
| | Title | 1 |
| | Abstract | 1 |
| | Method | 1 |
| *Participants* | | 3 |
| *Apparatus* | | 3 |
| *Procedure* | | 3 |
| | Results | 1 |
| | Discussion | 1 |
| | References | 1 |

*Note*: If any subsections are required under a Level 3 heading, a Level 4 (paragraph) heading would be used, as in the following (abbreviated) example.

*Participants*
The participants in this experiment were 30 adults. . . .

*Pre-testing.*    Before allocation to experimental groups. . . .

# Appendix H
## Headings and subheadings for a multiple experiment research report

| Subheading | Heading | Level |
|---|---|---|
| | Title | 1 |
| | Abstract | 1 |
| | Experiment 1 | 1 |
| | *Method* | 2 |
| *Participants* | | 3 |
| *Apparatus* | | 3 |
| *Procedure* | | 3 |
| | *Results* | 2 |
| | *Discussion* | 2 |
| | *References* | 2 |
| | Experiment 2 | 1 |
| | *Method* | 2 |
| *Participants* | | 3 |
| *Apparatus* | | 3 |
| *Procedure* | | 3 |
| | *Results* | 2 |
| | *Discussion* | 2 |
| | General Discussion | 1 |
| | References | 1 |

*Note*: If any subsections are required under a Level 3 heading, a Level 4 (paragraph) heading would be used, as in the following (abbreviated) example.

*Participants*
The participants in this experiment were 30 adults. . . .

*Pre-testing.*    Before allocation to experimental groups. . . .

# Appendix I
## An example of a research report

This fictitious example is provided to illustrate the logical sequence and some selected features of a research report. To achieve this required an example that is contrived, and so somewhat artificial. In addition, there is more than one way of organizing material in the parts of a research report, and individual writing styles differ. Not everyone, therefore, would write this report as it appears here. Another point is that the requirements of some lecturers and departments might necessitate variation from this example.

An important point to understand is that each experiment is unique, and so research reports must differ. Students should not, therefore, regard this example as a mould into which to force their own. Rather, they should use it as an aid to understanding the principles and conventions involved, and apply these to their own research reports.

### Notes

Notes on some aspects of editorial style are given in the left-hand margin of the body of the report, and some notes on content are given in the right-hand margin.

NB: Obviously, because of the page size, the dimensions of pages and of margins, and the number of words on a page, are not representative of the dimensions and number of words on an A4 page.

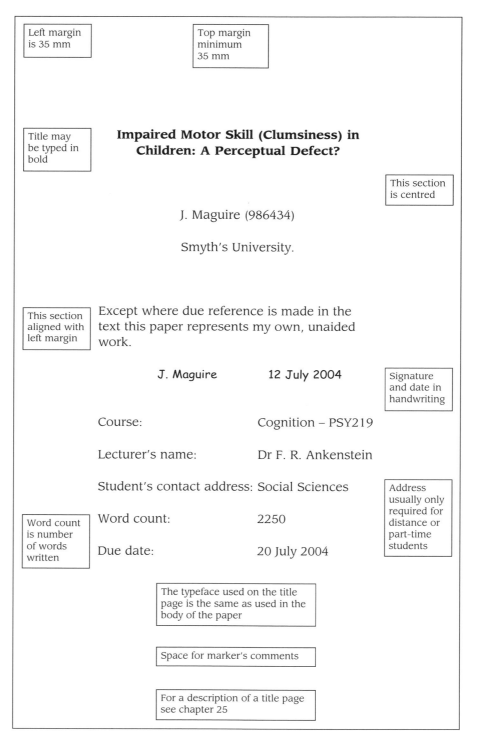

Left margin is 35 mm

Top margin minimum 35 mm

Title may be typed in bold

**Impaired Motor Skill (Clumsiness) in Children: A Perceptual Defect?**

This section is centred

J. Maguire (986434)

Smyth's University.

This section aligned with left margin

Except where due reference is made in the text this paper represents my own, unaided work.

J. Maguire      12 July 2004

Signature and date in handwriting

Course:      Cognition – PSY219

Lecturer's name:      Dr F. R. Ankenstein

Student's contact address: Social Sciences

Address usually only required for distance or part-time students

Word count is number of words written

Word count:      2250

Due date:      20 July 2004

The typeface used on the title page is the same as used in the body of the paper

Space for marker's comments

For a description of a title page see chapter 25

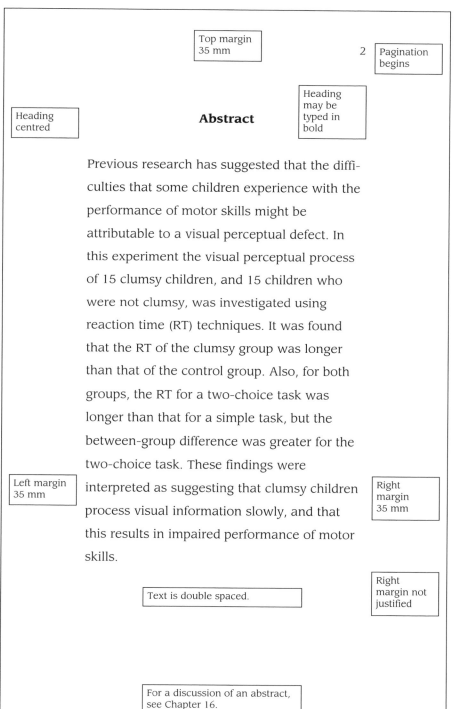

Top margin
35 mm

2

Pagination begins

Heading may be typed in bold

Heading centred

## Abstract

Previous research has suggested that the difficulties that some children experience with the performance of motor skills might be attributable to a visual perceptual defect. In this experiment the visual perceptual process of 15 clumsy children, and 15 children who were not clumsy, was investigated using reaction time (RT) techniques. It was found that the RT of the clumsy group was longer than that of the control group. Also, for both groups, the RT for a two-choice task was longer than that for a simple task, but the between-group difference was greater for the two-choice task. These findings were interpreted as suggesting that clumsy children process visual information slowly, and that this results in impaired performance of motor skills.

Left margin
35 mm

Right margin
35 mm

Text is double spaced.

Right margin not justified

For a discussion of an abstract, see Chapter 16.

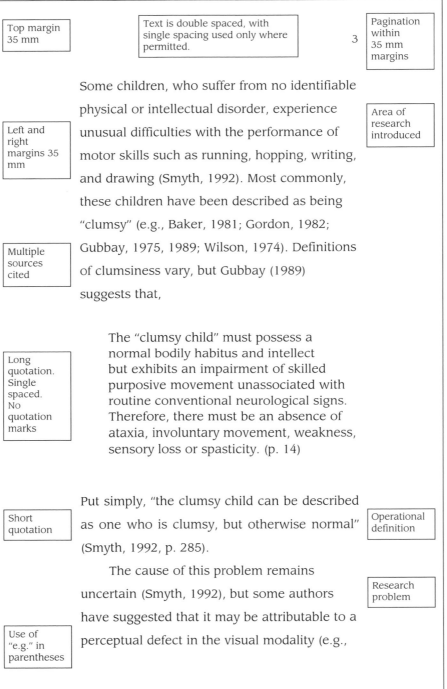

Top margin
35 mm

Text is double spaced, with single spacing used only where permitted.

3

Pagination within 35 mm margins

Some children, who suffer from no identifiable physical or intellectual disorder, experience unusual difficulties with the performance of motor skills such as running, hopping, writing, and drawing (Smyth, 1992). Most commonly, these children have been described as being "clumsy" (e.g., Baker, 1981; Gordon, 1982; Gubbay, 1975, 1989; Wilson, 1974). Definitions of clumsiness vary, but Gubbay (1989) suggests that,

Left and right margins 35 mm

Area of research introduced

Multiple sources cited

The "clumsy child" must possess a normal bodily habitus and intellect but exhibits an impairment of skilled purposive movement unassociated with routine conventional neurological signs. Therefore, there must be an absence of ataxia, involuntary movement, weakness, sensory loss or spasticity. (p. 14)

Long quotation. Single spaced. No quotation marks

Put simply, "the clumsy child can be described as one who is clumsy, but otherwise normal" (Smyth, 1992, p. 285).

The cause of this problem remains uncertain (Smyth, 1992), but some authors have suggested that it may be attributable to a perceptual defect in the visual modality (e.g.,

Short quotation

Operational definition

Research problem

Use of "e.g." in parentheses

4

Gordon, 1982; Wilson, 1974). Vision is
important in motor skills, and so a visual

Possible
explanation

impairment would be expected to be
detrimental to performance. For example, a
child who has defective vision would be
expected to have difficulty with ball skills
(Gubbay, 1975).

First citation
of multiple-
author
source

Hulme, Biggerstaff, Moran, and McKinley
(1982) tested the ability of a group of clumsy
children to judge, and to reproduce, the length

Previous
research

of stimulus lines in the visual modality, and
they found that the clumsy children were less
accurate than were children who were not
clumsy. This finding suggests that clumsiness
is associated with a visual perceptual defect,
but an association is not necessarily evidence
of causality. Another problem with attributing
clumsiness to a visual perceptual defect is that

Critical
comments

most clumsy children have normal vision
(Baker, 1981). On the other hand, it is possible
that clumsy children suffer from a perceptual
defect that is not revealed by normal testing of
visual acuity.

First line of
paragraph
indented.
No
additional
space
between
paragraphs

It is generally accepted that vision is the
predominant modality, and that individuals

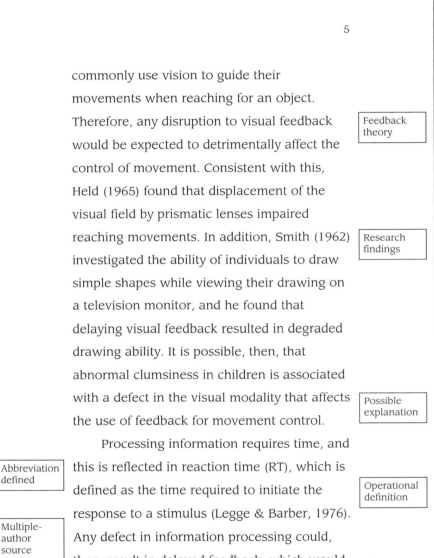

5

commonly use vision to guide their
movements when reaching for an object.
Therefore, any disruption to visual feedback
would be expected to detrimentally affect the
control of movement. Consistent with this,
Held (1965) found that displacement of the
visual field by prismatic lenses impaired
reaching movements. In addition, Smith (1962)
investigated the ability of individuals to draw
simple shapes while viewing their drawing on
a television monitor, and he found that
delaying visual feedback resulted in degraded
drawing ability. It is possible, then, that
abnormal clumsiness in children is associated
with a defect in the visual modality that affects
the use of feedback for movement control.

Processing information requires time, and
this is reflected in reaction time (RT), which is
defined as the time required to initiate the
response to a stimulus (Legge & Barber, 1976).
Any defect in information processing could,
then, result in delayed feedback, which would
be expected to have an effect on the
performance of motor skills similar to that
observed by Smith (1962). It is possible,

Feedback
theory

Research
findings

Possible
explanation

Abbreviation
defined

Operational
definition

Multiple-
author
source
cited in
parentheses
using
ampersand

Information
processing
theory

6

therefore, that clumsy children suffer from a
dysfunction in the processing of visual
information, and that this results in delayed
feedback.

| Theoretical hypothesis |

Donders (1869/1969) investigated the RT
of individuals using simple and choice RT
tasks. In a simple RT task, individuals are
required to respond to single stimulus as
quickly as possible. By comparison, in a two-
choice "go, no-go" RT task, individuals are
required to respond to one stimulus, but not
the other. Donders reasoned, therefore, that
the simple task involves no discrimination, but
that in the two-choice task individuals must
discriminate between the two stimuli.
Moreover, he found that the RT for a choice
task was longer than that for a simple task.
This finding, Donders argued, showed that
discrimination between stimuli requires time.
Moreover, he reasoned that the difference in
RT between choice and simple RT tasks
reflected the time required for the
discrimination process.

| Republished classic article cited |

| Abbreviation used after being defined |

| Donders' stage theory |

Sternberg (1969) adopted a slightly different
approach, arguing that "loading" a process –

7

such as perception – by increasing the amount of processing required, lengthens RT. In his view, the requirement to discriminate between stimuli loaded, or increased the demands on, the perceptual process. Following Sternberg's reasoning, the two-choice task imposes greater demands on the perceptual process than does the simple task, and so will result in a longer RT. The functioning of the perceptual process, therefore, can be investigated by manipulating the load on that process. In particular, if a process were defective, increasing the demands on that process would be expected to result in a greater increase in RT than if it were functioning normally.

It is possible, then, to investigate the visual perceptual process using RT techniques. The functioning of the perceptual process can be investigated by manipulating the load on this process, and this can be done by using simple and two-choice RT tasks. If clumsiness is associated with a perceptual defect, which impairs processing of visual information, then loading the perceptual process should increase processing time more for clumsy children than

| Sternberg's additive factors model |

| Source referred to without year in same paragraph after being cited in full |

| Research approach |

| Research design |

| Research hypothesis developed |

8

for children who are not clumsy. Therefore, it can be hypothesized that the RT for a two-choice task will be longer than that for a simple task, and that the difference will be greater for clumsy children than for children who are not clumsy.

Research hypothesis

## **Method**

Level 1 heading. May be in bold.

### *Participants*

Level 2 heading. May be in bold

The participants were 30 children, of whom 15 had impaired motor ability and who could be described as clumsy, and 15 who had normal motor ability. The mean age of the *clumsy* group was 8 years 5 months (range 7 years 11 months to 8 years 9 months), and that of the *normal* group was 8 years 4 months (range 7 years 10 months to 8 years 7 months). There were 11 boys and 4 girls in each group.

Use of numbers

Years and months not abbreviated

Participants described

Children in the clumsy group were drawn from a larger group of 27 children who were participating in a remedial programme for children who had impaired motor skills. Selection was made on the basis of

Selection of participants

9

willingness to participate and the children having no identifiable physical or intellectual disorder to which their impairment could be attributed. Those in the normal group were selected from children in a local school, on the basis of willingness to participate and of their motor ability being normal. The normal children were matched for sex and age with those in the clumsy group.

Matching

All of the children were tested for motor ability using the Gubbay (1989) five-item version of his test of motor impairment. The mean score on this test for the clumsy group was 4.2 items at below the 10th percentile (range 3 to 5), and that for the normal group was 0.4 items (range 0 to 1).

Preliminary testing

One boy in the clumsy group withdrew from the experiment after completing the first condition. He and his matched control were deleted from the study.

Loss of participant

Normal double spacing before subheading

### *Apparatus*

Abbreviation defined

Two red light emitting diodes (LEDs) were used to present visual stimuli. These LEDs, together with a start switch and a response

10

Apparatus
described

Reference to
figure

switch, were mounted on a 200 mm × 100 mm
panel. (See Figure 1.) The LEDs were mounted
50 mm apart, the start switch was centrally

Switch
labelled

located 60 mm in front of the LEDs, and the
response switch was mounted 100 mm to the
right of the start switch. The LEDs and the two
switches were interfaced with a personal
computer (via an 8-bit input-output card),
which was used to control presentation of
stimuli and to measure and record RT scores.

### Experimental Tasks

Two tasks were used in the experiment: (a) a
simple RT task, and (b) a two-choice "go, no-
go" RT task. In the simple task only the right
LED was used, and the children were required
to respond to illumination of this LED by
releasing the start switch and depressing the
response switch. In the two-choice task either
the right or the left LED was illuminated, in
random order (with the restriction that left and
right stimuli were presented on an equal
number of trials), but a response was required
only to the right stimulus. As in the simple
task, the children were required to respond to

Experimental
task
described
under
subheading

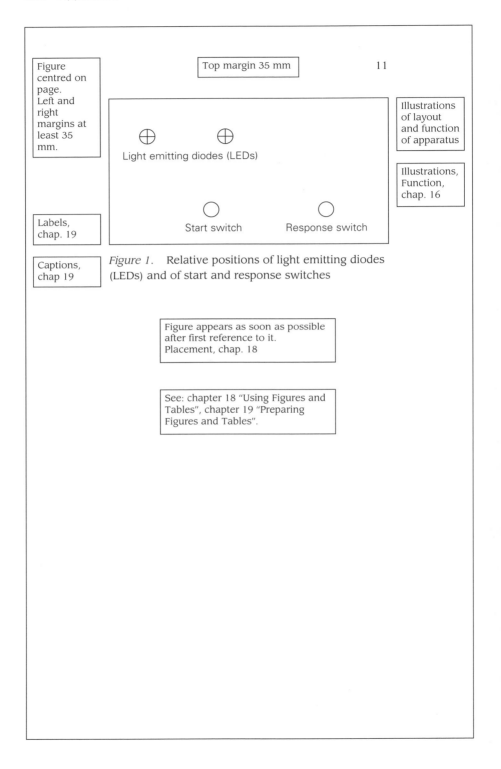

Figure centred on page. Left and right margins at least 35 mm.

Top margin 35 mm                    11

Illustrations of layout and function of apparatus

Illustrations, Function, chap. 16

Light emitting diodes (LEDs)

Labels, chap. 19

Start switch        Response switch

Captions, chap 19

*Figure 1.*    Relative positions of light emitting diodes (LEDs) and of start and response switches

Figure appears as soon as possible after first reference to it.
Placement, chap. 18

See: chapter 18 "Using Figures and Tables", chapter 19 "Preparing Figures and Tables".

12

illumination of the right LED by releasing the
start switch and depressing the response
switch.

Prior to illumination of the LED, a warning
tone was presented, using the built-in speaker
of the computer. The period between presentation of the warning signal and illumination
of the LED (i.e., the foreperiod) was randomly
varied between 1 and 3 seconds.

| "i.e." used in parentheses |
| --- |

| Numbers less than 10 for units of measure-ment |
| --- |

### *Procedure*

In both conditions, the children were
instructed to depress and hold down the start
switch, to listen for the warning tone, and to
be prepared to respond to the visual stimulus
as quickly as possible. For the simple task, the
children were instructed to attend only to the
right LED and, when this was illuminated, to
respond as quickly as possible by releasing the
start switch and depressing the response
switch. For the two-choice task, the children
were instructed to attend to both LEDs, but to
respond only to the right LED. They were
instructed to do nothing when the left LED
was illuminated.

| Instructions to participants |
| --- |

| Use of hyphen |
| --- |

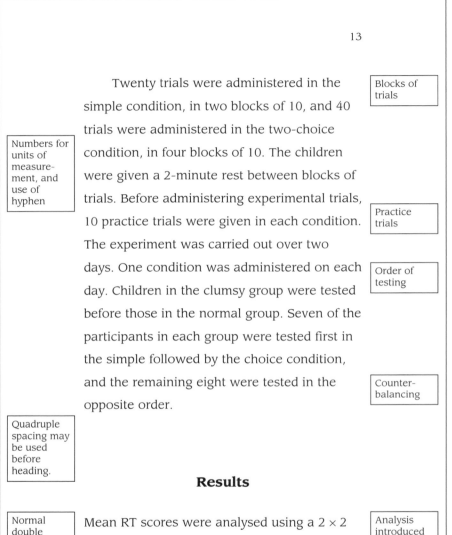

13

Numbers for units of measurement, and use of hyphen

Twenty trials were administered in the simple condition, in two blocks of 10, and 40 trials were administered in the two-choice condition, in four blocks of 10. The children were given a 2-minute rest between blocks of trials. Before administering experimental trials, 10 practice trials were given in each condition. The experiment was carried out over two days. One condition was administered on each day. Children in the clumsy group were tested before those in the normal group. Seven of the participants in each group were tested first in the simple followed by the choice condition, and the remaining eight were tested in the opposite order.

Blocks of trials

Practice trials

Order of testing

Counter-balancing

Quadruple spacing may be used before heading.

## Results

Normal double spacing after heading

Mean RT scores were analysed using a 2 × 2 (Group × Task) mixed design analysis of variance, with repeated measures on the second factor. An alpha level of .05 was adopted.

Analysis introduced

Alpha level given

The analysis revealed that mean RT for the

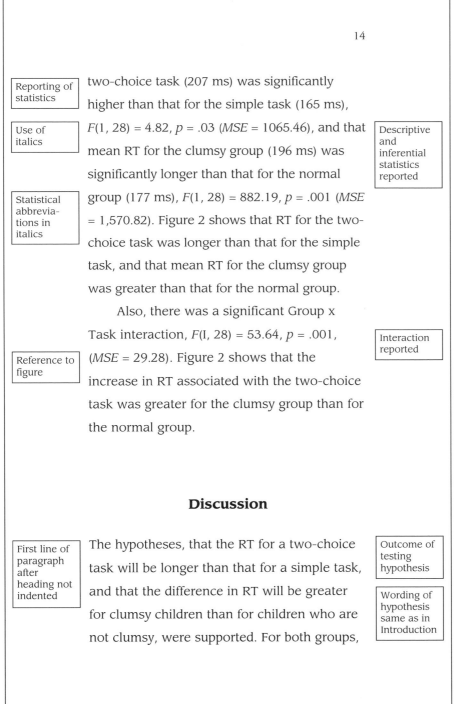

14

Reporting of statistics

two-choice task (207 ms) was significantly higher than that for the simple task (165 ms), $F(1, 28) = 4.82$, $p = .03$ ($MSE = 1065.46$), and that mean RT for the clumsy group (196 ms) was significantly longer than that for the normal group (177 ms), $F(1, 28) = 882.19$, $p = .001$ ($MSE = 1,570.82$). Figure 2 shows that RT for the two-choice task was longer than that for the simple task, and that mean RT for the clumsy group was greater than that for the normal group.

Use of italics

Statistical abbreviations in italics

Descriptive and inferential statistics reported

    Also, there was a significant Group x Task interaction, $F(I, 28) = 53.64$, $p = .001$, ($MSE = 29.28$). Figure 2 shows that the increase in RT associated with the two-choice task was greater for the clumsy group than for the normal group.

Interaction reported

Reference to figure

## Discussion

First line of paragraph after heading not indented

The hypotheses, that the RT for a two-choice task will be longer than that for a simple task, and that the difference in RT will be greater for clumsy children than for children who are not clumsy, were supported. For both groups,

Outcome of testing hypothesis

Wording of hypothesis same as in Introduction

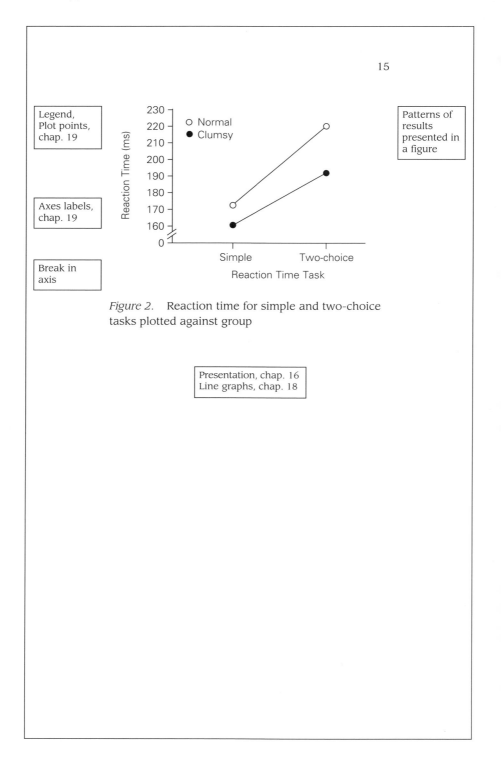

*Figure 2.*   Reaction time for simple and two-choice tasks plotted against group

16

RT for the two-choice task was greater than that for the simple task, and the difference was greater for the clumsy children than for the children who were not clumsy.

> Use of hyphen

In the two-choice task the children were required to discriminate between two visual stimuli, while in the simple condition no discrimination between stimuli was involved.

> Possessive apostrophe when author's name ends with "s"

In terms of Donders' (1869/1969) stage theory, then, the longer RT observed in both groups for the two-choice task, therefore, can be attributed to the requirement to discriminate between stimuli in this condition. This is

> Outcome related to Donders' theory

consistent with Sternberg's (1969) finding that

> Possessive apostrophe

increasing the load on a process lengthened RT. The present results, therefore, show that the requirement to discriminate between stimuli in the two-choice task effectively loaded the perceptual process.

> Outcome related to Sternberg's model

The finding that loading the perceptual process had a greater effect on the RT of the clumsy group, therefore, suggests that

> Subsequent citing of multiple-author source using "et al."

clumsiness is associated with a defect of visual perception. This is consistent with the results of the Hulme et al. (1982) study, which

> Outcome related to earlier finding

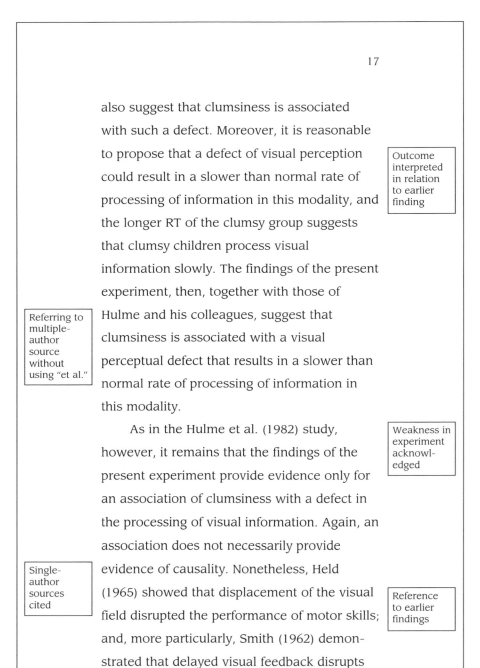

17

also suggest that clumsiness is associated with such a defect. Moreover, it is reasonable to propose that a defect of visual perception could result in a slower than normal rate of processing of information in this modality, and the longer RT of the clumsy group suggests that clumsy children process visual information slowly. The findings of the present experiment, then, together with those of Hulme and his colleagues, suggest that clumsiness is associated with a visual perceptual defect that results in a slower than normal rate of processing of information in this modality.

Outcome interpreted in relation to earlier finding

Referring to multiple-author source without using "et al."

As in the Hulme et al. (1982) study, however, it remains that the findings of the present experiment provide evidence only for an association of clumsiness with a defect in the processing of visual information. Again, an association does not necessarily provide evidence of causality. Nonetheless, Held (1965) showed that displacement of the visual field disrupted the performance of motor skills; and, more particularly, Smith (1962) demonstrated that delayed visual feedback disrupts

Weakness in experiment acknowledged

Single-author sources cited

Reference to earlier findings

18

drawing ability. The present results suggest that clumsy children process information slowly; which, in effect, would be expected to result in a delay in visual feedback. It is reasonable, then, to argue that it is at least possible that in clumsy children a perceptual defect results in a slower than normal rate of processing of visual information resulting in delayed visual feedback, which disrupts the performance of motor skills.

> Outcome interpreted

In summary, the findings of this experiment suggest that clumsiness is associated with a perceptual defect in the visual modality. This is consistent with earlier suggestions that clumsiness may be attributable to a visual defect (e.g., Gordon, 1982; Wilson, 1974), and the findings of the Hulme et al. (1982) study that clumsiness is associated with such a defect. Moreover, the present findings add to those of Hulme and his colleagues by suggesting that the visual perceptual defect associated with clumsiness results in a slower than normal rate of processing of information in this modality; and hence, in effect, delayed visual feedback. Such

> Summary and conclusion

> Multiple sources cited

> Source cited first with year and then without in same paragraph

> Contribution to present knowledge

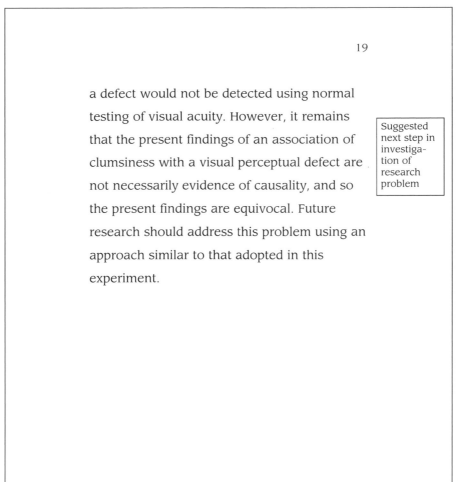

19

a defect would not be detected using normal testing of visual acuity. However, it remains that the present findings of an association of clumsiness with a visual perceptual defect are not necessarily evidence of causality, and so the present findings are equivocal. Future research should address this problem using an approach similar to that adopted in this experiment.

Suggested next step in investigation of research problem

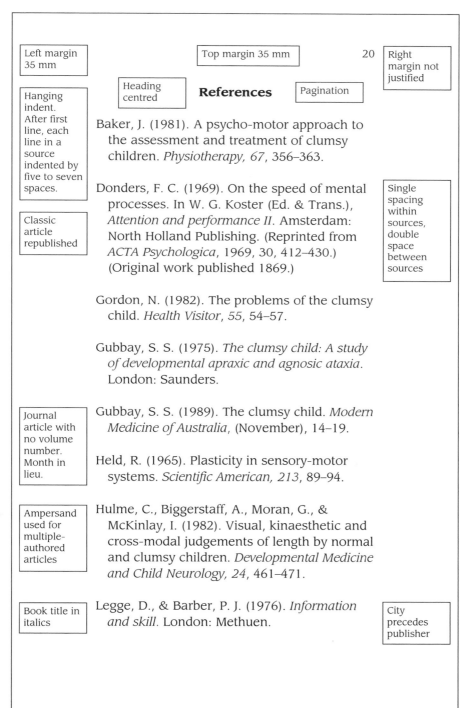

Left margin 35 mm

Top margin 35 mm    20    Right margin not justified

Hanging indent. After first line, each line in a source indented by five to seven spaces.

Classic article republished

Heading centred

**References**

Pagination

Baker, J. (1981). A psycho-motor approach to the assessment and treatment of clumsy children. *Physiotherapy, 67,* 356–363.

Donders, F. C. (1969). On the speed of mental processes. In W. G. Koster (Ed. & Trans.), *Attention and performance II.* Amsterdam: North Holland Publishing. (Reprinted from *ACTA Psychologica,* 1969, 30, 412–430.) (Original work published 1869.)

Single spacing within sources, double space between sources

Gordon, N. (1982). The problems of the clumsy child. *Health Visitor, 55,* 54–57.

Gubbay, S. S. (1975). *The clumsy child: A study of developmental apraxic and agnosic ataxia.* London: Saunders.

Journal article with no volume number. Month in lieu.

Gubbay, S. S. (1989). The clumsy child. *Modern Medicine of Australia,* (November), 14–19.

Held, R. (1965). Plasticity in sensory-motor systems. *Scientific American, 213,* 89–94.

Ampersand used for multiple-authored articles

Hulme, C., Biggerstaff, A., Moran, G., & McKinlay, I. (1982). Visual, kinaesthetic and cross-modal judgements of length by normal and clumsy children. *Developmental Medicine and Child Neurology, 24,* 461–471.

Book title in italics

Legge, D., & Barber, P. J. (1976). *Information and skill.* London: Methuen.

City precedes publisher

21

Smith, K. U. (1962). *Delayed sensory feedback and behaviour*. Philadelphia: Saunders.

Journal title and volume number in italics

Smyth, T. R. (1992). Impaired motor skill (clumsiness) in otherwise normal children: A review. *Child: Care, Health and Development, 18*, 283–300.

Sternberg, S. (1969). The discovery of processing stages: Extensions of Donders' method. In W. G. Koster (Ed.), *Attention and Performance 11. Acta Psychologica, 30*, 276–315.

Page numbers for journal article

Wilson, R. G. (1974). The clumsy child. *Midwife and Health Visitor, 10*, 53–56.

For a description of a reference list, see chapter 8.

# Appendix J
## An example of a poorly written research report

This example research report is provided to illustrate some of the flaws and errors found in students' reports. It is contrived to illustrate a number of these, and so is not typical. In particular, more flaws and errors are included than would be expected even in a very poorly written paper, and some are exaggerated.

Notes on some flaws in the content of the report and on writing are provided following it. A selection of errors in areas such as spelling, grammar, punctuation, and editorial style is indicated by superscript numbers, which relate to notes provided.

There are other defects that have not been commented upon or indicated by superscripts. This has been done to encourage students to read the report carefully in search of defects and mistakes. Doing so will draw their attention to a number of areas, and so help them to avoid similar problems.

*Note*: Although this example is a research report, many of the defects in the Introduction and Discussion sections are equally relevant to an essay or a literature review, or to any other formal or technical paper.

**An experimental envestigation of RT in a sample of children**

N. O. Good (9806435)

Smyth's University

Except where due reference is made in the text, this paper represents my own, unaided work.

Course:        Development and Cognition — PSY219

Lecturer's name:      Dr F. R. Ankenstein

Student's contact address:      Ancient Studies

Word count:

Due date:      18 July 2004

## Abstract

In this experiment the RT of children was tested. There were 15 children in each group. The RT for the choice task was longer than the RT for the simple task. Also, I found a difference in RT between groups. This shows that there is a defect of vision in some children. The children are tested using lights as stimulus and they respond by pressing a switch. However, there are weaknesses in the experiment because the sample of children is small and the experiment was conducted by university students. Also, there is a lot of variability in the RT. Therefore, the results might not be reliable.

## Introduction

The concept of childhood is relatively new to psychology, and can be traced to the work of Hall (1885). Since then, there has been alot of research in psychology on children. Children are obviously important to society, and so the psychological study of children are important. Therefor, it is important to study children. Educators, especially, are interested in child development. A particular area in which educators are interested is the development of motor skills. This is because children who have poor motor skills have problems with their schoolwork.

Clumsy children have difficulties with motor skills.

(Gubbay, 1975)[1] This has been known for many years, and many authors have wandered[2] about and written about this problem. Why is this important?[3] Obviously it is important for children to develop motor skills, and children can have difficulties with motor skills for many reasons, May[4] researchers have done experiments to find out why clumsy children have difficulties with motor skills, but we[5] still do not know why clumsy children are clumsy. The cause of clumsiness in children uncertain (Smyth, 1994). This is an important problem, because children in our[6] society need to develop motor skills.

Visual defects can result in difficulties with motor skills.[7] For example, you[8] would expect defective vision to impair children's ability in ball skills (Gubbay 1975). This experiment will try to find out if clumsy children have difficulties with vision. Hulme et al. (1982)[9] tested clumsy children and found out that they had trouble with vision. In their experiment, Hulme et. al.[10] (1982) showed the children lines asked the children to draw lines of the same length. Hulme et al (1982) found that clumsy children were not as accurate in judging the length of lines as normal children, who were more accurate than clumsy children. On this basis, Hulme *et al.*[11] (1982)[12] postulated that clumsy children have trouble with vision. Processing of information takes time and this is reflected in RT.[13] In simple RT tasks individuals have to respond to only one stimulus, but in choice RT tasks individuals have to respond to more than one stimulus.

Therefore, in choice RT tasks individuals have to discriminate between stimuli. For example, I think that in a two choice[14] RT task individuals have to discriminate between two stimulus (Barber and[15] Legge, 1976). Simple RT tasks and choice RT tasks, therefore, are different and so the outcome of experiments that use these tasks will be different and can be attributed to the differences in the RT tasks used, which means that these tasks can be used to test for differences.

In this experiment clumsy children and normal children will be[16] tested using RT tasks to try to find out if clumsy children have problems with vision. The clumsy and normal children will be tested using a simple RT task and a two-choice RT task. One or two red lights will be used as a stimuli and two switches will be used for responding. There will be fifteen[17] clumsy children and 15 normal children in the experiment. It can be hypothesized that clumsy children will have a longer RT than normal children.

## Method

### Participants

The participants were 15 clumsy children &[18] 15 normal children. There wsa,, therefore, a total of 30 participants in the two groups of participants in the experiment. The participants being voluntary participants in the experiment. The mean age of the clumsy children was 8 yrs 5 mths, and the mean age of the normal children was 8 yrs 4 mths.[19] In each group of participants there were 11 boys and four girls.

**Apparatus**

A panel with two red light emitting diodes (LEDs) and two switches.[20] A computer connected to the panel.

**Procedure**

The children will be brought into the room one at a time. The children will then be told about the experiment. The children will then be told what to do. A warning tone will be[21] presented before the stimulus. In the simple RT task one light will be presented and the children will have to release the start switch and press the response switch as quickly as possible. In the two-choice task one of the lights will be presented and the children will have to release hte[22] start switch and press the response switch as quickly as possible. There will be twenty[23] trials in the simple condition and there will be 40 trials in the two choice condition. There will be 10 practice trials. The foreperiod will vary from 1 to 3 secs.[24]

Results

The mean RT for the two-choice task was 207[25] which is more longer than what the mean RT was for the simple task which was 165. There was a difference in mean RT between the simple and the two-choice tasks, $F^{26}(1, 28) = 4.82$, $p > .05$. The mean RT for the clumsy children was 196 and the mean RT for the normal children was 177 ms. The mean RT for the clumsy group being longer than the mean RT for the normal group, $F(l, 28) = 882.19$, $p^{27} > .001$. There was a significant interaction, $F(l, 28) = 53.6$, $p < .001$.

|  | Clumsy | Normal |
|---|---|---|
| Simple | 169 | 161 |
| Two-choice | 221 | 193 |

Table 1[28]
Table of scores for the experiment[29]

## Discussion

The hypotheses[30] that two-choice RT will be longer than simple RT was proved. RT for the two-choice task was 207 ms and RT for the simple task was 165 ms. Discrimination being longer for two skills. Therefore RT was longer, which is sensical. These findings are similar to those of Smith (1996).

Also, the RT for the Experimental Group was longer than the RT for the Control Group.[31] This suggests that clumsy children have a difficulty with vision, and this is consistent with Gubbays[32] (1957) idea that defective vision would be expected to impair childrens' motor ability. You can see, therefore, that the experiment, therefore, proves that clumsy children have difficulties with vision. So, a clumsy child would have difficulty with their[33] motor skills.

However, there being some weaknesses in this experiment.[34] I think that the fifteen clumsy children used in the experiment were a very small group, and if a bigger group was used the results would have been more reliable. Also, I think there was a lot of variability in the scores and this would be smaller if a bigger group was used. Another problem is that the experiment was conducted by university students, and I think this could have effected[35] the results.

However, this experiment proves that clumsy children have problems with vision and that this makes their motor skills poor. We know, therefore, that a visual problem causes clumsiness. It is obviously necessary for children to have good motor skills. So the government should do something to help these children so that they have good motor skills. This would help clumsy children to play sport and make them more happier[36]. It would also help them with their schoolwork.

### Bibilography

Gubbay, *S. S. (1975). The clumsy child: A study of developmental apraxic and agnostic* ataxia. Saunders: London.[37]

Hulme, Charles, Biggerstaff, A., Moran, G., and McKinlay, 1. *(1982).* Visual, kinaesthetic and cross-modal judgements of length by normal and clumsy children. *Dev. Med. and Child Neur,*[38] 24,[39] 461–471.

Smyth, T.R. (1996). Clumsiness: Kinaesthetic perception and translation. Child: Care, Health and Development **22**, 1–9.

Legge, David., & Barber, P. J. *(1976). Information and skill.* England:[40] Methuen.

Gleitman, H. (1991). *Psychology* (3e Ed.).[41] W. W. Norton Ltd:[42] New York.

## ▶ **Notes**

### Title

The title does not give any idea of the central issues. In particular, there is no reference to clumsy children or impaired motor skills, and no reference to a possible visual defect. Another point is that the title includes the abbreviation *RT*, with which the reader might not be familiar. Although short, the title includes a redundancy (i.e., "An experimental envestigation [*sic*]") and a spelling error, and main words are not capitalized.

### Abstract

The abstract presents a poor summary of the experiment. In particular, there is no reference to clumsiness or impaired motor skill, and there is no reference to previous research. The reader would not be able to clearly understand what is meant by "simple" and "choice" tasks, and how the findings suggest a visual defect is not clear. Also, the abstract includes the abbreviation *RT*, with which the reader may not be familiar, and the first person personal pronoun *I*. There are also errors in the use of tense.

### Introduction

Overall, the Introduction is superficial and does not lead logically to the hypothesis with which it ends. From the outset, it is apparent that the paper reports an investigation of clumsiness in children, but "clumsy children" are not defined, other than by commenting that they have "difficulties with motor skills", and this would seem to be obvious.

The first paragraph of the Introduction, and much of the second, is irrelevant and a waste of words. A particular point is that the assertion made in the last sentence in the first paragraph is not supported. Moreover, the meaning of "poor schoolwork" is not made clear.

The third paragraph suggests that clumsiness *might* be attributable to a defect of vision. Rather confusingly, the following paragraph cites evidence from the Hulme, Biggerstaff, Moran, and McKinlay (1982) study that suggests that clumsy children suffer from a defect of vision. In the fifth paragraph, processing of information and "RT" are suddenly introduced, but RT is not defined, and the reader might not be familiar with this abbreviation. Moreover, how these concepts might relate to a defect of vision is not explained, except in so far as discrimination between stimuli is involved. A particular point to note is that no theoretical basis for the research has been presented.

The last paragraph of the Introduction describes the experiment. This description includes details that should be given in the Method section, and not in the Introduction. On the other hand, the description is vague, and the reader could not be expected to understand the experimental design.

Finally, the hypothesis that "clumsy children will have longer RT than normal children" is proposed. However, how this hypothesis was derived is not explained. Moreover, unless the reader is familiar with the abbreviation RT, and has some familiarity with experiments of this type, it would be difficult to understand the hypothesis.

## Method

### Participants
The description of the participants does not provide any information on how the "clumsy" and "normal" children were selected, other than that they were volunteers. Also, no information is provided on how motor ability was assessed.

### Apparatus
This section presents an inadequate description of the apparatus used. In particular, how the stimulus lights and switches were positioned on the "panel", and the contribution of the computer to the experiment, are not mentioned.

### Procedure
On the basis of the information provided the reader would not be able to understand which was the start or response switch, how the warning tone was presented, which of the two stimulus lights was presented in each condition and how this was determined, how many blocks of trials were used, how many trials were in each block, on what basis the foreperiod was varied, and exactly what the children were instructed to do.

## Results

Although it is not made clear in this section, it is evident that the data were analysed using an analysis of variance. Why this was done, in the light of the research hypothesis ("that clumsy children will have longer RT than normal children") is not clear. Such a simple comparison would be expected to be tested using the Student's $t$ test. Also, no measures of variability are provided (either in the text or in Table 1), and what the data shown in Table 1 are intended to illustrate is not apparent.

Another point is that, in the second sentence of this section, the author fails to comment on whether or not the difference in RT between the simple and two-choice tasks was statistically significant. Although the probability is given as $p > .05$, the alpha level adopted has not been given. Moreover, exact *a posteriori* probabilities should be given. In addition, the author fails to comment on whether or not the difference between the clumsy and normal groups was significant. Also, in this case the author has shown the symbol $>$ when it should have been $<$. Although the author points out that the interaction was statistically significant, no details of the interaction are given.

## Discussion

This section begins with what seems to be appropriate – a statement about the hypothesis. However, the hypothesis referred to (i.e., "that two-choice RT will be longer than simple RT") is not the research hypothesis given in the Introduction. A further point is that statistics, which were reported in the Results section, are unnecessarily repeated in the first paragraph. Notably, no attempt is made to interpret this finding. Moreover, a comment is made that the findings are similar to those of Smyth (1996), but no details of the Smyth experiment are given. This source was not cited in the Introduction. If it were relevant it should have been referred to in the Introduction, and how it contributed to the research being reported should have been made clear.

An important point is that, in the first instance, the author comments that the hypothesis "was proved". An hypothesis can never be proved – it can only be supported by the results. Similarly, in the second paragraph, the author comments that the experiment "proves that clumsy children have difficulties with vision". Again, the results of an experiment can never prove anything; they can only provide support for an hypothesis.

The second paragraph refers to the research hypothesis, and relates the findings of a longer RT for the clumsy children to Gubbay's (1975) suggestion that clumsiness can be associated with defective vision. However, how this finding suggests that "clumsy children have a difficulty with vision" is not explained. Moreover, no reference is made to the findings of the Hulme et al. (1982) study – mentioned in the Introduction – that suggest that clumsy children suffer from defective vision. Also, no reference is made to either Smyth (1992) or Legge and Barber (1976), both of which were referred to in the Introduction. A final important point to note is that the outcome of the research is not discussed within a theoretical context.

The remainder of the short discussion concentrates on weaknesses in the experiment. One suggestion is that variability in the data might have affected the results. However, no measure of variability was provided in the Results section, and so the reader cannot form any opinion on this. A notable omission is that no attempt is made to interpret the meaning of the significant interaction reported in the Results section.

An important point is that the Discussion does not end with any clear conclusion, and no suggestion about directions of future research is made. On the other hand, the conclusion section includes a recommendation that the "government should do something", which is based on a value judgement. It also includes two unsupported assertions with regard to children's happiness and their schoolwork.

## ► Sources

Only five sources are included in the reference list. One source included (Gleitman, 1991) is not cited in the text, and two cited in the text (Hall [1885] and Smyth [1994]) are omitted.

The first sentence in the second paragraph of the Introduction is followed by the reference "(Gubbay, 1975)". This reference follows the full stop at the end of the last sentence, and so does not form part of that sentence. To what the reference is intended to refer, therefore, is not clear.

The Gubbay (1975) reference is a book, the Smyth (1996) reference is a review article, and both are on the subject of clumsy children. It is surprising, then, that in the Introduction the author only cited Gubbay twice and Smyth once. It would be expected that the author might have found more material in these sources to which to refer. Together with the quite small number of sources used, this suggests that the author did not read either widely or carefully. This conclusion is supported by the lack of depth in the report.

## ► Writing style

The report is not written in a scholarly manner. There are numerous errors in grammar, punctuation and spelling. In some sentences the author's meaning is obscure. As an example, in the fourth paragraph of the Introduction the author comments that "in choice RT tasks individuals have to respond to more than one stimulus", but the meaning of this is not clear. Similarly, in the last paragraph of the Introduction the author writes that, "One or two red lights will be used as a stimuli", but what this means is not readily apparent. Also, the description of apparatus should have been written in normal English prose. A particular failing in this section is that neither of the two groups of words included form sentences. Another point is that the writing lacks "polish". For example, three of the first four sentences in the Participants subsection begin with "The".

## ▶ Tense

There are several errors in the use of tense. As an instance, the present tense has been inappropriately used in the Abstract. In the third paragraph of the Introduction, the author comments that, "This experiment will try to . . .". Also, in the final paragraph the experiment is described in the future tense. For example, the author writes that, "clumsy children and normal children will be tested . . .". Again, in the Procedure section, the procedure is described in the future tense.

## ▶ Other flaws

Although perhaps not of major importance, the title page is not well presented. It could have been spaced to give a more pleasing appearance, and the alignment of typing is poor. The Abstract should have been presented on a separate page. Similarly, the Reference list should have begun on a separate page, and it should have been typed using a hanging indent. In addition, the reference list was headed "Bibliography", which it is not. The correct heading is "References".

Other points are that the certificate on the title page was not signed or dated, and the word count was omitted. However, this comment is based on the requirements given in this book, and such requirements differ between institutions.

## ▶ Numbered errors

### Reference to text

1. Placing of reference
2. Spelling
3. Rhetorical question
4. Misspellings
5. Pronoun
6. Pronoun
7. Assertion not supported
8. Pronoun
9. First citation of multiple-authored source
10. Punctuation
11. Italics
12. Repetition of "Hulme et al. (1982)" in paragraph
13. Non-standard abbreviation
14. Hyphen

15. Ampersand
16. Tense
17. Number
18. Ampersand
19. Abbreviation
20. Sentence
21. Tense
22. Misspelling
23. Numbers
24. Abbreviation
25. Units of measure
26. Italics
27. Italics
28. Position of table title
29. Italics
30. Spelling
31. Capital use
32. Possessive
33. "Their" as a singular pronoun
34. Sentence
35. Spelling
36. Comparative
37. Order of city and publisher
38. Abbreviation of Journal name
39. Italics
40. City
41. Abbreviation
42. Unnecessary

# Appendix K
## Checklist

This checklist should be read in conjunction with chapter 10 (Drafts and Editing). It is not comprehensive, but it covers a number of important points.

The first part of the checklist is relevant to all papers. This is followed by short checklists that are specific to particular types of papers.

▶ **General**

### Title

| | |
|---|---|
| The title appropriately summarizes the topic in no more than about 10–12 words. | Chap. 13  The title. |
| If the topic has been limited, this is indicated in the title. | Chap. 12  Limiting the topic. |

### Body of the paper

| | |
|---|---|
| The paper presents a central idea. | Chap. 1  Information and ideas. |
| Everything in the paper is relevant and contributes to the argument. | Chap. 1  Selecting material; Chap. 12  Relevance. |
| The reason for including information and ideas is clear, and points are clearly made. | Chap. 9  Making the point. |
| Information and ideas included are accurate, and all necessary detail is included. | Chap. 2  Accuracy. |
| Relevant theories are considered. | Chap. 12  Applying theory. |
| Your own ideas are clearly distinguished from those of others. | Chap. 9  Your ideas. |
| Information and ideas included are analysed, synthesized, and critically evaluated. | Chap. 1  Critical thinking. |
| The basis of assertions made by others has been examined. | Chap. 6  Basis of assertion by others. |
| All assertions are supported. | Chap. 6  Support. |
| The source of information or ideas is acknowledged | Chap. 6  Acknowledgement. |
| An appropriate number of sources is cited. | Chap. 12  Number of sources. |

**Objectivity**

| | |
|---|---|
| The discussion is balanced, and no information or idea contrary to the author's argument has been omitted. | Chap. 1  Personal views. A reasoned and balanced argument. |
| Examination of information and ideas, and the argument advanced, are objective. | Chap. 2  Objectivity; Chap. 12  Objectivity, Perspective. |
| The discussion is value free. | Chap. 2  Values. |

**Structure**

| | |
|---|---|
| The paper has been well structured so that the information, ideas, and argument advanced lead logically to the thesis or conclusion. | Chap. 9  Thinking; Chap. 12  Planning; Chap. 13  Thesis or conclusion. |
| The logical progression of thought is clear, and easy to follow. | Chap. 12.  Art vs science. |
| There is no redundancy. | Chap. 9.  Concise writing. |

**Sources**

| | |
|---|---|
| All sources cited have been critically evaluated. | Chap. 5  Evaluating Sources; Chap. 1  Selecting material. |
| If an edited book is cited, the author of the relevant chapter is cited as the source. | Chap. 6  Edited book. |
| Sources are cited at the appropriate point. | Chap. 6  Discussion or description, Placing a source. |
| Abstracts are not cited as sources. | Chap. 5  Abstracts and secondary sources. |
| Secondary sources have not been used, or one has been used by first-year students with care. | Chap. 6  Using secondary sources. |
| Secondary sources are not used when referring to theories. | Chap. 6  Referring to theories. |
| General or introductory textbooks have not been used as sources. | Chap. 5  General textbooks. |
| Educational material such as course or subject handouts, or educational material available via the Internet, has not been cited. | Chap. 5  Educational material; Chap. 6  Availability. |
| Sources cited are permanently and publicly available. | Chap. 5  Permanence. |
| Any on-line source cited has been carefully evaluated. | Chap. 5  Evaluating Sources. |
| Sources are cited correctly. | Chap. 6  Citing sources; and Appendix B. |

The abbreviation "et al." is used correctly.                Chap. 6  Multiple authors.
The ampersand is used only within
   parentheses.                                               Chap. 6  The ampersand.
The possessive case apostrophe is used
   correctly.                                                      Chap. 6  Possessive case.
Multiple sources are cited correctly.                       Chap. 6  Multiple references.
Page numbers (or paragraph numbers
   in some electronic sources) are
   included where  appropriate.                        Chap. 6  Page numbers.

### Quotations
No, or few, quotations have been included.
Quotations have been appropriately
   acknowledged.
Quotations are enclosed within double
   quotation marks, but long displayed
   quotations are not.
The source of the quotation is given, with
   the page number following the
   quotation.                                                       Chap. 7  Quotations.

### Academic honesty
There is no suggestion of plagiarism or
   other academic dishonesty.                          Chap. 4  Academic Standards.

## The Conclusion

The Conclusion summarizes the evidence            Chap. 9  Conclusion;
   and reasoning presented.                            Chap. 13  Conclusion.
The author's thesis or conclusion is                   Chap. 9  Thesis. Conclusion.
   clearly presented.
Nothing irrelevant is included in the
   Conclusion.
The conclusion does not include any
   value judgements.                                           Chap. 2  Values.
Assertions are supported, and sources
   are cited as appropriate.                             Chap. 6  Citing Sources.

## The reference list

The reference list (not bibliography)
   includes all sources cited in the paper,        Chap. 8  The Reference List;

and does not include any source not cited.

Appendix C; and
Appendix I.

The reference list begins on a new page and is correctly presented.

## ► Writing

The paper is written clearly and concisely.

Chap. 9  Clear and concise communication.

Information and ideas are clearly expressed.

Chap. 3  Expression

First person personal pronouns are not used, or are used with care.

Chap. 2  First person personal pronouns.

Footnotes are not used.

Chap. 9  Footnotes.

The paper is written:

in a formal style;

Chap. 3  Formality; Textbooks.

at an appropriate level,

Chap. 9  Level of writing.

in a scholarly manner, and

Chap. 3  Scholarly style.

in a polished manner.

Chap. 9  Scholarly writing.

Rhetorical questions are not used.

Chap. 3  Polish.
Chap. 3  Rhetorical questions.

## ► Conventions

The paper is written in "standard" or "International" English

Chap. 3  English usage.

Appropriate tense has been used.

Chap. 3  Tense.

Paragraphs are well structured.

Chap. 9  Paragraphs.

Grammar is correct.

Chap. 21  Grammar.

Punctuation is correct.

Chap. 22  Punctuation.

Spelling and capitalization are correct and consistent.

Chap. 23  Spelling and Capitalization.

## ► Editorial style

The paper complies with the APA editorial style.

Chap. 3  Editorial style;
Psychology style;
chap. 9  Editorial style.

Abbreviations and use of numbers are correct.

Chap. 24  Abbreviations and Numbers.

The abbreviations "e.g.", and "i.e." are correctly punctuated and are used only within parentheses.

Chapter 24  Abbreviations and numbers
Appendix D.

Sources are cited correctly.

Chap. 6  Citing sources; and Appendix B.

## ▶ Typing and presentation

White A4 paper is used throughout.

Chap. 25  Typing and Presentation.

Margins are correct (usually 35 mm).

Appendix A.

Pages are paginated at the top right-hand corner within the 35 mm margins.
The title page is not paginated.
Times New Roman typeface is used for all text (possibly with the exception of text in figures and tables).
Typing is double spaced, except where single spacing may be used.
No additional space is left between paragraphs.
The first line of each paragraph is indented by five to seven spaces.
Text is not right-justified.
The title page is presented as required.
The paper is bound as required.
Double quotation marks are used.
Figures and tables are separated from the text, and are of good quality.

Chap. 19  Preparing Figures and Tables.

## ▶ Local requirements

The paper complies with any local requirements given.

Chap. 3  Local requirements; and Appendix A.

## ▶ Essays

The essay addresses the specific topic or question.

Chap. 12  Addressing the topic.

The topic or question has not been changed.

Chap. 12  Changing the topic.

| | |
|---|---|
| If the topic has been limited, this is made clear in the title and the introduction. | Chap. 12  Limiting the topic; Chap. 13  Limitation. |
| The introduction does not include irrelevant material. | Chapter 13  Introduction. Relevance. |
| Any assertions made in the Introduction are supported. | Chap. 13  Assertions. |
| The author's approach is not detailed in the Introduction | Chap. 13  Approach. |
| The author's thesis is not given in the Introduction. | Chap. 13  Thesis or conclusion. |
| Headings are not used, unless in very long papers. | Chap. 13  Headings. |

## ▶ Literature reviews

| | |
|---|---|
| The above notes with regard to an essay are equally applicable to a literature review if the word "topic" is replaced with "research problem", and "thesis" is replaced with "conclusion'. | Chap. 9  Conclusion. |
| In addition, the conclusion of a literature review should suggest the suggested next step required in the investigation of the research problem or question. | Chap. 11  A literature review. |

## ▶ Research reports

The general notes above and those relating to literature reviews are equally relevant to the Introduction and Discussion sections of a research report. The following notes are specific to research reports.

### Title

| | |
|---|---|
| The title summarizes the main idea in no more than about 10–12 words. | Chap. 16  Title. |

### Abstract

| | |
|---|---|
| The abstract summarizes the research report in a single paragraph of no more than 120 words. | Chap. 14 Abstract; Chap. 16 Abstract. |

## Introduction

| | |
|---|---|
| The Introduction clearly presents the research problem or question. | Chap. 16  Research problem. |
| Theoretical hypotheses are clear. | Chap. 16  Theoretical hypothesis. |
| The research design is described briefly, but in sufficient detail to allow for an understanding of the research or experimental hypotheses. | Chap. 16  Research design. |
| Independent and dependent variables are clearly identified. | Chap. 15  Variables. |
| Operational defintions are given as necessary. | Chap. 15  Operational definitions. |
| Research or experimental hypotheses are clearly stated. | Chap. 15  Research or experimental hypothesis. |
| The reasoning upon which research or experimental hypotheses are based is clearly explained. | Chap. 16  Research or experimental hypothesis. |
| The wording of experimental or research hypotheses is maintained throughout the report. | Chap. 16  Research or experimental hypothesis. |
| The development of multiple hypotheses is clear. | Chap. 15  Multiple hypotheses. |
| Multiple hypotheses are in a logical sequence. | Chap. 16  Multiple hypotheses. |

## Method

| | |
|---|---|
| The Method section is written simply, clearly, and concisely. | Chap. 16  Method; chap. 9  Concise writing. |
| This section is written in the past tense. | Chap. 16  Tense. |
| Participants (respondents or subjects) are appropriately described. | Chap. 16  Participants, Respondents, Subjects. |
| Apparatus or materials used are clearly described. | Chap. 16  Apparatus, Materials. |
| The procedure followed is cleary described so that someone else could carry out the research. | Chap. 16  Procedure. |

## Results

| | |
|---|---|
| The results are presented simply, clearly, and concisely. | Chap. 16  Results. |
| The Results section is written in the past tense. | Chap. 16  Tense. |
| The results are presented so that they are easy to follow. | Chap. 15  Results. |
| No unnecessary analyses are reported. | Chap. 15  Results. |
| The results are not interpreted. | Chap. 14  Results; chap. 16 Commenting on results. |
| Where appropriate, descriptive and inferential statistics are reported. | Chap. 15  Statistical analyses. |
| Statistics are reported correctly. | Chap. 17  Reporting Statistics. |
| Abbreviations used are correct. | Appendix E. |
| Analyses are correctly interpreted. | |
| Figures or tables are used only for a specific purpose. | |
| What a figure or table is intended to illustrate is explained in the text. | Chap. 18  Using Figures and Tables. |
| Any figures or tables are simple and easy to understand. | Chap. 19  Preparing figures and tables. |
| Figures or tables comply with the APA style requirements and are not simply photocopies of those printed by a statistical package. | Chap. 19  Statistical package figures and tables. |

## Discussion

| | |
|---|---|
| The Discussion follows logically from the Introduction. | Chap. 14  Introduction and Discussion. |
| The Introduction and Discussion sections make sense without reading the Method and Results sections. | Chap. 15  Introduction and Discussion. |
| The outcome of testing of hypotheses is reported. | Chap. 16  Discussion. |
| Statistics are not needlessly repeated in the Discussion. | |
| The outcome is: | |

- related to the research problem or question;

- related to the theories, ideas, and research findings referred to in the Introduction;
- discussed within the theoretical context of the research.

Any alternative explanations of the outcome are recognized, and any weaknesses in the research are acknowledged.

Implications of the results are discussed.

The outcome of the research is summarized.

How the research contributes to knowledge in the area is discussed.

The next step in the investigation of the research problem or question is suggested.

No new material is introduced.

No value judgements are included in the Discussion.

Chap. 2 Values.
Chap. 16` Value judgements.

## Presentation

The format of the report is appropriate.

Chap. 14 Format; Chap. 16 Format.

The abstract appears on a separate page, and the reference list begins on a new page.

Chap. 25 Format.

Other parts of the report do not begin on a new page.

Headings and sub-headings are appropriate.

Chap. 15 Subheadings; Appendices F, G, and H.

# Bibliography

American Psychological Association. (2001). *Publication manual* (5th ed.). Washington, DC: American Psychological Association.

Anderson, J., & Poole, M. (1994). *Thesis and assignment writing* (2nd ed.). Brisbane: John Wiley & Sons.

Bate, D., & Sharpe, P. (1990). *Student writer's handbook.* Sydney: Harcourt Brace Jovanovich.

*Collins concise dictionary and thesaurus.* (1991). Glasgow: Harper Collins.

Davis, L. & McKay, S. (1996). *Structures and strategies: An introduction to academic writing.* Melbourne: Macmillan Education Australia.

Dooley, D. (1995). *Social research methods* (3rd ed.). Englewood Cliffs, NJ: Prentice Hall.

Epstein, R. L. (2002). *Critical thinking* (2nd ed.). Belmont, CA: Wadsworth/Thompson Learning.

Eunson, B. (1994). *Writing skills.* Brisbane: John Wiley & Sons.

Fiske, S. T., & Taylor, S. E. (1991). *Social cognition.* New York: McGraw-Hill.

Gleitman, H. (1991). *Psychology* (3rd ed.). New York: W. W. Norton.

Goodwin, C. J. (1995). *Research methods in psychology: Methods and design.* New York: John Wiley & Sons.

*Hamlyn pocket guide to English usage.* (1983). London: Newnes Books.

Hoffman, A. (1996). *Research for writers* (5th ed.). London: Black.

Judd, C. M., Smith, F. R., & Kidder, L. H. (1991). *Research methods in social relations* (6th ed.). Fort Worth: Holt, Rinehart and Winston.

Leedy, P. D. (1993). *Practical research and design* (5th ed.). New York: Macmillan Publishing.

*The Macquarie dictionary* (2nd rev. ed.). (1987). Chatswood, NSW, Australia: Macquarie Library.

Neuman, W. L. (1997). *Social research methods: Qualitative and quantitative approaches.* (3rd ed.). Boston: Allyn and Bacon.

Pagano, R. R. (1990). *Understanding statistics in the behavioural sciences* (4th ed.). Minneapolis, St Paul: West Publishing.

Page, G. T. (1991). *The Wordsworth book of spelling rules.* Ware, Hertfordshire: Wordsworth Editions.

Renton, N. E. (1990). *Elements of style and good writing.* Melbourne: Schwartz & Wilkinson.

Rice, P. L. & Ezzy, D. (1999). *Qualitative research methods: A health focus.* Melbourne: Oxford University Press.

*Roget's international thesaurus* (3rd ed.). (1962). London: Collins.

Sommer, B. & Sommer, R. (1997). *A practical guide to behavioral research: Tools and techniques* (4th ed.). New York: Oxford University Press.

Trimble, J. R. (1975). *Writing with style.* Englewood Cliffs, NJ: Prentice Hall.

Walker, M., Burnham, D., & Borland, R. (1994). *Psychology* (2nd ed.). Brisbane: John Wiley & Sons.

*Webster's third new international dictionary.* (1976). Springfield, MA: G. C. Merriam.

Winterowd, W. R., & Murray, P. (1988). *English: Writing and skills.* Austin, TX: Holt, Rinehart and Winston.

# Index